THE DOULA BOOK

THE DOULA BOOK

*How a Trained Labor Companion Can Help You
Have a Shorter, Easier, and Healthier Birth*

Marshall H. Klaus, M.D.

John H. Kennell, M.D.

Phyllis H. Klaus, C.S.W., M.F.T.

A Merloyd Lawrence Book

PERSEUS PUBLISHING

A Member of the Perseus Books Group

Portions of this book appeared in an earlier edition entitled *Mothering the Mother,* published by Addison-Wesley in 1993.

Cataloging-in-Publication Data is available from the Library of Congress
ISBN 0-7382-0609-1

Perseus Publishing is a member of the Perseus Books Group.
Find us on the World Wide Web at http://www.perseuspublishing.com.

Perseus Publishing books are available at special discounts for bulk purchases in the U.S. by corporations, institutions, and other organizations. For more information, please contact the Special Markets Department at the Perseus Books Group, 11 Cambridge Center, Cambridge, MA 02142, or call (800) 255-1514 or (617) 252-5298, or e-mail j.mccrary@ perseusbooks.com.

Text design by Jeff Williams
Set in 12-point Bembo by the Perseus Books Group

First printing, November 2002

1 2 3 4 5 6 7 8 9 10—04 03 02

We dedicate this book to all the sensitive and caring women who have provided continuous support during labor for the mothers in our studies. They have helped us in immeasurable ways to evaluate, describe, and begin to understand the power of their presence. We also dedicate this book to all the doulas in the future who will enable mothers and their partners to have a less complicated and more rewarding birth with long-term benefits.

Doula is a Greek word whose definition has come to mean a woman who helps other women. The word has further evolved to mean a woman experienced in childbirth who provides continuous physical, emotional, and informational support to the mother before, during, and after childbirth.

ॐ

CONTENTS

ACKNOWLEDGMENTS

Our understanding of the needs of mothers during labor developed during our systematic studies over the last twenty-five years. Insights also came from discussions with doulas and with close colleagues Steven Robertson, Susan McGrath, Roberto Sosa, Manuel de Carvalho, Clark Hinkley, Penny Simkin, Nadia Stein, Roberta O'Bell, Susan Landry, Kenneth Moise, Marjorie Greenfield, Kathy Scott, Charles Mahan, and Debra Pascali Bonaro. We also thank the medical students, and, especially, Wendy Freed, who more than a quarter century ago sparked our interest in exploring the needs of women during labor through observations she made when she stayed with ten mothers during labor as part of another study. Apparently benefiting from her supportive presence, these mothers all had a remarkably short labor and a complication-free birth. These observations were a critical stimulus to our exploration of the effects of a doula.

We appreciate the major conceptual additions to this book by Kerstin Uvnäs-Moberg and the Swedish midwives, Ann-Marie Widström, Anna-Berit Ransjö-Arvidson, Eva Nissen, Kyllike Christensson; as well as Beverley Chalmers, G. Justus Hofmeyr, Wendy-Lynne Wolman, and their Johannesburg research colleagues; and Christina Smillie with her new information about the "latch-on" in breast-feeding.

The perceptive comments of Laura and David Abada, Susan and Bob Sholtes, Devi and David Borton, Kristin Brooks and Glenn Meyer, Humm Berreyesa, Tracy Fengler, and Frances Bachman were especially helpful.

We thank our secretaries for their excellent work and patience: in Cleveland, Susan Wood, and in Berkeley, Nancy Pino. We are greateful for Peggy Kennell's early contributions and her strong doula-like patience and support.

Finally, our heartfelt thanks to Merloyd Lawrence for her continuing encouragement, sensitive understanding, and remarkable editing skills.

1

The Need for Support in Labor

Continuous support from a doula during labor provides
physical and emotional benefits for mothers and health
bonuses for their babies. With less medical interventions,
fewer complications, and shorter hospital stays,
there may be financial savings as well.

HARVARD HEALTH LETTER

Women helping women give birth is an ancient practice that is still widespread today. For instance, according to anthropological data that we reviewed for 128 nonindustrialized hunting-gathering and agricultural societies, all but one offered mothers the continuous support of other women during labor and delivery. As childbirth moved from home to hospital, however, this vital ingredient in childbirth began to disappear. While efforts to involve fathers and to introduce other humane practices into hospital births have done much to improve this situation, an important link remains missing. Although the introduction of fathers into the birth room brought the couple together for childbirth, this practice tended to reduce the sensitive and individualized care of the obstetric nurse in their labor. Childbirth is usually now lonelier and more psychologically stressful for both parents. For some mothers, left to labor largely on their own, birth becomes "solitary confinement."

In the past twenty-five years, together with colleagues, we have studied the effects of restoring to the childbirth experience this important element of having women as helpers during labor. Continuous support from an experienced labor companion has proven dramatically beneficial.[1] In studies of over 5000 women involving comparisons of outcomes with and without such support, we have seen a major reduction in the length of labor, a greater than 50 percent drop in cesarean sections, a

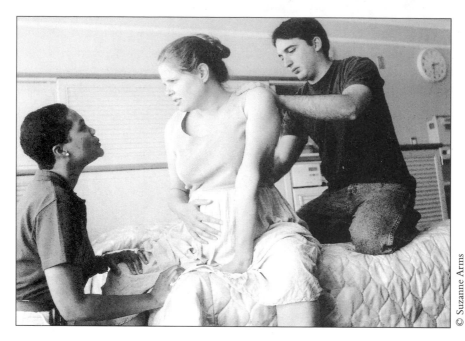

Getting acquainted and being reassured in early labor.

remarkable drop in the mothers' need for pain medication, and several other important and measurable benefits, which we describe in the chapters that follow.

This continuous support was provided by caring, experienced women we call *doulas.* In searching for a term to describe this role, we wanted a word with a nonmedical connotation that would stress the value of a woman companion as attentive and comforting. We turned to the Greek word *doula,* meaning "woman caregiver." Our first exposure to the word came from Dana Raphael's use of the term to describe "one or more individuals, often female, who give psychological encouragement and physical assistance to the newly delivered mother."[2] We use the word in the now widely accepted sense of an experienced labor companion who provides the woman and her husband or partner both emotional and physical support throughout the entire labor and delivery, and to some extent, afterward. Other people use terms such as *labor coach, monitrice, childbirth assistant, labor companion* or *mother assistant.* Whatever the term, we hope our readers will come away with an understanding of the vital shared ingredient that makes this role so powerful and beneficial. In this book we describe what a doula can provide both during labor and birth and in the postpartum period, and how she is trained. We discuss the results of our studies on labor outcomes and differentiate not only between the assistance of a doula and the equally vital help of fathers but also between the work of the doula and that of the nurse, physician, or midwife. We also offer guidance in finding and evaluating a doula, and give, in Appendix A, information on how a doula is trained.

We realize that a woman having a baby may be married or single and accompanied by the father, her own mother, or a close friend. When we use words such as *father, partner, couple,* and *parents,* we mean to include all types of family arrangements. Also, for simplicity, we use the words *mother* and *father,* rather than *mother-to-be* and *father-to-be,* for a woman and man as they share in the experience of labor and delivery.

TYPES OF LABOR SUPPORT

When embarking on one of the most meaningful experiences of their lives—the birth of their first child—a couple fantasizes about what the labor and delivery will be like. They may have a dream of how it will be—perhaps hoping that this pregnancy and birth will be all their own, something they do together without anyone else's interference. At the same time, they will have fears. On the one hand, they may picture being alone together, with the father being the main helper and support, and music playing in the background as they go through labor without interruptions or interventions and then have idyllic quiet time with their new baby. On the other hand, they may worry about pain, loss of control, problems for the baby, or life-threatening complications.

Given these hopes and fears, all mothers and fathers need emotional support and help during labor. Much of this support they can provide to each other. The mother needs to feel the father's care, love, sense of connection, responsibility, and sense of sharing in the intimate experience of bringing their child into the world. The father or other chosen partner has a strong desire to help, to participate, to feel useful and active, and to feel important and necessary for the mother.

But when two people share an emotional bond and an ongoing relationship, it is very difficult for that companion to remain continuously objective, calm, and removed to some degree from the mother's discomfort and, fears, or

Steady support helping the woman visualize through a contraction.

with labor and be a reassuring and constant presence for both her and the father. The doula gives a level of support different from that of a person who is intimately related to the woman in labor.

These two kinds of support complement each other. A doula can help a woman work with her labor and guide her on how to stay relaxed and comfortable at home until labor is well established. Prenatally, the doula can show the pregnant woman how she will have the ability and confidence to be an advocate on her own behalf. In the hospital the doula can help the father or other partner be less anxious. With her practiced skill, the doula serves as a role model for the less experienced person.

Very often the couple worry that an outside support person will take over and control the labor experience, as many individuals providing labor assistance have traditionally done. The training of a doula is quite different, emphasizing quiet reassurance and enhancement of the natural abilities of the laboring woman. A doula is constantly aware that the couple will carry the memory of this experience throughout their lives. As we discuss in Chapters 3, 7, and 8, the doula is there to help the parents have the type of birthing experience they want.

any danger to her. In most cases—and this cannot be stated too often—the father will have the unexpressed but deeply felt question, Will everything be all right? Also, a father often has had little or no experience with the birth process.

For these reasons, every woman in labor needs not only the father or other chosen partner but also a nurturing, experienced person—a doula—who can calmly and skillfully help her cope

For millennia the relationship of mother to daughter, of older experienced woman to younger birthing woman, was respected and understood. Today, although many women may want their own mothers' help during labor, most of today's grandmothers are not experienced around birth. The experience of women who gave birth in the 1960s and 1970s may not have been ideal. Also, many women are distant from their adult daughters geographically and some, psychologically. Many expectant women today prefer not to have their mothers at the actual birth, even if they have a caring relationship. Many prefer to have the father present, and it is often easier for the couple to have a nonrelated but caring person help them. Sometimes men who have become involved in birth through childbirth courses may feel their position is usurped if their mother-in-law or a close friend of the mother's is acting as the main support during labor. Though laboring women's mothers and friends can offer important support along with fathers, a doula's nurturing, helpful, and objective support relieves the family member chosen to be present from sole responsibility for the labor. It is not an attempt to interfere with the relationship between the woman and her partner or other family member.

THE NEEDS OF FATHERS DURING LABOR AND DELIVERY

In asking fathers to be the main support, our society may have created a very difficult expectation for them to meet. This is like asking fathers to play in a professional football game after several lectures but without any training or practice games. Couples sometimes get the mistaken impression from childbirth classes that by using a number of simple exercises, the father can be a main source of support and knowledge for the entire labor when the nurse is unavailable. This is true for a small number of fathers, but most fathers—especially first-timers—do not get enough opportunity in the classes to observe and practice. Often the dilemma for childbirth instructors is how to get fathers to be more a part of the experience and appreciate what actually lies ahead. Fathers entering into this new role often feel nervous, joke frequently, and consciously or unconsciously wonder whether they belong in this whole obstetrical arena. Dr. Martin Greenberg, an experienced physician who has done research with new fathers, commented: "I didn't realize until later how frightened and angry I felt at the staff for being left alone with my wife when having our first baby."

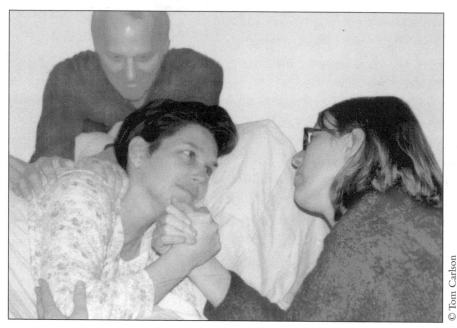

The nurturing presence of both the father and doula in early labor.

In no other area of the hospital is a family member asked to take on such a significant caretaking role as in childbirth. When working in the obstetrical unit, we have often been struck by how terribly relieved fathers are when an experienced nurse or midwife enters the room and remains with them. This feeling of relief enables fathers to be much more relaxed, loving, and emotionally available than when they bear the burden of responsibility alone.

We therefore want to enable the father to be present *at his own comfort level* and to remain emotionally connected to his partner and child. Few fathers want to be—or should be—the sole support person in the room. As we discuss in Chapter 8, the mother gains more assured, steady emotional support from her partner if he is less worried about what he is supposed to do and if they both can relax and trust the doula's expert care. As one father noted: "I've run a number of marathons, I've done a lot of hiking with a heavy backpack, and I've worked for forty hours straight on call; but going through labor with my wife was more strenuous and exhausting than any of these other experiences. We could never have done it without the doula. She was crucial for us." His wife added: "I want the doula there to assure me that everything is fine and to comfort me. I want my husband there for emotional support."

A laboring woman's rapid changes of mood may alarm an inexperienced father and compound the mother's fears. "If you leave the mother alone for even five minutes," a doula commented to us, "she begins to become distressed. She begins to fall apart and lose control, and when you return, it may take a half hour to get her settled down." Fathers express feelings of mounting anxiety. Underlying this anxiety is often an unexpressed fear of danger for the mother or child, as well as distress for the mother's pain. Although fathers have many positive feelings and great anticipation, these negative feelings can get in the way and, in turn, affect the progress of the labor itself. Over and over again we have been impressed by the calming influence the doula has for both the mother and father as she explains what is happening, uses her extensive experience to help the mother, and supports the parents in having the kind of experience they originally desired.

A Variety of Settings for Birth

Hospitals and obstetric caregivers, including physicians, nurses, and midwives, approach delivery from very different perspectives. The role of a doula or other provider of labor support will be affected by these differences.

On one end of the spectrum, childbirth is viewed as a normal physiological event that follows a natural course. Interventions needed for these natural deliveries are seen as minor, although the personnel must remain alert for any medical sign of complications. When childbirth is planned from this point of view, mothers are informed what to expect during the start of labor and, after checking with their caregivers, given the okay to stay at home during most of labor. They are guided to stay relaxed, take in fluids and light food as desired, rest, do distracting activities in early labor, and as labor progresses help with a variety of comfort measures. These include relaxation, visualization, massage, position changes, shower or bath. At the hospital they are further helped to work in a natural way, allowing their labor to continue without interventions (rupture of membranes, augmentation with pitocin). Minimal medications are used, and mothers attempt to give birth without an

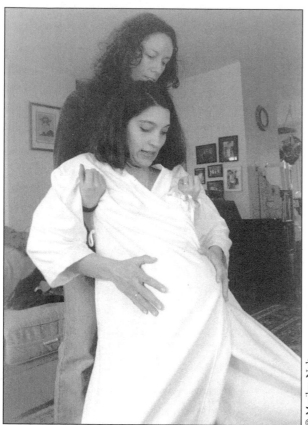
Supporting the woman in an upright position promotes the use of gravity.

© Marilyn Nolt

epidural. Episiotomies are kept to a minimum, and most mothers give birth vaginally.[3]

On the other end of this spectrum, childbirth is seen as a medical event fraught with potential danger. For many mothers giving birth in such a setting labor begins with an induction between Monday and Friday. Other women, whose labor begins at home, are usually asked to come into the hospital early. There, they are monitored and receive IV fluids, and they are often limited to bed and unable to drink or eat. Often the membranes are ruptured, an early epidural is given, and contractions are augmented with pitocin. These mothers have a higher rate of cesarean sections and a higher rate of episiotomies. Many maternity hospitals or obstetrical practices, of course, fall in between these two extremes.

In planning or thinking about their own delivery, expectant parents should know about the different practices of the physicians and midwives in their community. By knowing which approaches these professionals tend to adopt, they can make a more informed choice in order to meet the mother's medical, emotional, and physical needs.

PRESSURES ON THE HOSPITAL STAFF

Many people do not appreciate that an obstetrical staff of nurses and doctors provides care for a wide range of patients. In the United States, 90 percent of deliveries are normal and routine, but 5–10 percent require an intensive effort with the use of advanced technology, consultants, and additional ancillary personnel. When the special cases arise, this reduces the number of nurses available to work with the larger group of mothers who are having routine, normal deliveries. In addition, the numerous cesarean sections in most hospitals also tie up the nursing personnel.

Studies by Ellen Hodnett in Toronto noted that women planning a hospital birth rarely expected to have a nurse with them throughout labor.[4] The women usually felt the nurses would be busy or viewed their role as purely technical. She commented, "Recognizing that laboring women require psychological support and realizing that nurses have little time to give it, hospitals have increasingly permitted and encouraged husbands to assume active roles in the care of their wives during labor." In addition, in hospitals many different caregivers are often involved with one mother. A recent study found that women giving birth encountered an average of 6.4 unfamiliar professionals during labor. The presence of many strangers can disrupt the labor and confuse the mother.

At home and in some hospitals, midwives who care for only one mother at a time, continuously attending each from early labor on, meet both the medical and emotional needs of the mother and father. When a hospital or other birth setting provides such continuous one-to-one nursing or one-to-one midwifery care and that caregiver's goal is to reassure, relax, comfort, and inform the mother rather than to tend only to the needed medical interventions, that person takes the same supportive role as a doula. Many nurses who care deeply for the emotional as well as the physical well-being of their childbearing patients are happy when they can provide such uninterrupted care.

In most cases, however, nurses on the delivery floor and hospital-based midwives generally care for several patients at one time, monitoring the progress of labor; the vital signs of the mother, such as heart rate, blood pressure, and temperature; and fetal well-being, with heart-rate changes. In non-high-risk situations obstetricians and family physicians are not in constant attendance but check in and out until late labor. Then they manage the delivery and attend to any medical aspects, giving strong support when they are present.

Many parents expect to handle child-birth alone, but within the circle of a "safe" hospital setting where help is just outside the door. Many nurses believe they should not interfere with labor and, instead, just come in to check on how things are going. When they or the physician come in only intermittently, they may not always recognize the great need that parents have for information and reassurance. It may be difficult for the father to ask for help or to realize when or what type of assistance his wife needs at each stage of labor. He may be getting anxious, and he will often think of "help" only as a medical intervention rather than as assistance with the emotional needs of the mother as she works through contractions.

Two widely respected, experienced, and caring teachers of obstetrics, Drs. Kierin O'Driscoll and Declan Meagher, whose work in Dublin is described in Chapter 9, have recognized the negative effects that a lack of support has on women in labor.[5] When a woman does not have an experienced person to give her continuous personal attention throughout labor and when the father is uncertain, fearful, or becoming anxious himself, they note, "the scenario for many can be written in advance: the woman becomes progressively withdrawn from contact with her surroundings, closes her eyes and buries her face in the pillow, only later to become increasingly active, with contorted features and restless movements, interrupted by outbursts, until finally a state of panic is reached and self control is lost." In our studies we have encountered several occasions in which couples who were reluctant initially to have a supportive companion because they wanted to be alone for this significant event changed their minds completely in midlabor and pleaded with us to supply them with a doula. The role of a doula is still being refined, and as we said earlier, labor support can be offered by several other types of professionals. Its essence, as we will show, is a "mothering" role, mothering both the mother and father as they are born into their new family. In Appendix A we describe the basic ingredients of doula training.

Our studies have led us to the firm conviction that a doula—a person providing unobtrusive, compassionate, and experienced support throughout labor—is needed by every couple during the delivery of their child. With such help, parents can capture the special moments and priceless experience of their own unique childbirth. This in turn becomes the foundation for strong attachment as the new family comes into being.

2

The Special Role of the Doula

We form such a rapport that a woman can
ask anything of me.

A DOULA

To understand the special role of a doula, we must first distinguish it from that of the others involved in childbirth. A doula is not a doctor, a nurse, or a midwife. She is not trained to make any medical decisions. However, her training includes learning about the usual medical interventions so that she can explain them to parents in order to relieve some of their uncertainties and anxieties. As an example, fetal monitors may record a very low heart rate (1 to 2 beats per minute) for a few seconds, even though the actual heart rate is a normal 148 beats per minute. The doula who is knowledgeable about this phenomenon can reassure the mother that the low reading is a problem of the machine, not the baby.

A nurse or midwife can provide support in labor if she does not have other duties, time constraints, or other patients. Many nurses and midwives choose obstetric work because of their empathic interest in helping women during childbirth. But as we saw earlier, the demands of the labor and delivery service, hectic schedules, and a large number of laboring women make it extremely unlikely that nurses or midwives can be totally and continuously available to any one laboring woman for her entire labor.

Some hospitals have birth centers with one-on-one midwife assignments, but this is not common. Much more often midwives are expected to care for two or more mothers at the same time. When that is the case, they generally welcome the presence of a doula when they have to leave one mother alone to care for another.

It is assumed that a doula will be a woman, and several advantages probably account for this. A mother in labor can usually be less inhibited in the presence of another woman. The intimate aspects of bodily function are more easily expressed with a person of the same gender. In addition, the softer, quieter, gentler, sensitive, nurturing qualities of "mothering" have traditionally come from women in our culture.

Most doulas have had children of their own. A woman who has given birth has an innate sense of what the experience is like and provides a natural empathy. However, personal birthing experience is not essential. A number of women who have not been mothers themselves work very sensitively as doulas. Although they do not have the experience of giving birth, they relate to the birthing woman through their inherent psychological and biological kinship as women.

Doulas do not prescribe any set breathing pattern or labor regimen. They create an emotional "holding" environment for the mother, encouraging her to allow her own body to tell her what may be best at various times during labor. The doulas cooperate fully with any breathing pattern the couple is prepared to use.

THE DOULA'S ROLE

What does the doula actually do to help the mother? Ideally, her role begins when the doula has an opportunity to meet the mother and the mother's partner one and a half to three months before labor begins—that is, during the third trimester of pregnancy. At that time the doula can learn in detail what the woman or couple expects and wants during labor. She can also find out what the mother has found helpful when feeling tense in other situations and what kinds of soothing make her feel more relaxed or less anxious. For example, a mother may say, "I often feel very relaxed if somebody rubs my shoulders or back very softly and slowly." Then during labor the doula will try this and ask the woman if she finds it helpful.

A doula learns that she has to be willing to take anything for an answer and not be embarrassed or feel foolish. Sometimes an action a woman enjoyed before may not feel right or helpful during the actual labor. The experienced doula develops enough confidence and self-esteem that she is not offended by the woman's seeming rejection of that action. A woman cannot or may not always tell the doula what she likes. Sometimes the doula tries something for a short while, observes the woman, and "reads" her responses. A woman in labor may feel that she must perform and act in a certain way in front of her husband, mother, or mother-in-law. In contrast, the woman can be completely at ease with the doula and unconcerned about having to try to please her or put on a show for her.

This initial visit of the doula with the couple or the pregnant woman becomes a time to build rapport, and it allows the doula to learn what goals and wishes the parents have for the birth of their child. When the expectations are unrealistic, the doula will tactfully explain what she can and cannot do. Two or three visits of the doula with the mother and her partner during pregnancy will allow the relationship to develop. In some cases, these prenatal visits cannot always be arranged. When the doula must first meet the mother at the time of her admission to the hospital, the early period of labor usually allows time for the relationship to proceed.

The most important assurance that a doula can give in these initial visits is that she will remain with the mother throughout the entire labor and not leave her alone. If the doula has to leave to eat or go to the bathroom, she will have the father or nurse stand by for her. The relationship builds on this assurance; it makes the woman and family feel cared for, not alone.

For women in labor much of the birth process is about permission: feeling total permission to be themselves and feeling free to let down emotional and physical barriers and to release expectations—those yardsticks or measures of performance that women carry with them into the institutional environment. Feeling completely safe with another human being creates a kind of freedom that enables a woman to begin to test the limits of her own capacities and to experience capacities possibly not recognized before—or perhaps recognized but not risked. This freedom to be one's true self produces feelings of empowerment, of creativity. As a new mother said to one doula, "Your staying with me all the time and your total support, at the same time trusting me completely, gave me a sense of knowing that I was strong enough to handle anything in my life."

Nadia, an experienced doula, explains that mothers whom she first meets at the hospital are often out of control at the beginning of labor when they first start to experience pain. With each one Nadia asks whether she is

The doula senses the need for holding the woman through a contraction while the father massages the mother's back.

afraid, and the mother usually says yes. The doula sees in the mother's face a growing fear about not being able to stand the pain. She explains to the woman that the labor is a very natural process and a natural function of the body. Nadia tells the mother just to let her body do what it has to do. If the mother continues to be scared, Nadia says, "Don't be frightened. Remember to let your breath go through—let it go through. Just breathe it through quietly, and try as much as you can to be relaxed. That's it you see, that's the only thing you have to do." Usually when Nadia quietly and calmly repeats one of these phrases over and over again in a cadence, the mother becomes quiet and peaceful. During this process she begins to feel confidence in herself and in the naturalness of the process.

Another doula, Joyce, describes a different part of her role. In early labor she finds that she gains the confidence of the mother by being cheerful and friendly. She notes that this can be an enjoyable stage, as they get to know each other. This is especially important when the doula and the mother have not met before labor.

As labor progresses, doulas frequently cradle or hold the women in their arms. If a woman should cry, the doula may get a damp cloth and wipe her face. Regardless of the response of the mother to labor, a doula remains encouraging, never trying to discipline the parents and never putting the mother down.

When women experience back labor, a doula suggests a variety of methods to help relieve the discomfort—back rubs, hot cloths, pressure against the back, or sometimes no touch whatsoever. Each mother has differing needs. As labor progresses, the doula asks what the woman would like, and the mother responds. "We form such a rapport that a woman can ask anything of me" said one doula. By her presence, manner, and comforting touch, the doula creates calmness and the essence of relaxation.

In midlabor, as dilatation of the cervical opening increases from five to seven centimeters and labor pains become more frequent and painful, the doula becomes more supportive. At this time the woman's partner may become frightened and also need support and explanations from the doula. It is here that the doula's ability to encourage and verbalize what is happening is deeply reassuring. One father stated after delivery that when the doula said the bloody show was "good, good!" he felt very relieved. "You could never say that enough. It was so helpful."

As labor becomes more intense, the father may move slightly farther away from the mother. If this happens, the doula can move closer or encourage more closeness from the father, if appropriate. At this time the doula continues to reassure the mother and the partner that the labor is progressing normally. She stays on top of what is happening, explaining each stage and praising the woman about her excellent progress. It is not unusual for some women to ask the doula over and over again when and if she is leaving. When replying, the doula knows it is wise to offer reassurance that she will not leave the mother except perhaps for a few minutes to go to the bathroom.

For the actual delivery, the medical caregivers are in charge. The doula remains by the mother's side along with the father, and afterwards congratulates the parents and especially the new mother on her accomplishment. Even more important is her memory of the couple's prenatal wishes, making certain, for example, that mother and father have time alone with the baby and the mother breast-feeds early.

When the doula visits with the family the day after the delivery, she asks them what they remember about the birth and if they have any questions or concerns. The doula spends time discussing the birth experience, allowing the parents to share all their positive feelings and, if appropriate, their negative feelings. The doula encourages them to talk, and she can add what was forgotten. Almost all mothers gain from hearing the details that fill in many of the missing pieces of the experience for them. From this they gain a new perception of their own participation. Often mothers feel they failed to perform well and did not do something right. This retelling of the birth story helps them understand what actually went on during their labor and delivery. It is an opportunity to heighten the mother's self-image by pointing out the strength she showed and the way her body followed its age-old biological course. If there were complications, the doula helps the mother integrate and sometimes reframe the experience.

THE DOULA AND THE HOSPITAL STAFF

A doula's efforts are more effective when she is known and respected by the personnel on the delivery floor and other hospital staff. The laboring mother has a vastly different experience when the doula has worked with the same staff repeatedly, in contrast to when a stranger is working as a doula. The more knowledgeable the doula is about the unit, the more helpful she can be to the parents. The better the staff know the doula, the more likely they are to be supportive to her. Whenever possible, it is desirable for doulas to be familiar with, and in turn to be recognized and appreciated by, the staff at two or three hospitals in the community that her families use for childbirth. She may receive her training in one hospital but work regularly in several others.

A doula's success depends on her ability to get along with a diverse group of hospital staff members. When she is able to do this, her ability to become closely connected to the woman in labor, to pick up the woman's signals and calm her, can often shift a potentially difficult situation into one that is easily managed. Once they have seen a doula have this effect, nurses are generally delighted to have her on the labor and delivery floor. Physicians also recognize her value and respect her.

In advance of any work at a particular hospital, the doula will want to introduce herself to the labor and delivery floor, meet the head nurse and other personnel, and learn about the routines for labor, delivery, and the postpartum period. When you work in somebody else's kitchen, you need to know where they keep the flour and sugar and how they wash the dishes. Similarly it is also important for the doula to know the admitting and labor and delivery practices unique to a particular obstetrical unit so that she can ease the transition from home to car to hospital for laboring women.

In addition, a doula will sometimes meet the childbirth educators in her community and, if agreeable with them, attend some classes or review the material they present. What the doula discusses prenatally with parents who attend childbirth education classes will then complement what has been covered in those classes. A doula's instructions, however, will be individualized to the needs of the parents. The support she offers a sixteen-year-old expectant mother, for example, may start at a more basic level and require extra visits.

We believe that in most cases the doula should be engaged separately by the family and not considered a staff member of a hospital. This frees the doula to focus all her attention on the needs of the family. For families without funds, hospitals ideally could offer a list of experienced volunteer doulas or organizations that provide doulas. In certain hospitals the doula is formally part of the program. In any case, the doula has to maintain a delicate balance between respecting the protocol of the hospital and professional staff and at the same time keeping the autonomy of the parents uppermost in her mind. In that way she encourages the parents to advocate on their own behalf, especially during the prenatal period.

An experienced doula becomes respected as an individual who can hear the mother's needs and wishes and, when necessary, interpret them to the medical personnel. For example, if the mother is experiencing much discomfort but wants to continue at her own pace, and the medical personnel believe that a drug for pain relief might be helpful, the doula may help the mother voice her wishes, without becoming confrontative or interfering with the medical staff.

THE DOULA, THE FATHER, AND OTHER FAMILY MEMBERS

A doula often interacts with the father and with members of the mother's family. She needs to relate tactfully and sensitively to them, not invading their position and sometimes being an adjunct to them. But she also helps the mother express to her family needs that may differ from their expectations or their ways of helping or interacting with her. The doula must tactfully move away from the mother when a close family member such as the husband or the laboring woman's own mother arrives to take over the support. The doula then remains nearby, unobtrusive yet ready to provide information. By her words and actions, the doula models behaviors and attitudes that are almost always copied and appreciated by the father. At times a doula needs to be resolutely strong and firm, and at other periods in the labor, tender, soft, and loving.

Throughout the labor and delivery the doula monitors the father's changing relationship to the mother, noting his attitude, skill, and knowledge about labor, his own comfort in touching, and his desire to be useful. (See Chapter 8.) If he is being a good enough support person at meeting most of the mother's needs, the doula can prepare him for what is coming, give suggestions, provide encouragement when he needs support, or spell him when he is exhausted.

A doula has many opportunities to model supportive behaviors for the father. The doula may increase the effectiveness of his support by suggesting that he hold the woman's feet or press a certain area in her back. This gives him something concrete and supportive to do while not overwhelming him with unfamiliar techniques. The doula is sensitive to the fact that even though the mother and father have a good relationship, his touch at certain times may feel like an intrusion to the woman. One doula, having intuitively assessed where a mother felt strong pain and pressure, asked a father to place his hands on his wife and press in that area. The mother, with eyes closed, exclaimed, "That feels wrong." The father, withdrawing his hands, said, "Oh, I'm sorry." The mother replied, "Oh, I didn't mean to hurt you." The doula then had the task of repairing the father's loss of face, his feelings of rejection, and his wife's distress at having hurt him. The doula responded: "It takes time to learn exactly how much pressure to place there. Why don't you hold Sally's feet. It feels good to have someone to press against."

MOTHERING THE MOTHER

After training and experience, a doula often feels an intuitive sense of when to "mother" the mother. This is a vulnerable time when a woman is unusually dependent and open, as she prepares to move through the major maturational change associated with experiencing labor and delivery and with becoming a parent. However, while dependent, a mother still needs the freedom to turn into herself—to take charge at an instinctual level in response to what her body wants to do. It is a paradox, really. A woman in labor needs total support—in order to let go completely, to allow her own system to adapt and respond to the power of the birthing process. This mixed need can be confusing to the mother herself and may be difficult for others to appreciate. Often caregivers find it hard to understand this complex balance: the mother's need to be dependent and independent at the same time.

In certain situations a doula's emotional support may have a deeper therapeutic effect. During birth there is a psychological regression to a woman's own birth, to her essential vulnerability. If a woman has had inadequate or inappropriate mothering herself, the nurturing provided by a doula during this unique period may furnish an opportunity to remother the mother as a person and bring a type of healing to that earlier experience.

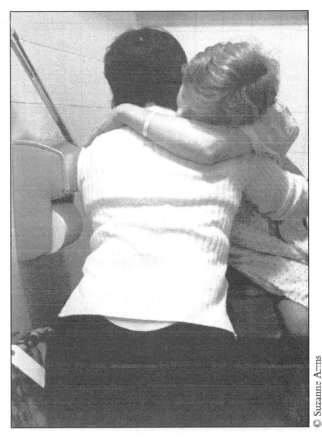

Many women find sitting on a toilet a most helpful position for labor.

To have this effect, a doula needs special skills and insights. A successful doula is comfortable with giving of herself and is not afraid to love. She also can enter another's space and be highly responsive and aware of another's needs, moods, changes, and unspoken feelings. At the same time, she is able to be flexible in this process, adapting herself to each mother's needs, and has no need to control or smother.

The doulas who have been most effective have been secure and confident women who touch easily, hold comfortably, and respond warmly and caringly, but at the same time acknowledge the mother's autonomy. Before she can help a woman in labor, a doula has to be comfortable with birth and not frightened by all the sights and sounds and emotional events that occur during labor and delivery—blood, sweat, screaming, defecation, vomiting, and sometimes crying. A doula must have strength and stamina because the labors are sometimes long and rigorous and may last all night. A doula must be able to remain supportive for the mother who is in pain, even if at times the doula is unable to relieve the discomfort completely. Although her efforts may not appear to be having the desired effect, she must not attempt to deny the pain or the woman's perception of her own experience.

To achieve calm and confidence, a doula needs a comprehensive knowledge of the normal birth process. (See Appendix A in regard to training.) She should be aware of the common situations and delays that occur during labor and recognize those that can be reduced or managed by simple nonmedical interventions, such as changing body position. Training of the doula will prepare her to understand situations that may require medical intervention so she can remain supportive to parents undergoing a difficult labor and birth, or when complications develop. She remains a link to "normalcy," helping the mother retain a sense of accomplishment and self-worth even if the birth does not go as planned.

A doula's presence can be equally valuable for a woman whether she is having her first or a subsequent baby. Mothers having second and third deliveries frequently and enthusiastically express their appreciation for the doula's emotional support. Those who did not have a doula during their first labor and delivery often say how much they wish they could redo that experience with the help of a doula. And most of those who have had a doula at the birth of their first infant insist they cannot go through another birth without that support. The special bond that develops between the mother and doula during the intense emotional and physical stress of labor and delivery creates a unique relationship. During this experience the woman may be able to move into a deep, safe, securely nurturing enfoldment without losing any part of her autonomy. The doula's support allows the mother's most powerful creativity to emerge in the safest way. This experience often overflows into other respects of a woman's life, enhancing the transformation that childbirth brings about.

As a doula gains experience, she learns how to assess a laboring woman more accurately and gauge both where the woman is in the course of her labor and just what degree of support to give her at that stage. For example, some mothers are so tuned in to their own bodies and trust their own systems so much that they are able to go about their labor in an internalized, self-directed manner. Just having the doula in the room is enough support for them.

Other women may seek the comfort and nurturance of a doula who stays very close, holds, caresses, murmurs encouragement, and initiates a variety of measures that enhance a feeling of security. At the right time the doula will sense a need and move in to hold a hand, caress a shoulder, massage the back, hold an arm or a leg, or support the woman's whole body through a contraction.

At the beginning of labor some women are very uncomfortable with touch by a stranger. The doula must recognize the mother's level of comfort and remain at whatever seems a respectful and comfortable distance. At that stage the doula's communication with the mother will be mainly verbal. As labor progresses most women eventually feel open to touch and then seek, welcome, and respond to more physical contact.

Regarding touch, if a doula is always present as a standard part of a birth program or protocol of the hospital, then even women who are less comfortable with touch are implicitly given permission to ask for it or accept it if they choose. Some women do prefer to labor "alone," in the sense of wanting to be in a quiet, dark, small, protected, and private space. In most hospitals the only such space may be the hospital-room bathroom, but all women want to know that some caring and knowledgeable woman is nearby—even if just outside the bathroom door—and ready to help.

Other women want to be held and comforted but are hesitant to ask for that intimacy. The laboring woman often relaxes noticeably when a doula calmly and rhythmically says—while touching the mother's hand or arm— "I'm here. I'm going to stay with you until the baby is born. I'm not going to leave you. We'll see this through together." The fear of the unknown is lessened and relieved. The doula's touch gives an added message of strength to her words. A number of doulas have

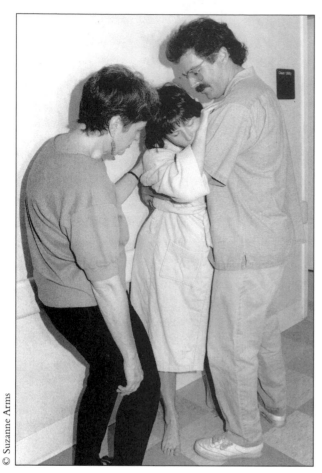

The doula is showing with her body posture how it will help if the woman lets herself sink into her husband's arms.

creates a palpable and comforting enclosure as the doula "mothers" the laboring woman. This reminds us of the literal and figurative holding environment that new mothers create for their infants. The doula's nurturing may somehow be internalized by parents and become a model as they care for their own infant.

Other women look to the doula to take the lead, at times wanting her suggestions and help for position changes, for relaxation, or for reminders to keep their throats open and breathe freely. Many women believe they can labor only when lying on their backs or sides, because they may not know about or appreciate the recent research studies showing shorter and often less painful labor when the woman is walking, especially when the cervix is dilated less than eight centimeters. Also, a hands-and-knees position with the head down helps many women find relief when their cervical dilatation is at ten centimeters. While a woman is laboring in such a position or is walking, the doula and the father give physical support as needed. For example, they may hold the woman's hand while she is

noticed that if they are holding a mother's arm while the woman has drifted off to sleep, and then lift their hand off the woman, she immediately awakens, saying, "Don't go"; sometimes, without opening her eyes, she grabs for the doula's hand. The power of touch

walking comfortably and then support her firmly, holding her during a contraction. They may also guide the woman with relaxation breathing throughout the contractions.

As we will see in Chapter 4 and Appendix B, doulas also support women who wish to use visualization and relaxation techniques. For many of the women who have practiced these techniques, this combination of mental, physical, and behavioral maneuvers appears to create a physiological change in the body that paves the way for the muscles to relax and open.

The experienced doula develops a special sensitivity to and an awareness of the different needs and progress of labor—sometimes very clear, sometimes rather subtle—in the women they serve. Often a doula can reliably predict the stage of cervical dilatation or descent of the baby's head as confirmed by direct examination by the midwife or the physician.

In some cases the woman has greater needs, as with teenagers or women who have been neglected, abused, or mismothered as infants or children. In such cases the doula assumes an extended support role; she will ideally start her work early in pregnancy and continue contact with the mother for as long as a year and a half after the birth of the infant. Some women may have had traumatic or sexually abusive experiences, and birthing may consciously or unconsciously retrigger feelings that stem from these experiences. A doula learns to work with the mother on language, gestures, and actions that do not restimulate these memories.

When she returns to visit the parents during the postpartum period, the doula is often greeted like an old and dear friend. Often parents bring the baby back to show to the doula six months or a year later. The doula finds it quite natural for the person to whom she has been so close to show pride and affection.

CHOOSING A DOULA

The personal characteristics of each doula will, of course, vary. However, the following qualities are most beneficial with any doula:

1. A warm, loving, enthusiastic, compassionate and caring nature, coupled with maturity and responsibility

2. Tolerance for people of different ethnic groups, social statuses, levels of income, and lifestyles

3. Good health and the endurance both to stand for long periods and

to work for long stretches in a crowded labor room in varied labor situations

4. The ability to deal with and remain supportive of women who may become unusually distressed during the final stages of labor
5. Experience of childbirth, personally and also through attendance at many births
6. Comfort with touch
7. The ability to communicate, especially to listen
8. The ability to submerge her own personal belief system about maternity practices
9. The ability to be flexible and to work in a variety of birth settings with changes in staff and care providers

In addition to considering the qualities just mentioned, parents may find the following questions helpful to explore when interviewing a doula:

1. What training and experience with birth does the doula have? Is she certified as a doula?
2. What is her philosophy about supporting mothers and fathers during labor?
3. Is she willing to meet with the mother and father, preferably in their home, and well before labor, to find out their preferences and hopes, and help them plan for the birth?
4. Is she available to provide support and reassurance close to the time of birth and during early labor—by close phone contact and later, her presence?
5. What hospitals does she work at in the parents' community?
6. Does she have a backup in case she is ill?
7. What are her fees?
8. At what point in labor does she like to be called?
9. What does she consider the most important elements of care when working as a doula?
10. Will she help parents develop a birth plan?
11. Can she help parents communicate with hospital personnel?
12. What comfort measures has she used for relaxation and pain relief?
13. What kind of help does she offer to husbands or partners of laboring women?
14. What is her experience and skill in teaching breast-feeding techniques?

As we mentioned earlier, the term *doula* has been applied to several different roles. In this book we primarily describe the labor-support doula or the childbirth assistant. In Chapter 10 we see another type of doula—the postpartum doula who provides support in the home to the mother after the baby is born, helping with both the house and the baby.

In some programs, as we mentioned earlier, the term *doula* is used for trained women who help pregnant teenagers and other expectant mothers with special needs, such as single, unsupported women. In this expanded role of the doula, each volunteer works with only one woman—meeting with her once or twice a week during the pregnancy; going with her to the prenatal clinic visits; acting as a support doula during labor, delivery, and the postpartum period; and helping with the multiple challenges and adjustments as the mother cares for her new baby.

In summary, the doula starts out developing a trusting relationship. Soon she becomes a quiet and calming presence. As labor progresses, she moves to a more intense, stronger nurturing role—pacing herself according to the mother's needs and the power of the birth process itself. Her own role with each mother has this developmental aspect and ends with a close tie, for she has shared one of the great moments in a woman's, and a family's, life.

3

Enhancing the Birth Experience

The family is born in the delivery room.

JOHNNY LIND, M.D., STOCKHOLM

After choosing a doula, a couple will find it especially helpful to have two or three visits with her well before labor begins, as mentioned in Chapter 2. These visits with the doula in a relaxed setting in their home permit the parents to discuss their expectations and make plans for labor and delivery. Parents have found this process valuable because they may not yet have shared with each other their personal wishes, thoughts, or feelings about labor and delivery. The visit with the doula creates an occasion to discuss these issues, and the doula adds her encouragement.

PLANNING AHEAD

An experienced doula will be familiar with the regulations of individual hospitals and the protocols of obstetricians. She may also be knowledgeable about the advantages and limitations of the different caregiving settings. It is extremely valuable to learn about these beforehand rather than in the midst of labor, when couples may learn that parts of their long-desired plans are not permitted and then may have their hopes dashed. For example, the hospital may insist on every mother having continuous fetal monitoring and staying in bed. Mothers who feel it is important (as we do) to be free to walk during labor need to know this regulation beforehand, to discuss it with their doctor or midwife, and, if necessary, change to a more flexible hospital.

By discussing their individual goals and various choices in advance, parents gain time to work out their options with their physician. Parents face many choices regarding labor, delivery, and the time afterwards. Not every hospital or birth center can provide them all, so parents may have to be flexible and to consider which are the most important arrangements. The doula can help them define their objectives. Childbirth education will also help in learning what to expect and how to prepare and plan. A doula by no means replaces such preparation. Couples may find that childbirth classes leave them with many questions to ask the doula or the physician, for instance, about the films shown, ways to evaluate the options discussed, or the effectiveness of relaxation and imagery techniques.

Meetings with the doula are the time to review step-by-step what will happen during labor and childbirth, and what the doula will be doing. In this way the couple can become familiar with the procedures while getting to know the doula. During these discussions, parents may on rare occasions find that they are not compatible with this particular woman. If that should be the case, they should make this clear and start looking for another doula more in rhythm with their personalities and styles.

With the selected doula a mother can actually practice various positions for labor and rehearse the relaxation, breathing, and visualization techniques that will help her reduce pain and work through the contractions. This is a good time for the woman to tell the doula about what helps her reduce discomfort when she has pain. While acknowledging this valuable information, the doula can help the mother realize that those techniques may need to change completely during labor. A doula must be able to change with the mother's needs, and the mother must learn to feel safe enough to express her changing needs to both the doula and the father.

EARLY LABOR AND THE DOULA

We have found it helpful for the mother to have the doula come to her home sometime during labor. For some mothers it is helpful for the doula to come there at the beginning of labor, and then to remain in contact either by phone or in person. The exact nature of early labor for the individual mother will determine the timing. It is crucial to provide appropriate support at appropriate times—not too early and not so much as to overwhelm the family. Knowing the doula will be available anytime during labor lessens the parents' initial anxiety, and the couple can then remain at home longer with more productive labor and less pain. When the mother is being supported at home and relaxing in a familiar environment, this early, or latency, phase of labor may be shortened.

Often mothers expecting their first baby rush to the hospital too early in labor and miss out on the benefits of having most of the labor at home. It is not unusual for a mother who has been experiencing some contractions all night to arrive at the hospital and still be at two to three centimeters dilatation. Of course, the final decision to go to the hospital will be made by the woman and her doctor or midwife or the birth facility.

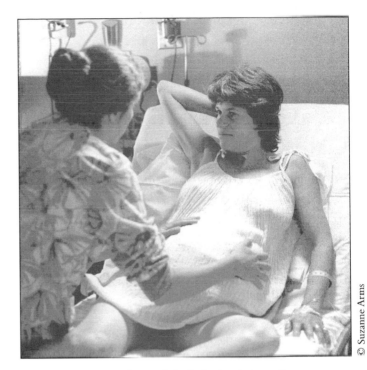

The mother and doula begin their work.

In early labor the mother herself needs to decide when she wants the doula to come. One mother said, "I was using the relaxation methods the doula had taught me for a number of hours, because my labor had started right out with contractions at seven minutes apart. We went to our midwife who said there were some cervical changes but no dilation and suggested we go home and rest and continue what I had learned, to help me through these early contractions. I thought I did not need the doula then because my partner and I got into a rhythm of walking and resting, and I used my breathing and visualizations for the contractions. But when the doula came a few hours later, I realized how relieved I felt. With her soothing words and her massaging me, I relaxed even more. In hindsight I would have had her come sooner." Although this mother was coping well and had a healthy first-stage labor, it lasted several hours, and the couple realized they would have benefited from the doula's help, taking turns with the father and adding her special knowledge of comfort measures.

In addition, this mother revealed that the doula had informed them in her prelabor sessions to ask the midwife if she noticed changes in the cervix, for a number of changes need to occur before dilation begins. In this way the mother did not become discouraged thinking she was in "false labor," but rather in "early labor." A doula can help the mother determine whether she is in real labor and not just having the so-called Braxton-Hicks contractions, which are a normal part of late pregnancy. (See also Chapter 7 in regard to the diagnosis of labor.) Information such as this can be useful for the mother who wants to have a normal labor without a lot of interventions, such as rupture of membranes or augmentation with oxytocin. For her, it is preferable to do most of the labor at home. But this mother needed to learn from the midwife about changes in her cervix.

If the mother stays in the hospital, there is a temptation for hospital personnel, not necessarily the mother's own physician or midwife, to become more active with interventions, such as rupture of membranes and large doses of oxytocin, which she may not want.

These interventions early in labor often create a path that leads toward a need for medical pain relief and instrumental delivery or cesarean section. These decisions are a delicate matter and need to be settled beforehand by the mother, her husband or partner, and her physician. Of course, the doula never interferes with the physician's advice, and the mother will need to follow that advice if there are other concerns. The doula's suggestions are made simply to enhance normal labor.

Coming to the hospital presents a paradox. For some women, arriving at the hospital in active labor causes a disruption in their labor. This may result from being in a strange place, from the chaos, unexpressed fears, or the attitude of worry from personnel. For other women, especially first-time mothers unfamiliar with labor, coming to the hospital relieves them of anxiety. The doula can then meet them at the hospital and continue the physical and mental relaxation activities together.

An anxious mother may feel more comforted that she's in a "safe" place and still take the time she needs to concentrate on her labor. However, even some first-time parents-to-be prefer to remain busy with routine or pleasurable distracting activities, such as watching a movie, cooking, or playing cards, rather than resting to while away the hours in early labor.

In the beginning of labor, the cervix is thinning and beginning to open; early labor can be a time for a woman to work with her body. Having practiced techniques in advance with the doula, the mother may feel more confident and empowered, able to trust her own ability to flow with and handle the early contractions. The time spent preparing reinforces this confidence. It is helpful for women to be supported in a way that enables them to tap into their own strength and resources.

Most mothers progress more rapidly in familiar surroundings, using comfort measures for relaxation learned in advance or suggested by the doula. During this period mothers have found the following suggestions helpful:

1. Walk as much as possible, because this appears to shorten labor and reduce pain.
2. If the membranes are not ruptured, a warm bath can help you remain more relaxed. However, early in labor a warm bath may slow labor; in late labor a bath may increase dilation.[1,2] If the membranes are ruptured, a shower is preferable because of the risk of infection.
3. Change positions at least every half hour.
4. Drink plenty of liquids (fruit juices, soup) and eat light foods if recommended by your doctor. Urinate frequently.

THE ENVIRONMENT OF LABOR

There are many factors in a woman's surroundings that can interfere with her concentration and comfort in labor. These can often be altered by the doula's attention to them. For example, the doula needs to notice the quality of the environment of the room (whether this is a home or hospital birth) and the woman's immediate needs or comfort level. Is she cold? Is the temperature of the room right for her? Does she feel exposed, thirsty, or, in some other way, physically uncomfortable? One woman had wished that her midwife or doula (both present throughout labor) had noticed how cold her feet were, but the mother was in too much discomfort to tell them. She remembered only later how tense this made her.

A woman in labor has heightened sensitivity to aspects of the environment that affect her senses—temperature, sound, odor, space, and visual distractions. The doula can consider what may affect, or be affecting, the woman and

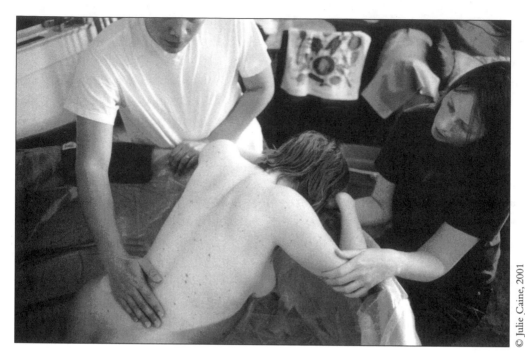

Late in labor, water in a tub or shower is helpful.

make changes in the situation, always keeping in mind the woman's own preferences or checking with her before making changes. During different stages of labor the woman's needs and preferences may change, even within a short period of time. Being flexible is key. Asking the woman if a suggestion is or isn't working can validate her sense of control and choice as well as help her recognize her own needs and give her permission to voice what is important to her.

Is the room too bright? Can one lower shades or lights to create more intimacy or aid concentration? For some women, too dark a room at night may feel lonely or frightening, especially if there are distressing memories from childhood. A doula will continually be 1) noticing, 2) asking the woman, 3) doing something to make an appropriate change, and 4) rechecking to see if the change is helping or not. A room temperature can often be adjusted; if too hot, by a thermostat change, a small fan, or opening a window. Cool cloths, a cold pack, or a cooling shower can help cool the mother. If the room is too cold, warm blankets, socks, and hot packs can warm the mother, or a thermostat change, or closing of a door or window can adjust the room temperature..

In some hospital situations the doula can help the woman create a more home-like environment by bringing some familiar elements of comfort with her such as food, music, and pillows to counter the strangeness or limitations that a typical hospital might provide.

The woman's taste in music may change throughout labor, so different choices should be planned, and the doula should verify that the woman still wants music during any particular stage of labor. Food and drink policies should be checked with the caregivers. A woman's mouth and lips may become dry, and a wet cloth, ice chips, as well as lip balm, can be soothing. Being well hydrated has been shown to help labor. Hospital sounds that are disturbing (televisions blaring, noises from other rooms or the hallway) can be toned down by keeping a door closed and also by helping the woman's inner focus of attention through visualizations or self-hypnosis or with headphones and music she likes.

PRIVACY

A woman's labor can be disturbed if she feels unduly exposed or interrupted. Thinking of how to protect her modesty may include having extra sheets, towels, large T-shirts or robes, or using two hospital gowns put on in opposite directions to help her feel less exposed during exams or protected while in a tub or shower. When using the bathroom, she should have the choice to be private. When she is laboring on the toilet with the doula's assistance, the door can be kept closed. Particular smells can be repugnant. The doula can reassure the woman that the smells and fluids of birth, like blood, feces, and amniotic fluid, are all normal parts of labor and are quickly taken care of by the staff. Some women may vomit during labor and can be reassured that this is normal and then be offered mouthwash or a toothbrush.

The presence and noise made by too many people can disturb labor. Perhaps the doula can remind participants to speak softly while the mother is focusing inward on her labor. Also, doulas can thoughtfully ask people or even extraneous staff (with the primary caregiver's permission) not to wander in and out unless it is medically necessary. The doula can check with the mother whether all the relatives or friends she has invited are still desired to attend. If not, the doula can be the one to have the somewhat difficult task to limit the number without offending anyone. If the mother has changed her mind, or if the doula notices the interruptive aspects of these visitors, the doula can simply say, "We've noticed that Mary can concentrate better if there are fewer people in the room. We'll call you as soon as anything changes. It's good that you want to be so supportive. I know that she will really welcome that support in a short while after the birth and when she's home later."

There have been situations where the woman's support people, unintentionally, have private conversations or nervous chatter. Without a definite role in helping her labor, they are not sure what to do. For example, at a home birth a woman later said that she felt bad, even lonely, that others were conversing with each other while she was struggling with labor, but she didn't know how to tell this to her loved ones.

Another woman in a hospital birth ended up with a number of medical interventions to augment labor because she could not relax into labor with all her relatives present. Later, she remembered feeling invaded by so many people and also upset that after the birth, the family was all involved with the baby, and she was left alone. It turned out that the family did not know what

to do and thought they were helping best by being with the baby. No one was communicating with the mother or asking her what she wanted.

The doula in this type of circumstance can be a liaison between the mother and the staff or family tending the baby or vice versa. The doula can also be a support to the mother going through tests or procedures, if permitted, and then let the mother know she will communicate to the family for her.

In these ways a doula fills a missing gap for the woman. As a doula becomes known and trusted in home or hospital births, the staff or midwife sees her as a member of the team helping the mother with support services that, because of their medical or midwifery concerns, they are not free to give her.

MOVEMENT

Does the mother have the freedom to move around? Movement is highly important in helping labor progress or enabling women to find more comfortable positions in which to labor. Walking, slow dancing, squatting, moving on a birth ball, being on hands and knees, leaning into a partner or doula, are some of the ways to encourage the progress of labor.

At different points in labor, the descent of the infant is aided by changing positions.[3,4,5] For example, when mothers are in the hands-and-knees position infants often rotate in ten to fifteen minutes from a posterior position. Most noteworthy is the use of squatting during second-stage labor with each contraction. This position increases the area of the bony outlet of the pelvis by 28 percent.[6]

TOUCH

The doula must be sensitive to the various ways in which touch can be experienced by the labor-ing woman. There are several aspects of touch during labor. There is medical touch—proce-dures such as checking the baby, the uterus, the progress of labor or dilation; administering IVs and blood-pressure readings; and so forth. There is also reassuring touch—calming, comforting, soothing. In addi-tion, there is touch related to pain-relieving techniques, such as massage, counterpressure touch to relieve back pain, as well as holding and hugging through contractions. Then there is touch used as reminders or cues, such as

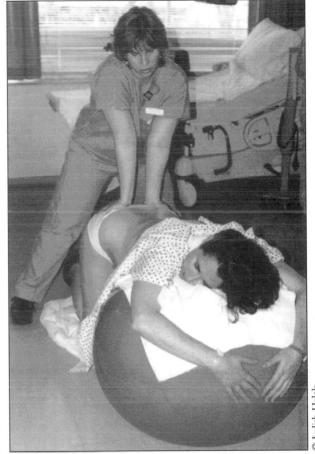

One of the many uses of the birth hall: a comfortable position that also relieves back pressure.

© Judith Halek

hand-holding or arm-stroking, to engage the woman to relax and go deeper into a visualization or self-hyp-notic state.

Massage and touch used according to the woman's comfort are especially effective pain-reducing techniques. They work by releasing oxytocin into

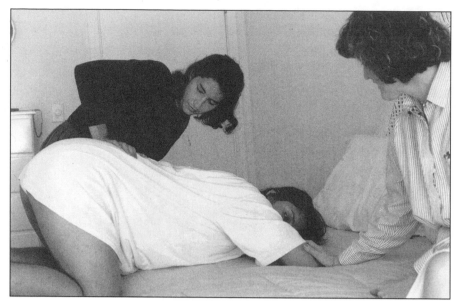

Hands and knees position helps a posterior baby rotate as the doula applies back pressure to relieve pain.

the brain itself, which raises the threshold for pain and produces calmness.[7]

What is the woman's perception of touch? Does the medical touch cause her to tighten up for fear that something might be wrong, or that a medical intervention is being taken out of her control or choice? Or does a painful procedure or touch activate a past memory of pain, trauma, or abuse? When a procedure is done without explanation, it leaves the mother uncertain of what is occurring. That uncertainty may create anxiety, which, in turn, can cause the mother to tighten up from fear and add to pain.

KEEPING THE MOTHER INFORMED

The doula's ability to keep the mother informed is essential. Lack of knowledge of what is happening or of the purpose of any intervention as well as lack of understanding or knowledge of how her own body is functioning or of what's happening with the fetus can all cause fear in the mother. When a doula continually informs the mother, asks her gently what her thoughts, worries, or concerns are, talks to her confidently with real information, the doula can help the woman shift her fear to more inner security. In addition, during any medical procedures, pain can be reduced when the doula remains with the woman, just holding her hand, reassuring her that she's doing well, and describing what each action or intervention means. The doula's constant presence and her reassurance of the normality of what is occurring can be enormously comforting.

SUPPORTING THE MOTHER'S CHOICES WITHIN THE HOSPITAL SETTING

It is also important for the woman to feel that she has control not only over her labor but also has choices about what sort of interventions will be used. Lack of choice and control can lead to a frightening experience and, possibly, to depression later.

What are the procedures and regulations of the hospital? Can the woman have nourishment, liquids, and choice of positions during labor and the second stage? Can she avoid arbitrary interruptions and interventions? One woman whom we interviewed was already pushing, and the baby was crowning, when to her surprise the doctor said, "I'm going to use the vacuum now." This was horrifying to the woman, and she had no control to stop him. Very upset, she left the hospital early. Mothers need to have answers ahead of time to many questions about a hospital's routine. Can she be assured that she won't be separated from the baby? Or that if she plans to breast-feed, that there won't be any bottle given to the baby? For instance if she puts on her birth plan not to have anything administered by bottle, will formula be given? If a hospital wants to do a PKU test, done for all infants to avoid brain damage from a metabolic disorder, and (since the mother's milk has not come in), the hospital might insist that the baby be given formula before the test. However, although the PKU test is very important, it can wait a few days until the mother's milk comes in. The test can be taken in the mother's home or at a clinic visit within the first week. Can the mother be assured that if she needs attention after the birth, that the father or other significant person can hold the baby? Uncertainty about these procedures can be distressing to the mother. Most of these situations can be planned for with the appropriate people beforehand, and a doula can help to remind all concerned of a mother's wishes.

CULTURAL AND EMOTIONAL SENSITIVITY

Some of the most significant elements of the environment surrounding childbirth are the behavior, attitudes, and attentiveness of the caregivers. The doula must be sensitive to the cultural traditions and emotions of the laboring woman and may need to protect the woman from insensitive actions by unsuspecting caregivers. How a woman is touched on certain areas of the body may be fearful to some mothers; for example, massaging the feet can be humiliating to a Chinese woman, whereas touching the head can be frightening to another group, such as the Hmong from Southeast Asia, because of their beliefs about where the soul enters or leaves. Some fathers and mothers can feel humiliated when the woman is having interventions that expose her body, whereas excluding some fathers from the procedures can make them feel left out and helpless. Doulas can inquire about these customs

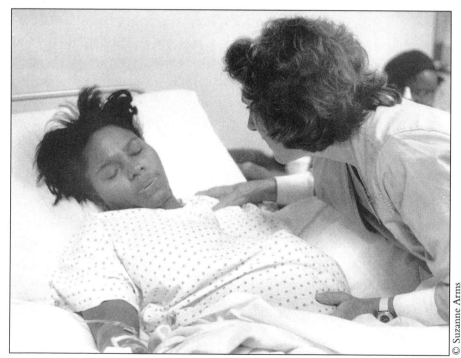

A doula uses her touch to support this mother, who is focusing on breathing slowly and evenly through a contraction.

from the families themselves, as well as read about cultural practices. Language barriers need to be addressed, of course. It is hard to help a woman who cannot understand what is happening or is being said.

When the woman is concentrating intensely and focused inward, inappropriate or loud words can disrupt her concentration. The doula may be able to remind others to approach in a softer manner or wait awhile if it is medically safe to do so. What is important to a laboring woman is sincere talk, not fake or glib reassurance. As the doula acknowledges the woman's real discomfort and does not try to placate her or minimize her experience, the mother learns she can trust the doula.

Being truly helpful in communication means listening to the woman, attempting to understand what she is feeling, what she needs to express, and then working with her to make a situation better or to continue what is already working well. For example, being encouraging to a woman writhing in pain, one would not say, "Oh, you're doing great!" The doula would be completely out of synchrony with her, and the mother would know she could not trust the doula to help her. Rather, by saying with sincerity and feeling, "Oh, that was a hard one. Let's see what we can do to manage the next one better. Right now, let out a sigh, take a big breath, and let your whole body go limp, that's right." The doula stays emotionally connected to the mother, and by joining in her reality, may be able to move her to a more comfortable inner place.

If the woman has a history of abuse or if the doula suspects such a background, the doula must be sensitive to phrases that can be retriggering, such as "open your legs," or "just let your body go." The doula can use more helpful phrases such as, "the baby is pushing the pain away," "The pain is leaving your body with the baby," or try helping the woman stay in the present, "I am with you. You are safe here." (See Appendix A, pages 205–208: Strategies to Help Women with a History of Abuse.)

LATE LABOR AND THE DOULA

Once the mother is at the hospital with labor progressing toward full dilatation of the cervix and delivery is near, the following signs may be noted:

1. Flushing of the face and body
2. An increase in bloody mucus
3. Longer and stronger contractions with little rest in between
4. Legs often becoming shaky

5. A feeling of nausea
6. Feeling of an urge to push

The mother, father, doula, and medical staff often then work as a team, using techniques that are most helpful. In the transition period when labor is most intense, and then when the cervix is fully dilated, the encouraging support of the doula becomes especially helpful. At those times the mother often believes she cannot make it through another contraction, and the father often experiences his most intense distress, feeling helpless at relieving the woman's discomfort. At this point the doula's support can give the mother the incentive to continue; the doula sometimes holds the woman, she reminds the mother (and the father) over and over again that she can continue and is doing great, and she helps the mother breathe through those last powerful contractions. A thirty-three-year-old woman, describing the birth of her third baby, said, "Bill was great, just great—but when I was losing it, I couldn't have done it without Virginia [the doula]!"

When necessary, if there is a change during the course of the labor, the doula will help parents redefine their objectives. The doula can help ensure that parents are informed about every-thing that is happening, step-by-step. When women know what is happening, they begin to realize that progress is being made and that there is an end in sight. If progress is too slow for some reason, they need to know what can and will be done. As Drs. Kierin O'Driscoll and Declan Meagher of Dublin, whose work we describe in Chapter 9, point out, everyone attending a woman in labor "has a responsibility to ensure that [she] genuinely understands the purpose of every medical procedure and the results of every examination."

As we said before, it is important for the mother to tell the doula which techniques particularly help in relieving pain, since each mother responds differently. The doula can then individualize her care. For instance, a woman in transition often finds it very helpful both to focus on the doula's face while breathing through a contraction and to hold the father's hand.

Sometimes during labor something may upset a mother's sense of security. For example, she may not fully understand why a medication or procedure was given and may wonder if this means that something has gone wrong. It is critical that the nurse, the physician, or the doula discuss this with the mother, to answer her questions, clarify her condition, and relieve her concern.

The doula's presence and knowledge can help the mother avoid many of the aspects of childbirth that later might be remembered as highly distressing to parents. A woman can feel traumatized if she has no control, no way to plan, no way to prevent something from happening. When a woman does not understand what is going on or believes her wishes are not being heard, she can feel betrayed, humiliated, or damaged in some way. Each mother may have differing needs; isolation and separation from loved ones are distressful to one mother, whereas being invaded by too many people can be counterproductive to another mother. Often labor stops when too many people are present. One of the authors was consulted about the problem of an unusually high rate of cesarean sections in a midwifery service in a commune in Europe. In this setting the birthing woman was observed routinely by ten to twelve members of the group.

Another of the authors has been consulted by several women suffering from postpartum depression that occurred because of the distress and anger they felt after ending up with a number of unwanted interventions resulting in cesarean sections. After processing their birth experiences, they realized they felt invaded, betrayed, damaged, exposed, and even emotionally abandoned as well as inadequate in themselves in not being able to give birth to their babies. Negative childbirth events sometimes underlie postpartum depression.

The doula's role is to help the parents avoid, as much as possible, events that could cause such severe stress reactions. The doula explains everything that is happening, and, by giving the parents accurate information, she helps the mother make her own choices and voice her own needs. Having a sense of control and a voice in decision-making avoids those feelings of helplessness and powerlessness.

The doula does not interfere with the medical management, but experienced doulas are respected by caregivers. When the doula thoughtfully suggests or asks the caregiver if the mother could try some position change or use another nonmedical comfort measure, most caregivers are willing to accommodate them.

During childbirth both the mother and the father may be stirred in ways they did not expect. Old fears, loneliness, and dependency needs may be triggered. Tearfulness may occur. Excretions, sounds, sights, smells, cries, or screams may trigger old memories of hospitalizations or elicit other unexpected reactions. The doula's sensitive listening can help parents express their feelings and sometimes get to the root of the problem. Then they become freer to move forward with the birth. Many times men feel dizzy and sick and need to leave for a short while to regain calm and control, after which they can return. With a doula present, this is not a problem.

At the end of the delivery, after certain vital assessments are made, the doctor, the nurses, and the doula leave both parents alone with the baby so the new family can get to know each other. Doulas can help parents insist on and protect this time. The infant is in an unusually alert state after birth. All sensory systems are operative, and the baby is particularly responsive.[8] Such an alert state seems programmed by nature so that newborns are ready to meet their parents, and parent and infant can begin to "take each other in" and become acquainted. Newborns often respond to their parents' voices at this early age.

With the UNICEF Baby Friendly Hospital initiative spreading throughout the country, almost all mothers shortly will be given private time in the first hour of life to get to know their newborn and for early suckling. Given this opportunity mothers will benefit from appropriate breast-feeding advice beforehand or at birth, enabling the baby to choose when to latch on.

When providing a quiet private time for parents and their newborn, caregivers need to take into account the mother's state and remain flexible to work with the mother's needs. Some women need more physical care and are not fully ready to take care of the infant alone but still want the baby near them or held by the father or partner.

A new mother told us how tired she had been after a long, but successful, labor, and how surprised she felt at being weak and sore. She had not expected the afterbirth uterine pain and discomfort. Her husband, after having given super care during labor, fell asleep. She did not want to disturb him, but during that postbirth period she felt quite alone as he slept. She needed help with toileting and baby care, but the hospital staff was not around, evidently thinking that the family wanted to be alone.

Another family had decided with their doula that as part of her service, she would stay for four hours after the birth because the doula had explained that the practice in that hospital was to leave the family alone after birth. This couple planned for the doula's presence in case they needed help. All doulas plan to stay at least two hours as part of their service.

On the other hand, a number of couples relish that private time to become acquainted with their baby, to start breast-feeding, and to rest together without having to pay attention to others' needs, demands, or expectations.

The important point here is for parents and their doula to make plans for that early period and to be able to make adjustments to their plan as needed. (See Appendix A, pages 202–205: Immediate Help for Postpartum Care in the Hospital.)

The day after the delivery the doula visits both parents to debrief with them on the labor and go over the labor and birth experience. Surprisingly, many mothers and fathers are concerned that they did something wrong, when actually their behavior has been absolutely normal and they have managed very well. It helps to go over all the details and be reinformed and reassured about the birth. (See Chapter 10 regarding a continuing role for the doula after birth.)

Few other events in the life of a couple bring them together in such a memorable and complex fashion. The strong need of both parents to be cared for during this momentous and demanding event may well be matched by an unusual receptivity. The presence of a nurturing, encouraging person throughout this entire intense experience may have both a conscious and a subliminal effect. In reassuring the parents and enhancing their sense of accomplishment, the doula may be modeling the parental role for them—mothering the mother and parenting the parents. As Professor Johnny Lind of Karolinska Hospital in Stockholm put it: "The family is born in the delivery room."

4

Reducing Discomfort, Pain, and Anxiety in Childbirth

Labor pain, like all other pain, is a function of the whole person, and we can go even farther than that and say that the experience of pain in labor is profoundly influenced by the values of the society in which the woman grew up.

SHEILA KITZINGER,
The Complete Book of Pregnancy and Childbirth

When a woman comes into labor, she brings her past with her: the stories she has heard about birth, any experiences of her own or other's childbirth, and her own early childhood events. She also brings her hopes and fears with her: about pain, about her ability to give birth, as well as about the health and safety of herself and her baby.

This chapter will examine many factors that affect how the mother will experience pain during labor. Central to these is the doula's role to help the mother relax and learn skills of visualization and self-hypnosis to reduce pain, discomfort, and anxiety.

EXPECTATIONS FROM THE PAST

Pregnant women have varied expectations of pain, based on what they have heard or experienced. One thirty-eight-year-old mother, expecting her first baby, said that her own mother described childbirth as one of the hardest experiences of her life. Another first-time mother-to-be became frightened watching a television special on birth in which everyone was rushing around, the mother was screaming and was finally silenced with medication and high-tech interventions. A third mother remembered that in her first birth, she was given pitocin to speed up her labor and found that she could never get on top of the contractions. She remembered begging for an epidural and for this current birth was planning to have one as soon as she started labor. However, when she began experiencing this labor with a doula, she had a very different outcome than she had imagined.

"I became so focused and in tune with the doula's voice and touch, I hardly noticed the pain. We were walking; she always had her hand on me. During each contraction, she showed me how to lean into my husband. He held me as he braced himself against the wall. I could let my whole body relax. She then guided me to breathe through the contractions. She counted backwards 20-to–1, slowly, three times, encouraging me to just breathe through it. By then, I could feel the contraction easing. I could value the power of my body and my baby working together. This was so different from the first birth. We continued this way in a kind of rhythm through each contraction. I depended on her every word. She added an image of ocean waves rolling through the contractions. I was amazed at how powerful I felt and yet safe and relaxed. I wasn't afraid, and I noticed no pain."

Though a doula cannot solve issues in the mother's past or erase the messages the woman has heard, with the future still unknown, she can begin her work being fully present with the woman to calm her fears, to validate her strength, to reassure her that she won't be alone, and to work with her on measures to alleviate pain.

It is helpful if the doula has some idea of the woman's history and beliefs about labor and pain. What are the woman's past experiences of pain? The doula needs to remember that stress, fear, loneliness, as well as the malposition of the baby, and lack of knowledge of how to work with her body, all result in tension that can produce pain. Right from the beginning, she can remind the woman that she will stay with her and work with her to help her manage labor. One woman was afraid that labor would be like the excruciating pain of menses that plagued her during adolescence. Another woman had a childhood memory of her father screaming in pain after an accident. For some women labor can be reframed as good hard work with a desired outcome, with a goal of staying relaxed through that work. One doula guided a woman in this way: "You've probably done hard work before. Can you remember a time you met a challenge and conquered it? Also, there are a variety of ways to help your body work positively with your labor." Does the woman have a history of past medical problems, injuries, or illnesses? Does she fear that labor will repeat some of those discomforts or damage her? She may need to express such fears and then be validated or reassured of the strength and health of her body now.

By asking a few sensitive questions between contractions early in labor, the doula may have an indication of specific fears or concerns the mother has, and, in general, how she is coping. If the doula has been able to meet the mother before labor, she could have learned then about any fears or anxieties that could potentially interfere with labor progress, as well as the mother's hopes for how the birth will happen. Using good listening skills, the doula encourages the mother to express her feelings. Once her fears, dreams, and feelings are truly acknowledged, the mother is often more open to work together with the doula to problem-solve or start planning in a realistic way.

Aside from the fear of pain mentioned above, some women fear damage to their body: torn tissues, danger to the baby, the rare condition of rupture of the uterus (especially when attempting a vaginal birth after a cesarean section [VBAC]), abandonment by their partner, loss of control with labor, discomfort with strangers, invasive procedures, and being inadequate to take care of a baby. If labor is slowing down, a doula might ask "How are you feeling right now?" and then when the mother answers, the doula should restate her answer to be sure she understands the mother's meaning. "I'm so afraid of ripping in the birth canal, and I don't want an episiotomy." "You're worried that pushing the baby through will cause a tear, but you want to avoid an episiotomy. Is that right?" If the mother confirms the doula's understanding of her concern, the doula can continue with potential ways to help, or at least show sensitive caring and attentiveness. "Other women express that fear, too." By validating the mother's fear, instead of dismissing it, the doula can offer new ways to think about the pushing stage. "Fortunately, we know a lot more today about how to protect the perineum and how to help the baby out to avoid a tear. A minor one will heal naturally or with a few stitches. Many women don't know that at this point in labor there is a wonderful hormone flowing through the whole area now called relaxin, which causes the tissues to be as stretchy, strong, and supple as soft elastic. The birth canal opens like a soft angora sweater over the baby's head." Here, information coupled with imagery and reframing can offer the mother an alternative way to perceive her body.

Another question a doula might ask is, "What was going through your mind during that contraction?" Depending on the woman's response, being troubled or just coping, the doula can determine what steps to take to help the mother.

© Marilyn Nolt

As the contraction starts, the doula quietly reminds the mother to breathe through it, adding her visualization of ocean waves.

mother put aside past fears. The mother might imagine putting those fears into a big container with a lid on that only she can lift off when she is ready, and then imagine placing the container outside or someplace far away. Or the mother may want to imagine a special inner guide or loving being who surrounds her as she gives birth to her baby.

MEDICATION AND PAIN

Over the years a major focus of obstetrics has been the management of pain. In the early 1930s childbirth was moved from the home to hospital in the hope of providing women with "painless" childbirth. Many drugs have been used to reduce pain, some of which have undesirable effects on the newborn. There has been a brisk discussion of a number of pharmacological methods, but not enough is yet known of the full impact of these on the newborn. Narcotics such as pethidine or Demerol have noticeable effects on the baby, for significant amounts pass from the mother into the infant's circulation. Babies born after the administration of such drugs may be less active, are less

She may need guidance on position change, massage, visualization, or other comfort measures. One valuable[1] study noted that a response of considerable distress early in labor frequently indicated a longer, more difficult labor.

Another reassuring technique doulas may use is called "emotional containment." This uses imagery to help the

likely to open their eyes immediately, show less hand-to-mouth activity, less seeking of the breast, and significantly less effective sucking within the first few days of life.[2]

Not much is yet known about the full impact or long-term effects of epidural analgesia on the infant. The majority of lactation consultants believe that epidural analgesia slows the ability of the baby to begin breastfeeding. They observe that the baby takes the nipple in his or her mouth but does not begin to suck, and that normal lactation may take several days to begin. However, there are no randomized trials comparing babies whose mothers have no medication with infants born following an epidural analgesic. We hope these important studies will be available shortly.

Epidurals given early in labor also numb and immobilize the mother, preventing her ability to work with her labor, often slowing the labor down, and have been shown to result in more "operative" vaginal (forceps, vacuum) deliveries. However, light and late epidurals after 6 centimeters often do not have this effect.

© Marilyn Nolt

Now in control with her breathing and imagery, the mother moves through the contraction.

THE DOULA'S ROLE IN HELPING A WOMAN WITH AN EPIDURAL

Although women in labor with an epidural anesthesia do not require the typical labor-intensive hands-on comfort measures through each contraction as with women in nonmedicated birth, they still require the skills and spirit of doula work—emotional support, reassurance, information, and appropriate physical help.

The mother has no pain, but depending on the level of the epidural the trade-off is no feeling in her lower body. She dozes, sometimes sleeps, then alerts, wondering how long it will take, is the baby okay, will it wear off, will she have any side effects, will it affect the baby later. She worries that her partner is bored, not involved, sometimes watching TV. She doesn't notice the contractions; it feels like a non-birth.

The father may also be unsure of what's happening, feel somewhat lost, having nothing to do. A number of partners just sit nervously, holding the woman's hand.

The mother's urge to push and ability to judge how to push in the second stage is reduced. Reduced muscle tone may require more instrumental deliveries by forceps and vacuum. Since the mother is so removed from the physical experience of contractions, caregivers depend more on the fetal monitor, and vaginal checks to assess labor progress. Up to 10 percent of women receive only partial pain relief. If the epidural goes too high, some women feel as though they can't breathe. Frequently, there is a rise in the woman's body temperature which reaches the level of a fever during an epidural. Since the

increased temperature in the woman could be caused by an infection and not the epidural, the newborn baby often requires a blood culture, sometimes a lumbar puncture, and could require an extended stay in the hospital for a course of antibiotics. This rise in temperature occurs in about 35–40 percent of women, usually those who had their epidural placed early in labor and had a prolonged course. During labor, some women complain of shivering and itching and experience urine retention requiring a bladder catheter.

Along with breast-feeding difficulties, which are a major problem after an epidural, newborns may be less responsive in the first several days, more irritable and inconsolable, have less ability to track objects or self-soothe, such as turning away from loud noises or sucking their hands. Parents may need help to recognize these reactions and allow their babies time to recover from the birth and the medication rather than assume or worry that the infant is compromised.

Although relieved of pain, women can still feel anxious, abandoned, unsure of their progress or the purpose of additional interventions, and helpless to function on their own. Right from the beginning, the doula can explain the procedures and be a liaison to the woman and partner as the epidural is placed. Some women have a fear of something placed in their back that they cannot see. The doula can remind the woman to stay relaxed, create positive images with her, help her with breathing and calming techniques, and validate how well she is doing. Some mothers feel disappointed that they needed an epidural and require support and reassurance for this decision.

During the hours of labor, the doula can indicate the contractions for the mother, even having the mother feel her abdomen with her hands during contractions. The doula can assist the mother safely into a change of positions if labor slows, if the fetal heart rate drops, or in second stage when she is ready to push.

The doula can help the mother avoid muscle or ligament injury by avoiding sudden jerks or movements. If a woman becomes frightened when the numbing sensation goes too high, the doula can help the mother stay calm, be reassured she is getting enough oxygen, and guide her through each breath. The doula has to be sure there is no threat to her breathing. If not sure, she must call the anesthesiologist or nurse since this situation can be life-threatening. With cool washcloths to the mother's face, neck, and chest, if all is well, the doula can cool the mother who is overheated or who develops a fever.

In addition, some women may tolerate letting the epidural wear off and will need knowledgeable doula support to increase their urge to push in second stage. Doulas can continue their role in facilitating breast-feeding after the birth if the mother needs this assistance. Thus, even with mothers having an epidural, doulas have an important role.

RELAXATION AND VISUALIZATION

Reducing pain in labor depends upon staying relaxed, working with one's body, and feeling confident, reassured, and in control. Physical relaxation methods include breathing and muscle-releasing exercises,[3] and visualizations of relaxing scenes, ideas, or processes of the body.[4]

Relaxation techniques and mental imagery play a significant role in self-hypnosis; the difference is only a matter of degree. Most women can learn some form of relaxation and visualization methods. We humans are visualizing or creating mental pictures of events all the time. Unfortunately, around childbirth many women have acquired a number of fear-producing or negative images and ideas. Therefore, creating more confidence-inspiring and positive images or thought forms can have a beneficial effect in reducing fear and anxiety. Whether or not one experiences the mental deepening or dissociative quality that is characteristic of self-hypnosis, the mother in labor can still benefit through the relaxation effects.

With visualization one creates a variety of internal sensory experiences that include sights, sounds, smells, texture, and a kinesthetic sense of body position and activity. Visualization is not just sight-oriented; it taps into the mind's whole array of memories and senses to enhance the inner mental and physical involvement. By doing this, one is distracted from the outer events or from discomfort in labor. Disturbing feelings and sensory experiences can be transformed or shaped into comforting ones. For example, feelings of pain and tension can be numbed, softened, even released. One can add colors of the rainbow, sounds of music, nature, waterfalls, or images or other sensations of water. These imaginative activities help the mind focus on an inner experience of relaxation and comfort.

Along with developing sensory changes in visualizations, one can add helpful verbal suggestions and then strengthen these words with appropriate images. The words and images can be adapted to the normal stages and progression of labor.

SELF-HYPNOSIS

When a woman is using visualization to facilitate self-hypnosis, she develops a series of physical and mental steps that help her mind move to an ever deeper level of relaxation and of inner-focused mental attention.[5] However, she stays in control of her own experience and chooses the level of mental experience she wants. She moves into this state knowing she can change any aspect of it at will.

There are several ways to induce self-hypnosis. Simply by going through the relaxation exercises and imagining oneself in a special place and then enhancing the experience with some sensory imagery, one can move into a light trance.

Another way to put the mind into this trance state is to focus one's eyes on a spot on the ceiling or rotate up toward the forehead, take a deep breath, let the eyelids flutter closed, and let a feeling of relaxation flow through the body when releasing the breath. By continuing the relaxation breathing and muscle releasing, combined with a variety of engaging images, one can shift one's external attention into this inner state of awareness and away from discomfort.

Some people use metaphors in their visualizations such as going down a beautiful stairway, or a lovely path to a

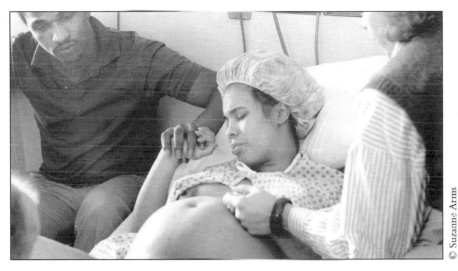

Deep in concentration, the mother maintains her inner focus
with support from both the father and doula.

safe and beautiful and peaceful place. Others simply give themselves the suggestion of drifting deeper and deeper and deeper with every easy breath out, or when descending down each step. Still other people use a counting method to guide themselves into a relaxed state. "As I count slowly and easily from ten to one, I can feel myself going deeper and deeper, getting more and more relaxed . . . ten . . . deeper and deeper . . . nine . . . even more relaxed . . . etc. I can enjoy becoming even more relaxed . . . my arms and legs heavier and heavier . . . more and more relaxed . . . "

Suggestions for self-anesthesia or developing a numbing sensation have the most effect when in a trance state.[6] In this inner state, the mind is open to a myriad of sensory impressions that can help create comfort and maintain healthy labor progression. "As I get more deeply relaxed, the cervix is opening and opening . . . "

Suggestions using positive words and metaphors with their figurative meanings often tap into the right brain and bypass the critical left side of the brain, so that one's sensory experience is enhanced and not stopped by rational thought. Here is where creative thinking comes in. One woman chose the following self-suggestions: "With each surge (contraction), I swim deeper and deeper into the beautiful changing colors of the tropical waters with my friendly dolphin. I am protected and safe . . . and then I rest and float . . . and rest and float. As I go deeper and deeper and become more relaxed, the surges are stronger and stronger, and I ride through them, and I breathe through them . . . and then I float and rest . . ." Through each contraction, she simply imagined herself in the water.

Women benefit by exploring images and suggestions that individually suit them, then using them or having the father or doula repeat them during practice sessions or in labor.[7] When women practice these or put them on tape, they develop their own rhythm and inner imagery and then find that they have these readily available during labor to help them work through the contractions.

Some other choices women have used are the following:

- "With every contraction, I become more and more numb.
- "I am in charge of my own experience, and I can trust more and more the wisdom of my body."
- "With each wave, the cervix is opening and opening . . . like a flower . . ."

- "The pain gathers in a big pink balloon and then floats away."
- "I can relax and let go and swim even more easily through the comforting waters, knowing others are watching and taking care of whatever I need."
- "With each surge, my baby is coming closer and closer."
- "My baby is being hugged as he goes down the water slide to my waiting arms."

It is important to add to any suggestions during labor that the woman can always ask for whatever she needs or talk with her caregiver, and then when whatever is necessary is taken care of, she can go back to being even more relaxed.

Self-hypnosis is an acquired skill. We instruct people to practice moving into the inner state and bringing themselves out of the state by a similar metaphor. For example, if one counts oneself into the relaxed state, use the opposite count to feel oneself coming back to the present state of awareness; or if one walks down an imaginary stairway to a peaceful place, imagine oneself coming back up the stairway. Whatever method is used, one should bring oneself out of the state gently and slowly so that all bodily systems are integrated and balanced and centered. Just as one would not jump out of bed too quickly, allow the system to return from the inner focus to the outer reality slowly and comfortably.

To summarize, self-hypnosis is a natural state of mind, an altered state of consciousness away from external awareness. This dissociative quality of this state can enhance relaxation as well as generate some desired physical responses. It is well known that mental imagery can affect physiological changes in the body. When people think of something frightening, the heart beat and breathing speed up and muscle tension increases and stress hormones can be activated. By thinking of something calming, peaceful, soft, safe, the quieting response of the body is released, and the person can become calm again.

We go in and out of this spontaneous trance state several times a day, when we are intensely focused on a book or a movie, or concentrating on a memory. In labor that ability to focus attention on positive and comforting images or inner experience can divert one's attention away from the pain and onto the inner imagery or sensation of relaxation.

Some people experience this state in deep prayer or meditation. In fact, some women prefer to use the soothing and comforting images and words of spiritual figures to help them in childbirth.

A woman is able to move easily in and out of this state as she wishes, but the more practice she has, the easier it is to go into the state in order to stay relaxed throughout labor.

In labor, hypnosis helps a woman feel in control and take in or hold in her mind a series of suggestions to stay relaxed and focused during the changing aspects of labor. Many of these processes are similar to or overlap with other methods of relaxation training. As we've said, the ability to stay focused and to move fairly deeply into this mental trance state versus simple relaxation is only a matter of the depth of imagination. One can be, for example, daydreaming in a relaxed state, but quite aware of the neighborhood children playing outside. But one can be so engrossed in inner thoughts and images of the daydream that the outer sounds appear to fade away from awareness. However, in both cases there is a dual level of consciousness: one part of the mind in the peaceful daydream scene, the other part relaxing but also keeping an awareness of the present outside situation. If there were a problem in either case, one would simply become alert, because in a trance one is not asleep, not unconscious, but simply absorbed in inner thoughts and images. Some have called self-hypnosis a type of "controlled imagination." This state can occur spontaneously without any formal method of induction. Contrary to common myths, there is nothing mystical or magical about hypnosis. A common fear is loss of control, or giving up one's power to the caregiver. Another myth is that people who can be hypnotized must be gullible. People fear that they will be influenced to do whatever is asked of them or that under hypnosis they will reveal embarrassing or personal things. From stage hypnosis and TV, people fear they may also get stuck in hypnosis. All of these beliefs are untrue. With the skill of self-hypnosis, people can actually develop more sense of control and increase their awareness of inner and outer events.

It is important to distinguish the use of self-hypnosis for labor from that of clinical hypnosis or hypnotherapy. Self-hypnosis for pain relief in labor is not therapy. All hypnosis is in reality self-hypnosis, that is, to enter this state is a voluntary choice, and one allows the mind to experience this state. Ideally, one learns the process from a skilled guide or therapist. The learning can be reinforced by appropriate self-help books.

It is interesting that a century ago hypnosis was a principal technique used for pain relief in childbirth. Self-hypno-sis may not only help shorten labor, and reduce fear and anxiety, but also increase comfort in the postpartum period. The use of relaxation, imagery, and suggestion has also been helpful in enhancing breast-feeding in mothers with both full-term and premature babies.[8]

One cannot be relaxed and tense at the same time, so as the mother learns to couple images and sensory experiences of releasing tension with the contractions, relaxation can ensue. These mental activities send nonstress hormones and other neurological and physiological messages throughout her body. Paradoxically, the deeper the state of relaxation, the more the mother's contractions become productive, and labor makes better progress. Self-hypnosis helps a woman separate her attention from discomfort and change distressing sensations to more comforting ones. This in turn helps her feel more in control of her labor and more confident in her body. However, even with this inner absorption, women should be reassured that they will always be able to respond to anything they need to and will always be able to become alert and express their needs, and to reenter the state at will.[9]

All women can benefit from relaxation techniques because labor works better when the woman is not stressed.

But self-hypnosis may not be for everyone. Some people are more confident or comfortable than others in using their imagination. Certain obstetrical events may interfere with or preclude self-hypnosis. There may be discomfort with the relaxed trance state, for the dissociative aspect of hypnosis may remind the mother of an earlier time of having felt "spaced out." Dissociation is caused by a variety of situations and may have originally occurred as an emotional defense mechanism to remove oneself mentally from painful experiences. Children as well as adults learn this automatic way to defend themselves. Even in childbirth classes, some women do not feel comfortable lying down and doing simple visualizations. They fear losing control in the trance-like state. However, once a woman understands her feelings, she may be helped to imagine herself in a safe place in her mind, or imagine being protected by loving real, imaginary, or spiritual figures.

It is hard work to stay so focused through the power of contractions, through disruptions, interruptions, and the chaos of delivery suites. When women feel they have accomplished this, they feel incredibly empowered and strong. The entire goal is to learn to stay mentally focused on an inner positive image, experience, or on chosen suggestions so as to feel mentally separate from pain or discomfort. This process is greatly helped when someone takes the role of protector. The father or partner can help the mother maintain the self-hypnotic state in the midst of interruptions. The doula can also do this or spell the partner. For example, if someone comes in and asks the woman a question while she is in her inward focused concentrated state, and the question is not medically essential, the doula can answer the question politely or offer to ask the mother when she is not involved in her self-hypnosis.

The use of voice is important. A woman in labor is already naturally in an altered state, a spontaneous trance, so words are taken in at a subliminal level of consciousness and can have much power and effect. Most doulas already use a comforting tone of voice, a rhythmic cadence to help the mother through contractions, such as, "That's right, just breathe through it . . . Gooooood." By offering a continuous ritual of rhythmic words, breathing with the mother, helping her stay focused on the images she has chosen, the doula is already using a hypnotic method to keep the woman in her concentration. The woman herself and her partner can develop suggestions to help her return to her self-hypnotic state with different

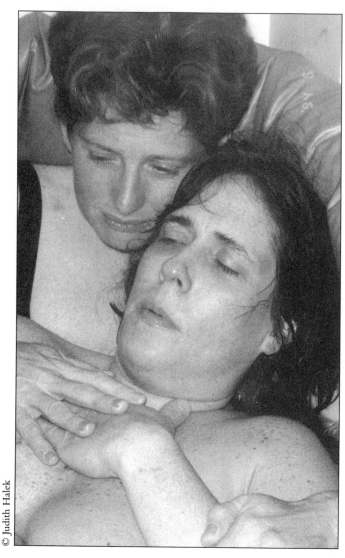

With her soothing voice and touch, the doula combines imagery with water to enhance the mother's relaxation.

When using self-hypnosis for childbirth, it is important to have a knowledgeable partner or doula with experience and understanding of the hypnotic state. Because many people give themselves negative messages or suggestions about birth without realizing it, understanding the power of the mind can counteract this tendency. Through self-hypnosis, the parents-to-be can learn to clear away or erase negative messages or fears. With hypnosis, they can use the power of their minds with visualization to enhance their inner connection to their unborn child, and women can develop trust in their bodies to release the baby into their waiting arms. (See Appendix B, pages 211–225 for visualizations and self-hypnosis exercises.)

FEELINGS AND SOUNDS

Helping women express feelings and utter sounds may relieve tension. The doula can work with women who are comfortable with this, or make sounds along cues so that she is not dependent on any one person's voice.

with the woman, encouraging the mother to let tension go with each sound. Many women fear that they will sound out of control. It has not been uncommon for a caregiver to admonish a laboring woman who is moaning or uttering a guttural sound while giving birth. Women have described how humiliated they felt. Making low sounds or groans deep in the throat through a contraction has an effect parallel to opening the birth canal, and some women feel supported if the birth companion joins them or encourages them. Some cultures use song or chants to bring the baby into the world.

Some women worry about their behavior in handling the pain of labor or their ability to do so. Other women fear that if they can't handle the pain, something is wrong, or they feel shame or anger that what they prepared for is not working. Here is where the doula can ask the mother what she is thinking or feeling as she went through a contraction: "What was going through your mind during that contraction?" The doula can acknowledge the mother's experience, giving her permission to give voice to her feelings and fears, so as to help her shift to a more positive response. "I feel as though it's a ball of fire." The doula might respond, "With that next contraction, change that ball of fire to a snowball cooling you." Changing negative thoughts or comments to more positive ones or creating appropriate affirmations along with visualizations or guided imagery helps women focus on the power of their bodies to give birth or conversely distract them from discomfort. "I'm hugging my baby through the contraction." "I'm swimming with the dolphin through the wave." "I'm going deeper and deeper, relaxing into this surge of energy."

Some years ago a doula had an experience with a laboring woman that surprised her. During the whole labor, the mother was bossy, negative, even yelling at the doula, but was extremely sweet and pleasant-sounding to everyone else, including her partner. Her persona to the outside world was thus quite different. It was a façade of being perfect. She showed much gratitude to everyone's efforts, but to the doula the mother remained quite demanding. Shortly after the birth, the woman said to the doula, "Thank you so much for letting me say everything I was feeling. You were the only one I could be real with. I felt safe to be myself." The doula related that through the difficult birth, she remained steady for this woman even though the woman's hostility was apparent. This experience reaffirmed for the doula the importance of being the emotional safety net for anything the mother needed to express without taking it personally.

When a woman is in labor, she is coping with a demanding, difficult, potentially frightening, and painful experience that brings out needs she may not have been aware of before. Most women are socialized into certain kinds of public behavior and hold back out of fear of embarrassment. Women apologize for making sounds, for the labor taking too long, for not doing everything they thought they could or should, even though in labor their behavior would be considered absolutely normal. In our culture, birth sometimes seems like a performance, or a TV show in which women are expected to act a certain way, and if they don't, they feel humiliated, out of control, or judged. This judgment is often directed at the woman by herself.

When a woman feels protected and safe in the arms of the doula, literally or figuratively, she realizes, perhaps intuitively, that she can be herself. The woman described above recognized that the doula was strong and would not collapse if the woman were her true self. Again we might point out that when a doula remains accepting, nurturing, competent, and strong, the woman can

internalize a model that might help her remain both nurturing and strong with her own child during tough moments.

In this regard doulas need to understand the power and potential of their role. Each must search within to find her own true self in order to be available at this deep level for a woman giving birth. It is essential that doulas examine their own motives for doing this work, take it seriously, show up promptly and prepared for the birth, not leave or disappoint a woman, but remain engaged and appropriately involved throughout the labor.

RECOGNIZING A MOTHER'S CHANGING NEEDS

Remembering that each labor is different even for the same mother, a doula's support must be guided by the immediate needs of the woman. One doula described for us three very different births with the same woman. During the first birth, she never left the woman's side, holding, massaging, guiding the woman's visualization, walking with the woman. The woman wanted help with every contraction. They moved from tub to toilet, to using the large "birth ball," to walking, and back again. The doula brought the partner in as he wished, but with the intensity of the contractions, he was only comfortable massaging his wife's hands. The mother revealed that even though the labor was an intense twelve hours, she felt totally safe, in charge, and to her, time passed quickly. She described a trance-like mental state. With the second birth a few years later, the husband worked more closely with his wife and the doula. In the third birth, the mother wanted the doula just to be there in the room with occasional guidance or turn taking, while she and her husband handled the majority of the labor. The woman later said, "Just your presence was calming and made me feel secure. I knew you'd help if I needed you to."

Letting the woman say what she wants is a cornerstone of doula care. For instance, at a home birth during a period where the mother wanted to rest on her bed, the doula remained at the woman's head, breathing with her, and gently guiding her with the woman's chosen images through each contraction. After a time the midwife suggested the woman be left alone for awhile, thinking

© Suzanne Arms

The upright position and movement help the baby descend.

that the mother needed to get more into her labor solo. Her doula did not feel comfortable suggesting otherwise to the midwife who was the primary caregiver. Two years later the mother told her doula that this was the worst moment in labor for her. She felt totally abandoned and betrayed but helpless to contradict the midwife's plan.

The doula needs the confidence to help the mother express her needs to the caregiver especially before and during any intervention. How a woman is listened to and responded to can affect her stress level and subsequently her experience of pain. The doula's presence, touch, and voice, coupled with her knowledge of labor, can calm the mother and diminish her perception of pain. However, the doula needs to know her limits, and occasionally when a fetal malposition does not change, or a woman is not progressing as expected or feels great discomfort, medical help can give her relief. When this is necessary the doula must validate the woman's courage as well as her decision to have such help.

REDUCING STRESS

Every aspect of support must start with the idea of reducing stress—mental, emotional, and physical. The goal is to enhance the woman's ability to relax. The body's stress system is called the sympathetic nervous system, which produces what we call the "fight-or-flight response." The opposite of the sympathetic nervous system is the system that creates calm and a feeling of well-being called the parasympathetic nervous system. The hormones of the sympathetic nervous system are epinephrine and norepinephrine. The parasympathetic nervous system produces a hormone called oxytocin. Reducing the stress response enhances the body's own production of oxytocin, as well as natural opiates called endorphins.

When the woman can relax, oxytocin strengthens the contractions of the uterus. It also allows the muscles to function properly, the longitudinal muscles to expel the baby and the lower uterine muscles to relax, stretch, and open to release the baby. When a mother's body is tense, the opposite occurs; the upper muscles of the uterus loosen and stop contracting, and the lower muscles tighten to retain the infant. This is perhaps nature's way of stopping labor if the mother has to flee from a frightening experience. Obviously, stress hormones have their place when one is in real danger. The goal of a doula and all those involved in childbirth must be to lessen the feeling of both danger and stress in labor. Fear puts the body into alert with the production of stress hormones. The fight-or-flight response occurs and the body gears for defense, sending blood to other organs of the body. If blood flow is reduced to the uterus, the uterine muscles constrict, causing the circular muscles of the cervix to tighten up, and dilation is impeded. Also, there may be less oxygen sent to the fetus. When the vertical muscles of the uterus continue their attempt to expel the baby, and the cervix resists, the baby's head pushes against tense muscles. This causes more pain and lengthens labor.

When labor is not impeded by undue stress and fear, the woman's own natural oxytocin is secreted from the posterior pituitary gland into the bloodstream. At the same time, her brain also secretes oxytocin to other areas within the brain itself. This has four effects. First, it markedly increases the pain threshold, so that the mother has reduced sensitivity to pain. Second, it results in drowsiness. Third, it results in some relaxation or calming, and finally, after the birth it helps the woman feel closer to the baby. The synthetic oxytocin (called pitocin), which is injected into the woman's bloodstream to stimulate labor, cannot reach the pain-relieving area of the brain, since there is a barrier to this substance passing from the blood to the brain. The synthetic pitocin results in stronger contractions for the woman. This usually results in her desire for pain medication or an epidural. In contrast when the mind and body relax, and natural oxytocin is produced, the system works more efficiently; the circular muscles of the cervix draw back gently, the cervix opens, stretches easily, the vertical muscles draw up and aid the opening, so that the baby can maneuver and the uterine muscles can push the infant out.

Fear, tension, and pain create a negative feedback loop. Any one of these elements can trigger the others and keep the stress response active. For example, a mother's negative beliefs about her body or the baby may activate fear and tension and cause her to hold back in labor. Lack of knowledge of birth may activate fear of the unknown, increasing tension. Negative memories of past events may activate post-traumatic stress reactions causing fear. Uncomfortable positions, as well as insensitive or negative treatment, can increase pain, adding to stress.

The doula can develop a variety of skills to enter into and interrupt the woman's stress cycle at any point. Using a variety of nonpharmacological and nonmedical methods, the doula's comfort measures can work in an active manner or sometimes in a more delicate or subtle way to lessen distress.

Comfort measures can be divided into five categories: 1) actions and behaviors that give emotional and psychological support; 2) mental activities that divert attention from pain or focus attention on thoughts or images that increase mental and physical relaxation; 3) physical activities such as relaxed breathing, muscular relaxation exercises, movement, position changes, use of water, heat, cold; 4) touch, including massage, acupressure, pressure, and counterpressure; and 5) rhythmic activities, music, chanting, singing, etc.[10]

Over the years experienced labor-support women and caregivers have developed movements, positions, massage, and caring techniques that facilitate the descent of the baby and ease discomfort. There is strong evidence that having freedom of movement and changing positions, using touch and massage, judicious applications of coolness and warmth to areas of discomfort, and counterpressure to relieve back labor pain all help relieve pain during labor.[11]

Helping the mother to stay relaxed is a cornerstone of all these techniques.

Apart from the skills and knowledge of these movements, positions, and activities, it is essential that the medical staff be willing to explain their diagnosis of the mother's stage of labor, the position and well being of the fetus, as well as willing to allow freedom of movement and time to make choices as labor progresses.

THE IMPORTANCE OF TIME

In labor time is a friend. The cervix needs time to ripen; the hormones need time to kick in. The baby needs time and space to maneuver. The woman needs time to go into a laboring mind. Those supporting her need to respect all the time this takes. Mothers who feel rushed into decisions will naturally grow tense, leading to a cycle of pain and fear. Mothers who are allowed to work with the contractions, with time to understand what is happening and to ask for the help they need, will feel empowered and recognize the strength and wisdom of their own bodies.

5

Obstetric Benefits of Doula Support

[The mother] is in the grip of natural forces and of a
process that is as automatic as ingestion, digestion and
elimination, and the more it can be left to nature to get
on with it the better it is for the woman and the baby.

D. W. WINNICOTT,
Babies and Their Mothers

Over the past decade, evidence for the benefits of doula support has been accumulating dramatically. There are now sixteen published, randomized controlled studies including more than 5,000 women. These trials, in Belgium, Botswana, Canada, Finland, France, Greece, Guatemala, South Africa, and the United States, have examined whether emotional and physical support in labor by an experienced woman altered length of labor, need for pain medication, epidurals, and other obstetric interventions, and what effects such support had on the well-being of the baby and later maternal behavior. The mothers in all the studies were healthy women at term who had a normal pregnancy. Almost all the women were having their first pregnancy. In evaluating the benefits of any particular medical procedure, it is important to know whether the results are statistically significant or whether they could have occurred by chance. The studies of the effects of doula support have been analyzed by precise statistical methods and published in peer-reviewed medical journals.

Mothers in each of the studies, except two, were invited to participate when they arrived in labor at the hospital and were told they might or might not have a woman (the doula) who would stay with them continuously during their labor and delivery, but they would all receive the same medical care whether they participated or not. In two studies, in Cleveland[1] and Oakland,[2] the mothers gave approval for participation in the study in the prenatal period but were not randomized to the control or doula group until they were admitted to the hospital.

A COMPARISON OF INTERMITTENT AND CONTINUOUS EMOTIONAL SUPPORT

One of the interesting questions raised in the labor-support trials is whether continuous or intermittent support is more beneficial. A recent study, conducted by one of the authors with colleagues, compared five trials in which the doulas were continuously with the mothers in labor, except for a very brief snack or toilet breaks, with six trials where the supportive woman had to leave the mother for long periods during labor because of other duties.[3] Appendix C lists the five intermittent trials and adds five new continuous trials to the five previous continuous support studies for a total of fifteen. The characteristics of the doulas and the women in each trial are noted. Continuous labor support from a doula in the ten studies reduced the odds of receiving analgesia by 31 percent, decreased the use of oxytocin to stimulate labor by 50 percent, forceps deliveries by 34 percent, and cesarean sections by 45 percent. The findings indicate that the presence of a doula on an intermittent

basis, when compared with no doula support does not confer the benefits seen in the mothers who received continuous support.

Because the labor attendants in the group of intermittent support studies were primarily experienced midwives or midwifery students while the women providing continuous support were mainly lay doulas, this difference rather than the duration of support could also explain the differences in the results. Another possibility is that the quality of support given by the lay doulas is more helpful because they have a strong interest in their task, are able to focus entirely on one person during the entire labor, and believe that the provision of emotional and psychological support is an important activity. Because the intermittent support group of studies were conducted in settings that had low baseline levels for the use of forceps (6 percent) and cesarean sections (7 percent), it may have been unrealistic to expect any improvement in these particular practices. However, it should be noted that the baseline percentages of oxytocin augmentation and analgesia were higher than in the continuous support group of studies and yet changed insignificantly with the presence of the intermittent doula. This study strongly supports the clinical observation of Dr. Kieran O'Driscoll at the National Maternity Hospital in Dublin. He noted that if the student midwife providing continuous emotional and physical support leaves for just five minutes, when she returns, it takes nearly an hour to get the mother back to her earlier calm state.

As a result of the data from this study, as well as other clinical observations, we recommend that the doulas leave the mother as briefly as possible, even when there is effective pain relief due to epidural analgesia.

Doula Support for Couples

The first six randomized trials of doula support, described later in this chapter, were carried out in hospitals where mothers labored alone or contact with the male partner and other visitors during labor was limited to brief visits. Up to this point, the studies had not addressed the effect of the father's presence during labor on obstetric outcomes, such as cesarean deliveries. A more recent randomized study was carried out in a university medical center obstetric unit in Cleveland.[4] The design of the study that looked at the effect of doula support for couples was different from our previous randomized doula trials. In the earlier studies the mothers learned about the study and were enrolled when they came to the hospital and were admitted in early labor. For the couples study, the research assistant explained the study either with the mother-to-be alone or with her partner at a childbirth education class or in the Women's Health Clinic at one of the prenatal appointments. The assistant also checked that this would be the mother's first baby, that she was healthy, and that she had no complications. The woman was asked for her consent to take part in a study and if she expected to be accompanied by her male partner.

Five hundred and fifty-five low-, middle-, and high-income couples were randomly assigned to have either continuous emotional support by a doula or to receive routine obstetric care. Thus, mothers in the doula group were accompanied by their partner and a doula, whereas couples in the control group labored alone. The mothers supported by both their partners and a doula had a cesarean delivery rate of 14.2 percent compared to 22.5 percent in the control group, a highly significant difference. In addition, those mothers who delivered vaginally and were supported by their partners and a doula had a significantly lower epidural rate (67.6 percent versus 76.8 percent).

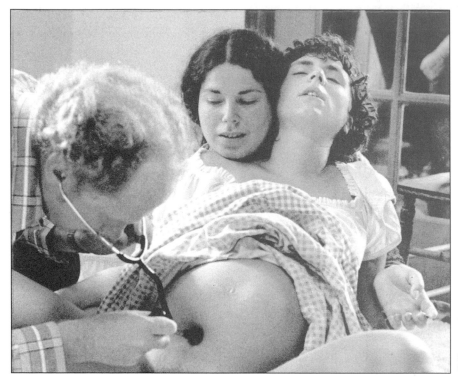

This mother is well supported during a contraction.

To simplify the evaluation of these studies, we have indicated with each of the following tables whether the results were:

- not statistically significant (no asterisk)
- statistically significant ★
- highly significant ★★

Before we started this study, we had some concern that the doula might displace the father, but this was never a problem. The doulas were asked to aid the fathers in deciding how best to help their partners. The doulas also explained to the fathers what was happening as labor progressed. The evaluation of the doulas by both fathers and mothers was remarkably positive with the frequent comment that they could never have gone through the experience successfully without the support of the doula. Providing continuous emotional support by a doula, even when the male partner is present with the laboring

CLEVELAND COUPLES STUDY		
555 women and partners		
	NO DOULA	DOULA
Cesarean section	22.5	14.2*
Mothers choosing epidural	76.8	67.6*
*Significant difference		

woman, has a positive effect on obstetric outcomes and a buoyant effect on the parents' psychological responses, as well as the possible influence on their relationship with each other and their new infant.

Judging from the many discussions we have had with parents, maternity units placed a real burden on many of the fathers when they were initially invited into the labor room in the 1970s after only a short course in childbirth education. Their anxiety increased when nurses withdrew, thinking the parents wanted private time together, not bothered by outsiders. (In some ways it was like taking six lessons in football and then the following Sunday being asked to play with a professional team.) Fathers are pleased to share their wives' labor room with a nurse, midwife, or trained doula who can explain what is happening, advise the father on support for his partner, and allow him to experience the birth without having to take on overwhelming responsibilities.

One-to-One Nurse Support of Women in Labor

A randomized controlled trial by A. J. Gagnon[5] et al. deserves special comment for it is the first study using nurses for continuous support. The trial did not observe any beneficial effects. In a carefully considered commentary about the report, Ellen Hodnett noted the trial was methodologically sound but underpowered, (not enough patients) and she asks a number of provocative questions. Was the failure to find a significant effect because the nurses were ineffective? She notes from her experiences that because nurses are hospital employees, "they are constrained by the formal and informal policies of the organization." When nurses "try to provide care that deviates from the norm, which seems to involve frequent, brief visits to their patients, arranging the epidural analgesia as soon as possible, and spending substantial periods of time with one's colleagues at the nurses' station, their associates exert considerable pressure to conform." A large multicenter trial involving hospitals in Canada and the United States is presently underway, which may tell us the role of the obstetrical nurse in the future in providing continuous emotional and physical support in labor.

LENGTH OF LABOR

A woman's first labor is on average much longer than all her subsequent labors. Women approaching their first delivery often worry about the prospects of a long labor. From a medical point of view, however, the length of a first labor is nature's way of gradually, and carefully dilating the birth passage. As the labor progresses, first the cervix opens and then the birth canal, and the baby passes through.

The results of two studies in Guatemala early in our research threw light on the length of labor for the birth of a first baby. The studies were carried out in an extremely busy obstetric facility. Almost all the women came to the maternity unit of this hospital in early labor when uterine contractions have started but the dilatation of the cervix is only one to two centimeters.

If the mother agreed to participate in the study, she was then assigned at random either to the no-doula or the doula group. The doula learned of her assignment after one of the researchers opened a sealed envelope prepared before the study began. From that moment on, the doulas began to work with the mothers in the doula group, while the no-doula mothers received the usual care. Mothers remained on the observation ward until the cervical dilatation was three to four centimeters. At that time they were transferred to labor rooms adjoining the delivery rooms. In these Guatemalan studies, hospital policies did not permit any family member or friend to be present in the labor rooms, apparently because of the large number of deliveries (an average of sixty per day) and the limitation of space. There were not enough nurses or aides for one nurse or aide to stay with one particular woman or even in one labor room with six or seven women. The no-doula mothers were thus "alone" for long periods of time during labor.

The exclusion of friends and family reflected the practices on maternity units in the United States twenty to thirty years earlier. It is surprising to reflect that as recently as the 1950s, mothers in the United States were laboring alone, usually in a sedated, semiconscious, amnesic state called twilight sleep, with the only support provided by a nurse who usually had responsibility for a number of laboring women. Almost universally, fathers were not allowed to be with their partners during labor and definitely were not allowed in the delivery room. It was this model, but without the twilight sleep, that was transplanted in the 1950s to Guatemalan hospitals by leading U.S. authorities in nursing and medicine. These routines and restrictions had remained frozen in time and were still evident when our studies were carried out in Guatemala City. (This was in striking contrast to the centuries-old customs of the Mayan Indians living only a few miles away. There a mother was supported by her mother, her mother-in-law, and a native midwife during labor and delivery in her home, and by her mother and mother-in-law in the first postpartum weeks. She was never separated from her family, her home, or her baby. One or more women she knew well were with her continuously no matter how long in labor.)

In the first study in Guatemala,[6] the average, or mean, labor length for women in the no-doula group who had routine care (that is, who did not receive oxytocin or have a cesarean section) was nineteen hours, in contrast to the women in the doula group whose labor was only nine hours. The only difference in obstetric care between the two groups of women was the continuous support provided for the doula group.

In a second study[7] the group of mothers in the no-doula group who received routine care again had a longer *average* labor length—15.5 hours, compared to 7.7 hours. As in the first study, the continuous presence of the doula was the only difference in care procedures. There were no significant differences in the age of the mothers, their income, or their living arrangements. However, there was a slightly greater cervical dilatation at admission in the doula group (an average of 1.9 centimeters versus 1.5 centimeters in the no-doula group). When analyzed statistically, a part of the difference in labor length could be explained by the difference in cervical dilatation, but the principal effect was due to the presence of the doula.

A third study was carried out in Jefferson Davis Hospital, a large public hospital in Houston, Texas.[8] We chose this hospital because it was a public hospital, and the care of patients by the resident physicians would not vary from mother to mother. That is, there would not be a different approach used by every obstetrician, as is sometimes the case with private obstetricians. Residents in this hospital were required to follow a uniform philosophy and care plan and to use the same indications in all cases for cesarean sections and drugs to relieve pain and to stimulate labor.

In this study, as with the two previous ones, first-time mothers were told about the study, and if they agreed to participate, they were placed by random assignment (sealed envelope) either in a group that would receive support from a doula or in a no-doula group that would have routine care. In this hospital a family member or friend might visit the laboring woman briefly if the labor room was not very busy.

The obstetrical care in this U.S. hospital differed from that in Guatemala in many ways. The study (1984–1987) was carried out a few years after the Guatemalan studies (1978–1982), and the differences reflected the rapid national and international dissemination of information about new obstetrical procedures and the subsequent changes in care. As was the case in most U.S. hospitals at that time, patients were confined to bed, and an electronic fetal monitor was placed on the abdomen of each mother as soon as she was admitted. Later on in labor, at five centimeters cervical dilatation, the mother's membranes were artificially ruptured so that the monitor could be attached to the baby's scalp, which gave a more direct connection to the fetus. In some situations a catheter was placed in the uterus to measure the strength and regularity of the uterine contractions. Oxytocin was used frequently to enhance the strength of the contractions. The obstetric staff expected mothers to follow a defined pattern or schedule for the dilatation of the cervix (roughly one centimeter an hour). If the labor did not progress according to this schedule, the obstetricians used measures such as intravenous oxytocin to speed up the labor.

When we began our study, the space limitations in this hospital made it necessary for the staff to require healthy women without complications to be in strong, active labor and to have a cervical dilatation of four centimeters or more before admission to the hospital. Given pressures to restrain hospital costs, most U.S. hospitals now have similar policies.

The average length of labor for the group of 212 women supported by a doula was 7.4 hours, in contrast to 9.4 hours for the 204 women in the no-doula group. The shorter labors in Houston compared to Guatemala were probably related not only to greater cervical dilatation and more advanced stages of labor on admission but also to the fact that many of the women were given oxytocin.

In spite of all the modern obstetric methods to speed up labor—which

© Suzanne Arms

Walking during early labor.

include the artificial rupture of membranes, augmentation of the strength of the contractions with oxytocin, and the use of forceps or delivery by cesarean section—the mothers with the shortest labor in our study were again those women who had a doula present throughout their labor.

NATURAL VAGINAL DELIVERIES

In the no-doula group in our Houston study a small number of women (only 25 out of the total 204 in that group, or 12 percent) delivered naturally (that is, vaginally without anesthesia, oxytocin, medication, or forceps), whereas in the doula group the number of women delivering naturally was a surprisingly large 116 out of 212, or 55 percent. It is fascinating to reflect that the presence of one caring woman continuously present throughout labor resulted in such a large difference.

PAIN RELIEF

A second randomized controlled trial in Houston compared the effects of three methods of managing the pain

HOUSTON STUDY

416 women (mothers given oxytocin or having cesarean section are included in this analysis)

	NO DOULA	DOULA
Length of labor	9.4 hours	7.4 hours**

**Highly significant difference*

HOUSTON STUDY		
	NO DOULA	DOULA
No. of mothers with natural vaginal deliveries	25	116**
Total mothers	204	212

**Highly significant difference*

of labor.[9] The mothers in one group received narcotic medication, another continuous doula support, and the third epidural analgesia. Pain relief reported by the mothers twenty-four hours after delivery was greatest for those who received epidural analgesia and the least was by those who had narcotic medication. The amount of pain decrease indicated by mothers who had continuous doula support was not as great as that by those who received epidural analgesia. But the doula-group mothers had better results in other ways than those receiving epidurals or narcotics.

The outcomes for the doula-group mothers compared to those in the other two groups showed fewer deliveries by forceps and vacuum-extraction and less need for oxytocin to stimulate labor. Mothers who had continuous doula support had a shorter average labor length of 7.8 hours, compared to 9.9 hours for the epidural group, and 9.5 hours for the narcotic group. Once again, there was a strikingly low cesarean rate in the doula group, 3.2 percent or 4 of 126 mothers, compared to 11.6 percent in the narcotic group and 16.8 percent in the epidural group.

Thirty-three percent of the epidural-group mothers, 26 percent of the narcotic-group mothers, and only 13 percent of the doula-group mothers developed a fever during labor. (We will discuss the implication of this later in this chapter.) Twenty-five percent of the mothers in the narcotic group went on to receive an epidural, but only 6 percent of the doula mothers did.

These data are especially interesting and suggest that the mothers receiving a doula had significant pain reduction. This occurred previously in another study where the mothers were randomized to a doula group, an observer group (a doula in the room who did not talk or touch the mother but stayed continuously), and a control group with neither a doula nor an observer. They received 7.8 percent, 22.6 percent, and 55 percent epidural analgesia, respectively. Thus, mothers who had a doula or an observer selected significantly fewer epidurals for pain, apparently showing the effects of a doula as well as the effect of a woman companion on the discomforts of labor.

Sitting through a contraction.

© Suzanne Arms

assistance to some mothers during labor. However, it causes contractions to become more forceful and painful so that mothers managing labor well without any medication often find they need an epidural or other pain medication after oxytocin is started.

In the first Guatemalan study the use of oxytocin was 2 percent in the doula group, compared to 16 percent in the no-doula group. Because it was used so infrequently at that time and the number of women in the study was small, there was not a large enough difference to show statistically whether a doula decreased the need for oxytocin.

In the second study, 2 percent of the doula-group women

When the two studies were carried out in Guatemala, there were no anesthesiologists prepared to administer epidural analgesia for obstetric patients. (This was the case up to 1982 in the majority of hospitals in the United States.)

The use of a doula also appeared to affect the need for oxytocin in one earlier study. Oxytocin provides valuable

HOUSTON STUDY			
Assigned Group:	EPIDURAL	NARCOTIC	DOULA
	n=150	n=137	n=126
Epidural analgesia*	87.5%	25%	6%
Cesarean delivery	16.8%	11.6%	3.2%

*Of the women who were assigned to an epidural, 12.5% did not accept it.

HOUSTON STUDY		
416 women		
	NO DOULA	DOULA
Mothers using oxytocin	44%	17%**
**Highly significant difference*		

needed oxytocin, in contrast to 13 percent in the no-doula group. Since a larger number of mothers were enrolled in this study, this was a statistically meaningful difference.

In the Houston study the percentages were also different. Forty-four percent of the women in the no-doula group were given oxytocin to increase their labor contractions, while only 17 percent of those in the doula group required this medication.

USE OF FORCEPS

Forceps are special instruments that were developed to provide a safe way to ease the passage of the infant's head through the birth canal. In the past a few babies were injured with the use of forceps when their heads were still high in the birth canal. Most of these unfortunate outcomes were the result of deliveries by physicians whose training and experience were insufficient to develop the skills and judgment needed to use forceps appropriately.

Our experience in an obstetric center where spinal, caudal, or epidural anesthesia has been used over a span of almost five decades has enabled us to appreciate that the use of low, or "outlet," forceps is often helpful, particularly when epidural, spinal, or caudal anesthesia has been used. When low forceps have been applied by well-trained, experienced obstetricians, there is no harm to the baby. At present, forceps are used in most hospitals and medical centers, but much less often than one or two decades ago.

In the Houston study, 8 percent of the mothers in the doula group had forceps deliveries, which was significantly less than the 26 percent in the no-doula group. These were all low-forceps deliveries. The higher incidence of forceps deliveries in the no-doula group was due in part to the more frequent use of epidural anesthesia. If the simple intervention of support by a doula can reduce the use of forceps to this extent, we must look favorably upon the influence of a doula, whether or not we consider delivery by forceps safe.

NUMBER OF CESAREAN SECTIONS

Statistics collected over many years show it is safer for a healthy mother to deliver her full-term baby vaginally

HOUSTON STUDY		
416 women		
	NO DOULA	DOULA
Forceps deliveries	26%	8%**
**Highly significant difference		

than by cesarean section. Both the mother and the baby face a lower risk of serious complications with vaginal delivery. However, there are some clearly defined reasons for a surgical delivery, such as disproportion between the baby's head and the pelvic outlet.

For several decades in the mid–1900s one measure of a good obstetrical service was that the number of cesarean sections did not exceed 5 percent of the total deliveries. However, after close scrutiny of outcomes when babies were in a persistent breech (feet–down) position, physicians proposed that delivering such babies by cesarean section was reasonable. In light of that conclusion, and some other ones regarding high-risk and preterm deliveries, physicians anticipated that the incidence of cesarean sections might settle at about 8 to 9 percent. However, the incidence of cesarean deliveries then skyrocketed to levels of 25 to 35 percent, with a few hospitals well above this. After a short period of decline, the pattern is upward again. The cesarean delivery rate in the United States was 22 percent in 1999, the latest year with complete records. This high rate is a matter of great concern to physicians, women of childbearing age and their families, as well as health insurers.

In our first study in Guatemala, 19 percent of the women in the doula group needed a cesarean section, in contrast to 27 percent of mothers in the no-doula group. The number of mothers in this study was too small to tell us whether this difference was significant.

In our second study in Guatemala, with a larger number of mothers enrolled, the mothers in the doula group had a 7-percent incidence of cesarean deliveries, in contrast to the 17-percent incidence for mothers in the no-doula group. This was a significant difference.

Hospitals in university medical centers such as the institution where we carried out our study in Houston often have a lower incidence of cesarean deliveries. In this Houston study the mothers in the doula group had a cesarean-section rate of 8 percent, versus 18 percent in the no-doula group— a significant difference.

In Guatemala City and Houston, with continuous labor support during labor as an integral part of care, the cesarean-section rates were remarkably

HOUSTON STUDY		
416 women		
	NO DOULA	DOULA
Cesarean deliveries	18%	8%★
Significant difference		

similar: 7 percent and 8 percent, respectively.

Aside from clear medical indications for cesarean section, some mothers choose a cesarean delivery for what they consider to be a pain-free delivery experience. A number of other women are extremely disappointed that they needed a cesarean, feeling that they have failed to deliver a baby the way nature intended and the way a majority of women manage this important life event. The postoperative discomfort and fatigue when the mother is attempting to meet the urgent demands of the new baby for care and attention have often led to depressed reactions in these mothers in the first weeks after delivery. The recovery time of a mother who has had a cesarean delivery is usually a matter of weeks, in contrast to days after a vaginal delivery.

Maternal Fever

With the high quality of obstetrical and newborn care provided for healthy mothers and infants in a teaching hospital in the United States, we did not expect that there would be a difference in the health of the infants in the two groups. In the Houston hospital, all full-term babies were routinely discharged home before forty-eight hours of age unless a medical problem arose. We were quite surprised to find a difference in the number of babies who had an extended stay in the hospital. Ten percent of the babies in the doula group and 24 percent of the newborn infants in the no-doula group were kept in the hospital. The difference was unrelated to the health of the mother and did not include babies who stayed when the mother had a cesarean delivery.

When we looked at the reasons for these babies being held for a longer stay, we did not find any actual differences in the health status of the infants in the two groups during their time in the hospital. Then, after examining the course of these babies more closely, we found that the main reason for the differences between the two groups was

HOUSTON STUDY		
	NO DOULA	DOULA
Infants kept more than 2 days in hospital	24%	10%★
Significant difference		

HOUSTON STUDY		
	NO DOULA	DOULA
Maternal fever	10%	1%*
Significant difference		

that more mothers in the no-doula group had developed a fever during labor. This occurred with 10 percent of the mothers in the no-doula group, and 1 percent of the mothers in the doula group.

When a mother develops a fever during labor, physicians recognize this as a warning the baby may have a serious and potentially fatal blood-stream infection called septicemia (sepsis). This is an uncommon occurrence, but because the risk of not treating a baby with sepsis is great, and because the diagnosis at the time of birth is difficult and existing antibiotics are effective, babies of mothers with fever are usually considered to have sepsis and are treated until the cultures are reported to be negative. Even though babies of mothers with fever may appear normal at birth, they will have cultures of their blood and spinal fluid taken immediately and will usually be started on intravenous or intramuscular antibiotics until their overall condition and the results of the cultures are known, usually within three days. As

there is no previous experience with the appearance and behavior of an individual newborn baby, maternal fever may be the only clue to a life-threatening infection. To wait until more clear-cut signs of infection appear is to risk the life of the baby.

When we investigated possible reasons for the fever, we found that the mothers who had a fever were significantly more likely to have had epidural analgesia. A probable explanation for this high incidence of maternal fever in the no-doula group comes from research in England.[10] This study shows that when a mother has epidural analgesia during labor, her temperature slowly but steadily rises; if labor is long enough, the temperature will reach the level of a fever. Long labors and epidurals were more common in the no-doula group, so chances were greater that mothers in that group would develop a fever.

It is difficult for physicians to be sure whether an individual mother's fever is due to epidural analgesia or to sepsis in the baby. In other words, the association of maternal fever with an epidural unfortunately does not help the obstetrician or pediatrician decide whether a specific mother's fever is caused by infection or by the epidural anesthesia. However, the decreased need for pain relief during labor when a doula provides support would lessen the number of epidurals and therefore the number of women who have fevers and the number of babies who have to be evaluated for illness.

CLEVELAND COUPLES STUDY		
Induced Labor	NO DOULA n = 22	DOULA n = 20
Epidural analgesia	16 (72%)	18 (90%)
Cesarean delivery	14 (63.6%)	4 (20%)**
***Highly significant difference*		

DOULAS AND INDUCED LABOR

Forty-two of the 555 women enrolled in the Cleveland couples study were admitted to the hospital for induction of labor for a variety of reasons that were similar in the doula, narcotic, and epidural groups. (Twenty-one women were past their expected due dates and ten had developed the condition known as pregnancy-induced hypertension, three had spontaneous rupture of membranes without labor, and no reason for induction was given for seven women.) For the women whose labors were induced, the overall rate of epidural use was 81 percent. The number of women being induced was too small to distinguish statistically between those who received epidurals and those who did not. The total induction group had a cesarean-delivery rate of 43 percent. The group of no-doula couples, had had over three times the number of cesarean deliveries.[11] These results from women who required an induction of labor high-light the importance of continuous doula support as an effective method for lowering cesarean-delivery rates in this group. There is a need for studies of labor support for women with other high-risk conditions.

DOULAS FOR TEENAGE MOTHERS

Doulas have been integrated into three separate long-term community-support programs focused on teenage pregnancy in Chicago: the Alivio Medical Center, Christopher House, and Marillac Social Center.[12] The project differed from other doula trials in the following respects: 1) The intervention began when doulas began working with the young mothers no later than the eighth month of pregnancy; 2) doulas collaborated with home visitors to provide a support team for mothers and infants; 3) prenatal education was given to all project participants; 4) in the last month of pregnancy mothers had weekly contact with their doulas; 5) doula support continued from before birth, during labor and delivery, as well as six to eight weeks postpartum, and (6) the trial ended with transition of the participant to the home visitor. A key element is the four-month training program for the doulas, which includes the development of listening skills, training in child development, the special needs of the pregnant teenager, extensive childbirth education, and skills in home visiting. The trial was not randomized.

The mothers ranged in age from 13 to 19, with an average of 16.9 years; 33.6 percent were African American, 63.4 percent Hispanic, and 3 percent non-Hispanic white. The table below compares the outcomes of these doula-supported births with those of U.S. teens.

Postpartum behavioral studies of this extended doula program revealed higher scores on mother-infant interaction when compared with short doula programs. The professional staff believe that the doula selection from women living in the target community who received four months of training and supervision is key to the success of the program. The Chicago Health Connection staff (the organizing institution) has developed interview guides to help in doula selection.

The support by a sensitive, caring doula from the same ethnic community—who starts in late pregnancy,

A COMPARISON OF THE PARTICIPANTS OF THE CHICAGO DOULA PROJECT WITH U.S. TEENS

	DOULA PARTICIPANT	U.S. TEEN
C-section rate	8.1%	12.9%
Breast-feeding at discharge	80%	45%
Breast-feeding at 6 weeks	60%	NA
Breast-feeding at 6 months	22%	12.2%
Epidural	11.4%	50% (U.S. urban Hispanic)
Inadequate prenatal care	10.5%	17.5%
Prematurity	7%	12.7%
Low birth weight	6.6%	11.5%

through the long hours of labor, and then continues seeing the teenage mother for six to eight weeks postpartum—can, in part, "remother the mother" raising her self-esteem and self-image. The more we care for the mother during this sensitive perinatal period, the more sensitively and appropriately she will care for her baby.

A PRACTICAL APPLICATION IN A U.S. HOSPITAL

There is global and robust evidence of the beneficial effects of continuous labor support by a doula in controlled trials from several research groups. More than eighty U.S. hospitals have organized in-hospital doula programs for their laboring women. The plan developed at the Danbury Hospital in Connecticut is of special interest because of its thoughtful and careful approach.

At the start, in 1996, thirty-two doulas were trained by DONA (Doulas of North America). There were also additional classes in childbirth education and breast-feeding, as well as bloodborne- and airborne-pathogen-safety training. In addition, each doula received a reference check, a screen for infectious disease, a hepatitis B vaccination, and a Danbury Hospital ID badge.

Information about the doula program was made available to all physicians. The program is open to all women delivering their babies at Danbury Hospital. During pregnancy, women can indicate their wish for a doula, request a prenatal conference with a doula (which is free), or decide when they enter the hospital in labor. Three doulas are on-call for each twenty-four-hour period and are required to arrive at the hospital within thirty minutes from when they are called. Patients are charged $50 for the doula service (Danbury Hospital subsidizes the cost of the program). Any woman who cannot pay the $50 can still enroll and will receive doula support. There are three written evaluations of the doula for each birth (birth parents, nurse, and physician).

The doulas are paid $275 per birth, regardless of the length of labor and are not compensated for call time, meetings, or prenatal conferences. All the doulas meet once a month to go over the difficult cases and discuss other procedures that might have been used. The program has been very successful, with doula-supported mothers reporting that they experienced much less discomfort and pain than they expected. At the beginning of the program, some nurses were concerned that the doulas were taking over the most interesting part of their work, but this changed as they noted how much more hands-on care and support mothers received from the doula's continuous attendance. In the last two to three years the physicians, nurses, and administrators have all strongly supported the program.

In the first year of the program, out of 2,400 total births, 123 women selected a doula. The cesarean-section rate for the mothers with a doula was 9 percent and use of epidurals 14 percent, while for all the mothers the cesarean-section rate was 18.4 percent and 21 percent requested an epidural. In 2001, 554 selected a doula, and their cesarean-section rate was 11.5 percent, yet it was 23.5 percent for all the mothers. It should be noted that these total figures include all women (single and multiple births) as well as women with a previous cesarean section. These data are of special interest, but this observation does not have the power of a randomized trial. For example, women who desired very little intervention may have chosen a doula. The hospital manager of the

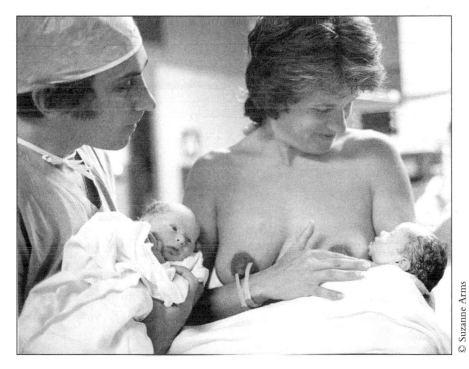

Proud father and mother of twins thirty minutes after birth.

doula program believes that what makes this plan work is "an awesome group of women committed to making birth a strong, wonderful, and positive experience for all the women they serve."

EPIDURAL ANESTHESIA RECONSIDERED

In the last decade the percentage of mothers who have had an epidural anesthetic during labor and delivery has escalated. The development and spread of the epidural technique in obstetrics has been of particular benefit for women who require cesarean delivery, because the mother is then awake and aware of what is going on.

In contrast to the agreement on the use of epidurals for cesarean deliveries, there are differing opinions about the effects of epidural anesthesia for healthy women likely to have a normal labor and delivery. Many anesthesiologists describe the epidural as the "Cadillac of anesthesias." They point out its ideal effect of providing control of pain throughout the long period while the cervix is gradually dilating. At times labor that has been progressing slowly may speed up after epidural anesthesia is started. For women who believe they cannot tolerate the pain of labor contractions, it is fortunate that epidural analgesia is available not only to relieve their pain and anxiety about it but also to allow them to be fully awake.

Many of the medical publications discussing the use of epidural analgesia have been positive. In addition, word-of-mouth communication from mother to prospective mother has also been favorable. As a result of these reports and other factors such as the availability of an obstetrical anesthesiologist around the clock in many hospitals, the incidence of obstetrical epidural anesthesia use has soared to 90-plus percent of deliveries in some institutions.

Many experienced nurses, midwives, and obstetricians report, however, that this anesthetic method often does not measure up to the ideal. Labor that has been progressing normally may slow down or stop when an epidural is started. The length of labor may be extended, as was the case in our Houston study. The pain relief is not always complete, and in spite of the development of continuous methods of administering the anesthetic, its effectiveness may fluctuate. When epidurals were first used, once the epidural was started, the mother was no longer able to walk around or change body positions easily. Since then, however, both the modification of technique and a decrease in the medication dosage have made possible what anesthesiologists call a "walking epidural." Several recent studies[13] have demonstrated the effectiveness of a walking epidural for pain and discomfort in early labor (less than 5 centimeters dilation). The dose of medication can be adjusted so as to give approximately two hours of analgesia without causing any detectable motor block.

However, attempts to start an epidural are sometimes unsuccessful. Frequently, the anticipated tapering off of the anesthetic's effects, which would reestablish muscle tone and the pushing reflex, is not achieved. Therefore, the descent of the baby's head through the birth canal is often slow and more difficult because of the lack of the normal reflex responses in the mother's body that turn the head into the optimal delivery position and push out the baby. This stage of labor consequently is often prolonged, and delivery by forceps, vacuum extraction, or cesarean section is often required. In the past ten years, a debate has continued on the obstetrical complications of epidural analgesia. Fortunately an analysis of eleven randomized trials involving 3,159 laboring women recently compared the effects of epidurals not involving a regional block with no intervention.[14] Epidural analgesia was associated with greater pain relief than nonepidural methods, but

also with longer first and second stages of labor. In addition, there was an increased incidence of fetal malposition, increased use of oxytocin, and an increase in instrumental (forceps or vacuum) vaginal deliveries. When new trial data were included, however, there was no statistically significant effect on the cesarean-section rate.[15]

Before women tell their physicians or midwives that they insist on an epidural for pain relief, they would do well to pause and reflect on these and other considerations. Although the drug used for an epidural goes into a small space just outside the woman's spinal cord, the medication does get into the mother's bloodstream and then into the baby. Babies therefore have mild to moderate changes in their behavior in the first hours and days. As we said earlier, a woman who has an epidural has a progressive rise in temperature as labor proceeds. This does not occur with natural childbirth or with other pain medication. The mother's rising temperature is associated with an increase in the baby's heart rate, which could incorrectly be interpreted as distress in the baby associated with, for example, an interference with the supply of oxygen. Together with the concern that the baby might have a serious infection, these signs put pressure on the attendants to deliver the baby as soon as possible. This may result in a cesarean or forceps delivery, because the baby's condition may remain unclear until after delivery and close examination.

In addition, as suggested earlier, a number of mothers have told us about their disappointment that they failed to go through labor without medication. They were "unable to do what any uneducated peasant mother could do." The percentage of mothers disturbed by this varies with different populations and appears to be related to their expectations and their view of the birthing experience. Because they had an epidural, these women express their sadness that they have missed out on the sense of accomplishment that they had expected.

The directors of some obstetrical services have been concerned about these side effects of epidural anesthesia and its influence on mothers' behavior with their babies. There has been relatively little study of the effects of epidural anesthesia on the normal shifts and surges of hormones thought to be associated with unmedicated mothers' intense desire to hold and interact with their infants after delivery. Some experienced obstetricians have concerns that the usual ecstatic enthusiasm of mothers toward their new infants common after

an unmedicated delivery has been lost, delayed, or minimized. They comment that the mothers who have had epidural anesthesia do not get the same feeling of accomplishment or boost in self-esteem as those who deliver without an epidural. While anesthesia, including epidurals, has been a godsend in complicated deliveries, a well-conducted, unanesthetized delivery can provide a new mother with special enthusiasm and a great burst of ecstasy for the "birth of her family."

FINANCIAL CONSIDERATIONS

In addition to the psychological and physical benefits of labor support, there are important financial ones. Anesthesia costs could be cut significantly if more doula-supported women labored and delivered without anesthesia or with a local anesthetic. Expenses could be reduced as fewer infants born to doula-supported women required an extended hospital stay.

In 1999 cesarean sections were performed in 22 percent of all U.S. births each year. Let us assume, on the basis of the Houston study, that the cesarean rate with a doula could be cut to 10 percent. This decrease and the accompanying shortening of maternal hospital stays and reduction of operating room

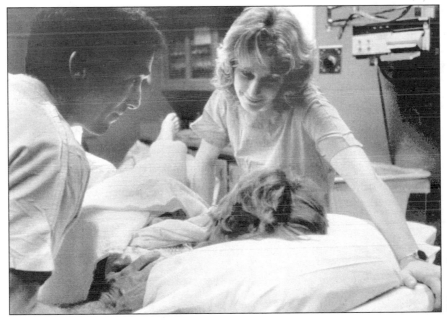

A mother, supported by the father and doula, just before delivery
(a vaginal delivery after cesarean).

expenses, need for skilled delivery and postpartum staff, and medication use would mean a considerable savings for families and insurance carriers. Even when the additional cost of the doulas' services are included, the reduction in total medical care costs for the nation would be in the billions.

A reduction in the use of epidural anesthesia to 20 percent from the current 80 to 90 percent in some hospitals could mean savings to the parents of about a thousand dollars per delivery—

a mammoth saving nationwide, given that more than four million births occur each year in the United States.

CONCLUSIONS

As mentioned earlier the authors have completed an analysis that draws together ten randomized trials of continuous doula support with a technique known as a meta-analysis. When the results of these studies are calculated together, the presence of a doula reduces the overall cesarean rate by roughly 45 percent, length of labor by 25 percent, oxytocin use by 50 percent, pain medication by 31 percent, the need for forceps 34 percent, and requests for epidurals by 10–60 percent.

These convincing research findings about the many benefits of doula care confirm our overall conclusions: doula support enhances the well-being of mothers and babies, leads to fewer medical interventions in the process of labor and delivery, and saves money. The findings provide a strong argument for expansion of doula services. Not all women will choose doula support in place of epidural analgesia, but all laboring women should be provided with continuous doula support.

6

Longer-Term Benefits of Doula Support

The mother is . . . the one person who can properly
introduce the world to the baby. She knows how to do
this . . . because she is the natural mother.

D. W. WINNICOTT,
Babies and Their Mothers

The period around childbirth appears to be a unique time when mothers are unusually open to change. It is a formative developmental stage and has the potential for either a positive or negative outcome. Because of the new mother's physical and emotional sensitivity, the care she and her infant receive during this time can have a beneficial or detrimental long-term effect on her self-concept, her relationship with the father, their care and image of their infant, and their own emotional well-being. Although the period of labor is a relatively short interval in a family's life, it is also an occasion of high stress and need, with no turning back.

A SENSITIVE PERIOD

New available data strongly demonstrate this sensitive period in the mothers' lives during labor, birth, and the following several days. During this special period the mother, and possibly the father, are especially open to improving their later behavior with their infant, depending on the caregiving and environment that surrounds them.

A number of well-designed studies show that humane, sensitive, and individually appropriate caregiving practices—such as keeping the mother and baby together as much as possible, right from the start with rooming-in, suckling in the first two hours[1] (with infants deciding when they take the first drink), demand-feeding, mother and infant skin-to-skin contact,[2] and the father[3] holding and learning about his infant in the early period—have produced four important benefits. They have resulted in decreasing abandonment in the maternity hospital,[4] decreasing rates of infant abuse,[5,6] increased success in breast-feeding during the entire first year of life, (including increased breast-milk production) and increased father involvement in the first three months of the infant's life. In addition, helping the parents discover the abilities and responses of their newborn[7] and showing them how to carry the infant in a cloth carrier on their chest in the early months of life have improved parent-infant interaction at three months, increased immunization rates at one year, and resulted in an increased incidence of secure attachment at thirteen months.[8]

The first doula study in Guatemala described in the previous chapter[9] provided subtle but distinct differences in how mothers perceive or respond to their infants after being supported or not supported emotionally during labor. Through a one-way mirror, two groups of Guatemalan mothers were observed with their babies in a standardized situation in the first twenty-five minutes after leaving the delivery room. The observers were blinded to the mothers' previous care during labor. The mothers who had been supported by a doula showed more affectionate interaction with their infants, with more smiling,

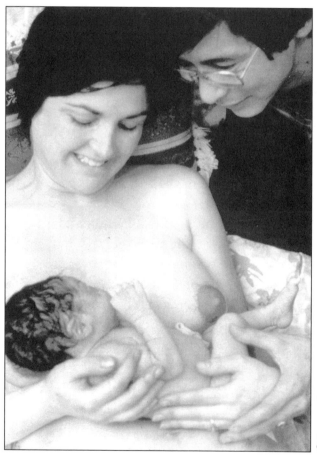

© Suzanne Arms

First inspection.

talking, and stroking than the mothers who did not have a doula.

EFFECTS ON THE MOTHER AFTER THE DELIVERY

Another excellent example of the remarkable effects doula support in labor can have on the responses of the mother during the first weeks of the baby's life can be seen in a doula study in South Africa.[10] The mothers' responses illustrate how early care during the sensitive period has the potential to alter later maternal behavior. Justus Hofmeyr, Wendy Lynne Wolman, Beverley Chalmers, and colleagues at the University of Witwatersrand in Johannesburg, South Africa, studied 189 women having their first babies. The patients were Indian urban mothers familiar with the hospital. The doulas in this study were laywomen (with a short weekend of training) who were asked to remain with the laboring women and used touch and verbal communication focusing on three primary factors: comfort, reassurance, and praise.

The results showed remarkably favorable effects of constant support during labor on the subsequent psychological health of the women and infants in the doula group in the following areas.

Mothers' Reports of Pain at Twenty-four Hours

The one-day postpartum interview results indicated that the doula group mothers reported less pain during labor and at twenty-four hours after labor. The two groups of mothers had similar levels of anxiety before labor, but the doula group had less at twenty-four hours. Fewer doula-supported mothers considered the labor and delivery to have been difficult, fewer thought it was much worse than they had imagined, and more believed they had coped well during this experience.

Behavior with the Infant by Mother's Report at Twenty-four Hours

When the mothers were asked about their experiences with their babies, the doula-group mothers spent less time away from their infants. These results suggest that doula support during labor has effects similar to those of mother-infant contact directly after delivery; both appear to increase the mother's interest in her baby and her interaction with the newborn.

Mothers' Reports on Feeding Behavior and Infants' Health at Six Weeks

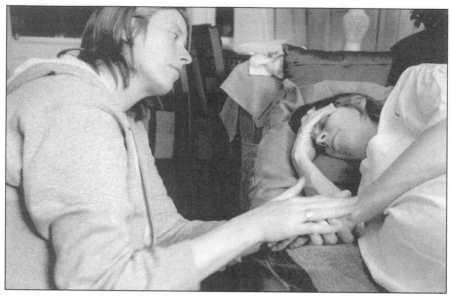

A doula touches or holds a mother during much of labor.

Reports given by the mothers in the doula and no-doula groups six weeks after delivery showed a significantly greater incidence of breast-feeding and of feeding the infant on demand in the supported group, and of giving food other than milk in the control group. They indicate a striking difference in the mothers' attitudes and behavior toward their babies. For nurses, pediatricians, and others who care for the health and feeding of children it is most impressive to see a marked difference in the reported incidence of feeding problems: 16 percent in the doula group, versus 63 percent in the no-doula group. What a difference this could mean to parents in terms of worries and doctors bills!

JOHANNESBURG STUDY		
Feeding Behavior at Six Weeks	NO DOULA	DOULA
Breast-feeding only	29%	51%★★
Demand feeding	47%	81%★★
Feeding food other than milk	53%	18%★★
Feeding problem ·	63%	16%★★
Average number of days breast-feeding only	24 days	32 days★★

Note: Modified from Wolman[11]
★★All highly significant differences

JOHANNESBURG STUDY		
Infant Health Problems at Six Weeks	NO DOULA	DOULA
Vomiting	28%	4%★★
Colds or runny nose	69%	39%★★
Cough	64%	39%★★
Poor appetite	25%	0%★★
★★*Highly significant difference*		
Diarrhea	33%	19%★
★*Significant difference*		
Note: Modified from Wolman[11]		

The information given by the mothers in the doula and no-doula groups about the health of their infants six weeks after delivery is noted above.

These results are striking. There were no differences in hospital admissions and no reasons to expect such differences in the babies, who were similar in all respects at birth. Can the presence of a doula during labor reduce a mother's anxiety sufficiently and give her such a boost in self-esteem that she considers her baby healthier? Or does the mother without a doula perhaps develop a more negative and depressed view of herself and her baby that leads her to look at her infant as more sickly? Certainly a portion of these differences could be related to the increased incidence in the doula group of breast-feeding, which is known to decrease gastrointestinal and respiratory infections.

When the mothers were asked about the amount of time they were away from their baby in a week and the number of days required to develop a relationship, there were again significant differences between the two groups.

Mothers in the doula group said they spent 1.7 hours a week away from their baby, in contrast to the no-doula mothers, who were away 6.6 hours. The doula-group mothers said it took them an average of 2.9 days to develop a close relationship with their baby, compared to 9.8 days for the other group of mothers.[11]

These results suggest that support during labor expedited the doula-group mothers' readiness to fall in love with their babies and that this attachment

MATERNAL OUTCOME AT SIX WEEKS		
	NO DOULA	DOULA
Mother brought baby to postnatal visit	47%	64%★
Mother always picks baby up when crying	40%	80%★★
Hours away from baby/week	6.6	1.7★
★*Significant difference*		
★★*Highly significant difference*		

made them less willing to be away from their babies. These findings fit with the observations of mother-infant interaction after mothers left the delivery room in the first Guatemalan study and the reports of mothers who had early and extra contact with their newborn infants after delivery.

Emotional State of Mothers

There were impressive differences in the average scores on psychological tests of the mothers in the two groups.

On these measures the doula-group mothers showed significantly less anxiety, fewer signs of depression, and a higher level of self-esteem.[12] Although these measures are not sufficient for diagnosing depression, the possibility is suggested by these results. Postpartum depression harms the mother and those who live with her—particularly the

infant. If fewer mothers develop this state when supported by a doula, there will be great benefits for the mothers themselves, their babies, and the other family members. Mothers who feel better about themselves and are less anxious create a more positive environment for their infants to grow and flourish.

The no-doula-group mothers were more likely to seek medical advice or treatment, a finding consistent with the measure of their emotional state—more anxiety, more depression, and lower self-esteem. Also, they were less likely to bring their babies with them for the six-week postnatal clinic visit. This fits with the doula-supported mothers' reports that they spent significantly more time with their infants than did the no-doula mothers. The doula-supported group of mothers almost always picked up their crying babies, while the no-doula group sometimes picked up their babies and sometimes let them cry. The fact that more of the doula-supported mothers in this South African study were breast-feeding, may account for some of the differences.

Relationship with Partner at Six Weeks

There were no significant differences between the two groups in the wom-

PSYCHOLOGICAL OUTCOME AT SIX WEEKS		
	NO DOULA	DOULA
Anxiety	40%	28%★★
Self-esteem	59%	74%★★
Depression	23%	10%★★

★★Highly significant difference
Note: Modified from Wolman[12]

ens' reported satisfaction with their partners before and during the pregnancy. However, some aspect of doula support resulted in doula mothers reporting a great increase in satisfaction with their partner since the birth of the baby and a much greater percentage of mothers who reported their relationship was better right after the birth—more than double the percentage of that in the no-doula group.[13]

Perception of the Baby at Six Weeks

At six weeks the doula-supported mothers' perceptions of themselves and their babies were clearly more favorable. Wolman reported that "support group mothers were more positive on all dimensions involving the specialness, ease, attractiveness and cleverness of their babies." A higher percentage of

Satisfaction with Partner	NO DOULA	DOULA
Before pregnancy	63%	65%
During pregnancy	48%	49%
Since the baby was born	49%	85%**
Relationship better right after the birth	30%	71%**

Note: Modified from Wolman[13]
**★★Highly significant finding*

supported mothers not only considered their babies beautiful, clever, and easy to manage but also believed their infants cried less than other babies. Grace Manning-Orenstein[14] noted in another study that doula-supported mothers reported that their babies were less fussy, compared with reports of mothers who gave birth without a doula. In fact, the supported mothers believed that their babies were "better" when compared to a "standard baby," whereas the no-doula mothers perceived their babies as "just slightly less good as" or "not as good as" a "standard baby." Wolman said that "support group mothers also perceived themselves as closer to their babies, as managing better, and as communicating better with their babies than control group mothers did." A higher percentage of the doula-supported mothers reported that they were pleased to have their babies, found becoming a mother was easy, and felt that they could look after their babies better than anyone else could. In contrast, the no-doula group of mothers perceived their adaptation to motherhood as more difficult and felt that others could care for their baby as well as they could.

In another study,[15] the results indicated that "Mothers who received doula support were also more likely to feel

MATERNAL PERCEPTIONS AT SIX WEEKS		
Perception	CONTROL GROUP	DOULA-SUPPORTED GROUP
Of baby:		
Cries less than others	17%	55%★★
Special	71%	91%★★
Easy to manage	27%	65%★★
Clever	47%	78%★★
Beautiful	67%	89%★★
Regards baby as a separate, sociable person by 6 weeks	80%	100%★★
Of self:		
Feels close to baby	80%	97%★★
Pleased to have baby	65%	97%★★
Managing well	65%	91%★★
Communicates well	68%	91%★★
Becoming a mother was easy	11%	45%★★
Can look after baby better than anyone else	31%	72%★★

★★ *Highly significant difference p<0, 01 on 1-tailed tests from Wolman*[15]

that labor had a very positive impact on their feelings as women and on their body strength and performance."

Mother–Infant Interaction at Two Months

In a study of 104 mothers over several months, normal healthy women expecting their first baby were randomly assigned to either a doula support or narcotic or epidural analgesia group. To evaluate later mother-infant interaction, observers were specially trained in home observations. The observers did not know the labor experience of the mothers. When each of the infants reached two months of age, a home visit was made to give a test of infant development and to observe the mother's interaction with her infant.[16] The interaction was scored on a scale of one to seven based on the mother's physical contact, visual attention, and affectionate behaviors toward the infant. The mother's interaction with her baby was rated on five occasions during the visit: 1) when the examiner entered the mother's house; 2) while a developmental test was being set up; 3) while the test was being scored; 4) during a feeding; and 5) while the mother changed the baby. Scores on the developmental test were not related to the social support or analgesia the infant's mother received during labor.

As expected, there were no significant differences on the developmental test results across the three groups of infants. However, the mother-infant interaction scores showed exciting and significant differences. The doula-supported mothers' score was significantly higher than the score of the no-doula group of mothers for four of the five observation occasions—a surprisingly robust finding (p<.001). Overall, these results indicated that mothers who had the support of a doula during labor had a remarkably positive level of affectionate interaction with their infants compared to the other mothers two months after delivery.

When trained observers use a carefully designed test and find significant differences between the behavior of two groups of randomly assigned mothers, researchers sit up and take notice. Since the mothers were not given instructions about how they should interact, the effects are remarkable and significant. It is still unclear, however, what physiological and/or psychological mechanisms could explain this powerful and long-lasting effect of doula support. Does the doula's continuous presence and sensitive support during labor release and sustain natural hormonal and behavioral responses? Are these responses restricted or inhibited by factors such as anxiety and stress associated with a hospital birth without the continuous support of a doula?

This sustained effect on mother-infant interaction is consistent with other evidence of the unusually powerful effects of early mother-infant contact and interaction during a brief period around the time of birth that we have labeled the "maternal sensitive period." In this period—the time in the first minutes, hours, and days after birth—parent-infant contact, as we said earlier, may alter the parents' later behavior with that infant. The remarkably strong and persistent effects associated with the doula suggests that the sensitive period starts during labor. Donald Winnicott, a pediatrician and psychoanalyst, made some remarkably astute observations about the period just following birth. He proposed that a healthy mother goes through a period of what he termed "Primary Maternal Preoccupation."[17] He noted, "Only if a mother is sensitized in the way I am describing can she feel herself into her infant's place and so meet the infant's needs." He noted that in this mental state she has a greatly increased sensitivity to the needs of her baby. To develop and maintain this state, a mother needs support, nurturing, and a protected environment.

PARENT-INFANT BONDING

The route to a secure attachment starts very early in a child's life and involves

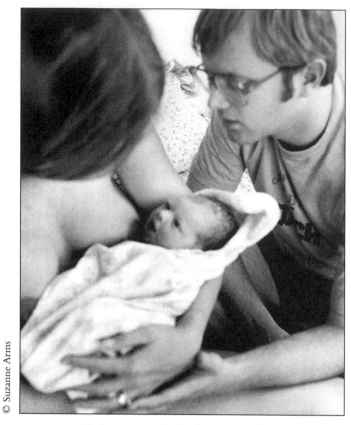

© Suzanne Arms

*Beginning to take in their new baby in
the postpartum period.*

early parent-infant bonding. Bonding refers to parents' emotional investment in their child. This is a process that builds and grows with repeated meaningful and pleasurable experiences. Parents feel this bond or emotional connection to their infant as much more than just an interest in feeding or tending the infant. It is caring—feeling oneself in the infant's place—sensing and responding to the infant's needs, physical and emotional. When parents are well bonded, the infant is powerfully influenced by their emotional investment. The apparent effects of doula support on the mother—rendering her more responsive, attentive, and sensitive to the unique needs of the baby—are highly likely to enhance long-term attachment of the infant to the parents.

Two long-standing human practices, early mother–infant contact and rooming-in (usually with breast-feeding) and continuous emotional support during labor, abandoned in the middle of the last century but restored in recent decades, have similar effects on maternal behavior. If these age-old practices can be provided for all mothers, we predict that there will be a higher percentage of securely attached one-year-olds than the present estimate of 60–65 percent. Other long-standing practices such as breast-feeding and carrying the baby on the caregiver's body during the first year and cosleeping would further increase mother–infant contact and interaction and might further increase the number of securely-attached children.

7

Birth with a Doula

I knew she was there and she just melted into the action,
whispering in my ear, reminding me at every turn how
strong I was and simply that I could do it.

A NEW MOTHER, SPEAKING OF HER DOULA

A Hospital Birth with a Doula

To make clear the real-life role of a doula, we followed the labor and delivery of two different couples expecting their first babies. The first couple, Lydia and Dan, found the doula's help beneficial in their hospital birth, whereas the second couple, Kay and Bob, engaged a doula to help them at a midwifery-assisted birth in their home. Each shared their birth stories with us in the following interviews.

Two to three months before the birth of their first child, Lydia and Dan began to consider engaging a doula. Lydia, thirty-three, is an administrative assistant in a large company, and Dan, thirty-six, is an electronics engineer. Both were delighted about having a baby and related their experience in detail.

Initially they had a difference of opinion about a doula. Dan was not sure he saw the benefits of having a third person, saying, "The drawback was in my mind that a doula would take away from the intimate experience of having this baby by ourselves— only us and the baby. It looked like an interference to me."

Lydia saw the issue differently. She was concerned about the possibility of pain. She did not view the birth as an intimate experience but rather "as being something that could conceivably be pretty painful, and you should do everything you possibly could to make it better."

In the next month Lydia saw Dan's decision change when during a childbirth class they viewed a film depicting the last ten minutes of delivery for five or six mothers. Lydia said afterwards it looked to both of them like a very intense experience. "I saw his mind wonder that maybe it might be more helpful to have somebody there, because it seemed like a pretty difficult thing to do."

Dan began to see the labor as a potentially very painful experience for Lydia and thought that a doula "might make it a bit easier by having more security. She might make the whole experience last a shorter time, and this way you'd experience less pain."

When he learned that the doctor arrived only in the last hour or so, that the nurse would be taking care of two or more patients, and that consequently they would often be left by themselves, they both then agreed that a doula was a good idea.

After interviewing three doulas, they chose Mary Frances, an experienced doula in her early fifties. They felt she was warm, caring, gentle, and friendly. She had a child of her own and had assisted in a large number of births, which made Lydia feel more comfortable.

The doula made arrangements to visit them four times in the two months before the due date to learn about their expectations and to discuss various aspects of labor and delivery with which first-time parents may not be familiar. This allowed them to talk in more detail with their obstetrician. The biggest issue was that Lydia wanted to try to have an unmedicated birth, but if she decided on an epidural during labor, she did not want any argument about it. In these discussions Mary Frances recognized that Lydia was "a strong person. I felt pretty confident that she was going to be okay and could make her needs known in either case."

At the first meeting the doula discussed the couple's plans and wishes in general. At the next visit she demonstrated visualization and relaxation techniques. At the third visit she showed Lydia and Dan a series of birth positions that might be useful during labor; during the fourth visit they toured the hospital together. Mary Frances also introduced her backup doula to the couple. Mary Frances taped a progressive relaxation and birth-visualization sequence and asked Lydia to listen to it several times. Mary Frances would then use many of these phrases during the actual birth, which would activate many of the suggestions already taken in at an unconscious level.

During one of the visits, Lydia had many questions for the doula about the birth. This was now near the time of labor, and Lydia was feeling especially tired. She wanted to know what types of things the doula would do if she were feeling pain. Dan was interested in the doula's perception of what might happen during the entire birth. Lydia noted that it was very helpful to her to talk to an experienced woman about some of her worries. Lydia, Dan, and the doula gained from these visits, each learning about the other. The doula noted, "I really like these prenatal visits. You get to know the couple, and then you can build up some trust."

The doula made plans to come to Lydia and Dan's home during early labor. Lydia also mentioned that her sister Lynne, to whom she was close, would be coming to the labor. Lydia was concerned, however, about the potential for her sister to become very anxious during times of stress. Lydia told her sister that if she became too anxious during labor, she would have to leave.

Labor began two weeks after their last visit, very nearly on the expected date, at 5:30 A.M., with rupture of the membranes. Dan and Lydia, both excited, called Lynne at 6 A.M., wanting to catch her before she left for the day. She drove over soon afterward.

Lydia took a long shower, which she found relaxing, and then she and Dan had a nice big breakfast, "because I'd heard that you needed to keep your strength up." They timed the contractions, which were getting stronger. They talked to the doula, Mary Frances, at 7:30 A.M., and she said to call the doctor. The doctor told them to come to the hospital when the contractions were three to five minutes apart and a certain length. Within a half hour it was time. They quickly called the doula to meet them there, since there was not time for her to come to their home. When they arrived at the hospital, the doula was waiting for them.

Dorothy, the nurse, took Lydia's blood pressure, asked her many questions, and checked her cervical dilatation. Lydia noted, "She said I was 100-percent effaced* and three centimeters dilated. I thought we were pretty far along. I knew I had to go to ten centimeters, but I thought three centimeters was a pretty good number to come in with.

"Dorothy, the nurse, started to ask me questions while I was having a contraction. I remembered from my childbirth class that if somebody's talking while you're having a contraction, the husband should say, 'She's having a contrac-

---

*Effacement is the thinning out of the cervix, expressed as a percentage of its full thickness. At 100 percent, it is completely flattened out.

tion. Could you please wait.' He didn't pipe up with that, so I said, 'I'm having a contraction—I'll answer you when I'm finished.'

"She asked me the question again; she had ignored what I'd said, which worried me. She was a knowledgeable person—she did give good suggestions—and sometimes she tried to be nice. But she must have had some kind of chip on her shoulder, because when we first walked in and she saw my sister Lynne, she said, 'Oh, you have Mary Frances, and you have your sister, too'—as if this other person was an extra burden on her, or was going to be. She couldn't believe we had three people, even though this hospital said it's okay, and my doctor said it's fine. I thought that the hospital should be able to handle it when a couple had more people.

"Dorothy then said, 'You may need to have an epidural. It's a first baby; it's going to be a long labor. I want you to see the anesthesiologist.' I mentioned that I'd had an epidural for knee surgery and knew what it was. She said, 'But I want you to have a pleasant experience.' This was a strange thing for me to hear.

"It seemed to me that everything was progressing very rapidly, and I didn't see any point in it. I thought, If we can do it without the epidural, why not? I can

tolerate a lot of pain. It's only for one day. It's worth it. The doula, Mary Frances, was in the room, and she was watching and being supportive. Everybody was there."

Mary Frances's recollection of this period adds a similar perspective. "I never got the feeling that the nurse was really with Lydia. When the nurse came in, she had a list of questions and a form to fill out. At one point Lydia started to have a contraction, and she indicated for the nurse to wait. I was watching the nurse, and she just was impatient—'Let's get on with this.' I thought, Oh dear, this isn't looking good.

"I don't see myself as somebody who should intervene, if the communication is something that is working. I need to stay out of it, because otherwise, I'm taking away the mother's power if I get in there.

"The nurse checked her at that point, and she was three centimeters. Then the nurse left. Early on, nurses are mostly out of the room, which is one of the reasons I think that a childbirth assistant is necessary in a hospital." Mary Frances pointed out that many nurses are much more supportive, but that pressures in hospitals can make it hard for them to remain attentive.

From 9:30 A.M. until 11:00 A.M. Lydia reported she was most comfortable when she was walking around the room or sitting in the shower. Dan mainly accompanied her in walking. Lydia said that breathing through the contractions with the doula was the most helpful tool, whether walking or in the shower. When she was lying in bed, she changed sides often and continued the breathing with Mary Frances. "At this time the doula was very useful to me. I felt she was very calm, and I felt I wanted to look at her face and I wanted to breathe with her. Around 11:00 A.M. the doula noticed that my legs were shaking and my skin was flushed. She suggested that I might be much further along in transition."

When the nurse came in to check at 11:00 A.M., Mary Frances vividly remembers what happened next.

"The nurse proceeded to tell her how great she was doing. 'You're really on top of your breathing; you're really doing wonderfully.' And then she paused for a minute and said, 'But you really don't have to experience all this pain if you don't want to.' I thought, What is this?

"And she said, 'You know, you can have an epidural, and it won't have any effect on you or your baby whatsoever.'

"I told an anesthesiologist friend of mine that a nurse had said this, and he was concerned because it's not the facts.

I was annoyed because Lydia was feeling a lot of pain and she was on top of it, but it was there. To have this carrot held out to you: that you don't have to feel this pain, and that it's not going to affect you or your baby! Lydia said to the nurse, 'What I'd like to do is have an unmedicated birth.' It was like the nurse didn't hear it. She said, 'I'd like you just to talk with the anesthesiologist,' and left to fetch him."

The doula noted: "It's easier for nurses if the mother has the epidural, and then she's on the monitor, and then they see everything from their station. Not all nurses recommend epidurals like this. I don't think that those who do really understand what they're taking away from the mother.

"Lydia said she'd talk to the anesthesiologist if the nurse wanted her to. But she said again, 'I'd really like to have an unmedicated birth.' I thought, God bless her, just to be able to get that out in the face of all this pain and this woman.

"The nurse came back fifteen minutes later to check Lydia and found that she was in transition at eight centimeters, having made great progress. The anesthesiologist came in but didn't push the epidural. He said to Lydia. 'It's up to you.' He did talk about the possible side effects. He mentioned that the urge to push could be diminished."

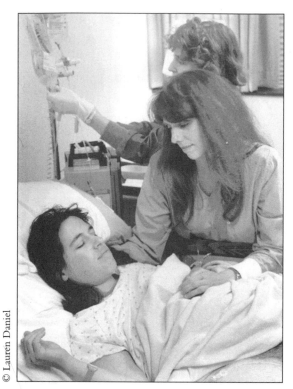

© Lauren Daniel

The doula uses quiet support to help the mother relax.

really helpful when I was pushing and I needed her also to hold my leg."

In the pushing stage, from that time until the birth of the baby, Lydia alternated between two positions: either squatting and supporting herself by holding onto a bar or propping up in bed with Mary Frances at her side helping her breathe, and Dan and Lynne holding her legs so she could push against them. The doctor was now present, checking and encouraging. They remember it as a real team effort.

Lydia described it thus: "During the pushing, Lynne and Dan sort of jumped in and started helping, and I felt they were being more effective. We were trying to figure what was the best way to progress in pushing. They brought a mirror in. The three of them, especially Dan and Lynne, were so excited. When I finally saw it in the mirror, I thought it was slow. I thought it was going to be faster than that. It was very hard. It was very difficult and painful.

"I felt I was directing them by saying, 'Here it comes again.' Then they would come and lift my legs up. We were sort of chatting in between the contractions. They weren't very far apart. No medicines. I had a little bit of water. Mary Frances was wiping my forehead occasionally.

The doula remembers offering Lydia support in whatever choice she made. Mary Frances said, "I wanted her to know that she was doing great—that she was really doing well."

The doula noted that Dan and Lynne were both helpful. "Dan never left the room," Lydia remembers. "He had a good expression on his face that made me feel good. It was also helpful when he held my hand or leg. My sister was

"I liked my team. They were great. Afterwards I think we all felt like a team—that we did a good job, that everybody had played an important role, a good part. I felt good about Mary Frances.

"Everybody would sort of comment on how good the pushing was: 'Oh, you're doing great. Keep going.' They were always very encouraging, partly, I think, because we had discussed that we wanted to always have encouraging thoughts going on. 'Things are going well.' 'That was a good push'— repeating those things over and over again. 'You can see the head crowning. Look at the hair.' So usually I had a good gauge on how my pushing was going. But at one point, listening to them, I couldn't tell whether I was effective or not.

"I thought, If I got up off this table and started to leave, these people wouldn't let me leave the room. I said to Dan, 'I want to go home.' The doctor at that point said, 'Give me your hand.' She took my hand and put it

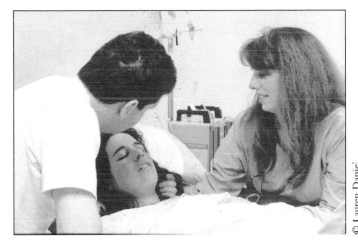

The father and doula work together to keep the mother reassured during a stong contraction.

on top of the baby's head. I could feel her head coming out even though it wasn't all the way out. The doctor said, 'One of my laws is, If you can touch it, you can push it out.'"

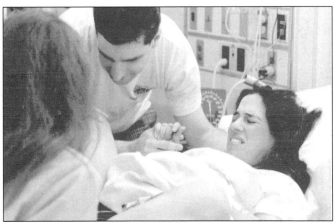

The mother is pushing, supported by her husband and the doula.

Lydia continued: "The birth of the baby took only another five or eight minutes. At 1:45 P.M. an eight-and-a-half-pound healthy baby girl was born. During this time the doula never left my side. She wiped my forehead. She was the one who noticed how I was feeling. Lynne and Dan were more interested in the baby. The doctor kept leaving and coming back, since she had two other deliveries that day. The doula was more caring about how I looked, if I was hot; she was concerned that things were taken care of for me quickly, whatever I asked for. She took care of me."

The next day the doula came into the hospital to visit Lydia and Dan. Together they went over how the labor and birth went. Lydia noted: "Mary Frances said I did a good job, I was very strong. I wasn't sure I had done a good job. I didn't feel bad about it, but she confirmed I did a good job. It was really kind of amazing how well it went. I think the doula kept me from having medication. She kept my resolve up. It's hard to say if she speeded up the labor or not, but she certainly made me feel more comfortable."

Dan added at this point: "It was a good experience. I was able to be more relaxed because some of the pressure was off me. We needed the extra person

physically to help Lydia and emotionally because the nurse didn't provide that help. The doula's presence was critical to the atmosphere because the nurse was very pessimistic."

A HOME BIRTH WITH A DOULA

Kay and Bob had made plans for a birth at home and had engaged a doula as well as a midwife. When Kay's contractions began, she and Bob spent the day doing some planned chores around the house. A visit with the midwife confirmed that Kay was in labor. Kay remembers somewhat minimizing the fact that she was in labor and worrying that she would not dilate. Her own words best describe her thoughts and early labor experience.

"Anyhow, after a late and wonderful meal at a restaurant we went home, and the contractions were mild—a little bloody show but nothing major. In fact, I think I was in denial of sorts—I think I thought I was never going to dilate—which was totally unreasonable, but it is amazing how powerful negative suggestions can be—and I heard a few times from my older sister that she 'didn't dilate' with either of her children and then an offhand comment my Mom made a few days prior to our birth stuck in my head. I expressed that I was worried that for some reason my labor would be like my sister's and that I wouldn't ever go into labor and she replied, 'You might not. I never did. I needed pitocin for all of my deliveries.' She meant to be supportive, but I think we have to be really careful of the things said to pregnant women. There are so many subtle and overt things that can be very disempowering. This offhand comment coupled with an image I was building in my head made me completely deny my own progress in early labor—in fact, I think I minimized everything until about 12:30 A.M. when I was nine centimeters and contracting like mad! I didn't actually believe I was in labor until it was almost over.

"So, denial going strong, we got ready for bed, and I dozed for about two hours. Things really intensified at about 2:30 A.M. I woke Bob up and headed for the shower where I stayed until 4 A.M. when we called our midwife, then the doula. Our midwife listened to us for a few contractions and said to call her back—but I wanted to call Deb (the doula) right away because, things were intensifying. So at about 5 A.M. we called our doula. She arrived at about 6:15 A.M. and found me laboring in the bathroom—in and out of the shower, on all fours—leaning on the toilet—just getting by. It was a huge relief to have her there. Kara, the midwife, came about the same time, so we felt we were immediately in good hands."

When asked about the choice of a home birth, Bob explained: "While so much of my concentration and energy was absorbed in dealing with the labor, it was nice not to have to worry about creating "our" environment in a foreign place. We were in our own place and, therefore, had all the comforting benefits and securities that come with being at home."

Kay described her experience in labor: "It was very different from what I had imagined. I thought I would be much more social—more communicative with the people around me, but as it was, once my labor got started, I was completely internal, struggling to reach out during every contraction. Thank goodness the contractions begin and end every few minutes and there is some break. I was more focused on just making it through than I imagined. Being at home cut out countless distractions and concerns right off the bat—no papers to sign, unnecessary procedures, new faces to confront. Everything was familiar so I could sink in and face what I needed to do to get to the place I needed to be to give birth.

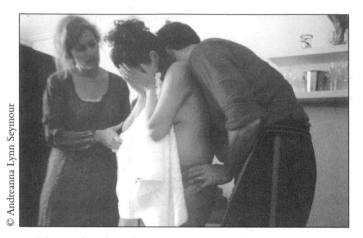

The mother closes her eyes to maintain her concentration, while the father relieves back pain with the Hip Squeeze, and the doula continues to hold the mother.

"It turned out that pain for me was very isolating in a way—from about 3 A.M. (and I gave birth at 7:30 P.M.), my contractions were one and a half to two minutes apart, and each one took my breath away for sure. It was all I could do to somehow announce to my husband, doula, or midwife—whoever was right there—the start of a contraction and then just concentrate on staying with it. It took all my energy to lean, or close my eyes, listen, or to bend and rock. I spent most of the labor in the hot shower with my husband, midwife, or doula right there to help with each contraction. I needed to be in a quiet, dark environment with absolutely zero distraction. It is difficult to imagine going through all of this in a busy hospital room with a million distractions.

"I feel so lucky to have been able to stay at home and have Griffin. It ended up being a difficult labor and it took him a long time to get into position where he could come down and be born. He was pretty big (ten pounds, four ounces) and stayed very high in my pelvis until very late in the day, but the contractions never let up. By about 1 P.M. I really was getting almost no break, and I never felt a lot of the sensations I was expecting to feel, like the urge to push! And so it felt to me like I was sailing with no compass in a way. As a result, I really needed *every ounce* of support from each person with me. I needed a fearless and experienced midwife to make complex 'medical' decisions and to remain focused on the health and safety of Griffin and me. I needed constant positive reassurance and almost a 'Pollyanna' attitude from our doula during each and every contraction, and I needed the physical support and love from my husband. Because they were a team, all giving 100 percent of their own unique role—everyone doing their best—and leaning a bit on each other, it all seemed to work out. I'm not sure all of that would have evolved in a hospital where caregivers have many people to take care of and lots of different roles to fill.

"Hands down, the best thing about being home was staying with our son from the moment of his birth and making all our own choices. It felt really great to have him with us from the second he was born, on through his first hour, day, month, and now year; he has been with us! And, for example, something as simple as the first bath. I guess I thought we'd bathe him the first day, but actually we waited about a week or maybe even a little more because it just felt right. And feeding is a whole other story. He was able to scooch up, latch on, and nurse from the get-go, and I think being skin-to-skin with both of us for those first few days at home, calm, and just being together, and having constant access to my breast minimized distraction for him and maximized our chances to get off to the right start. I am so grateful

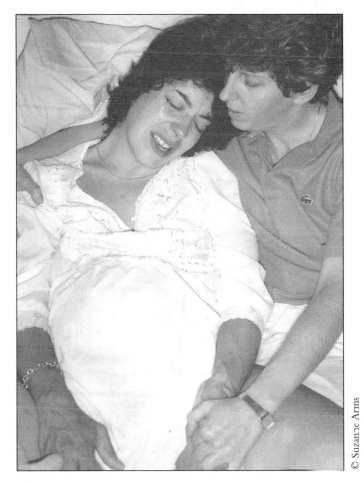

The doula encircles this mother with strong support late in labor.

and still filled with a sense of awe and wonder at my own power, the strength and sheer skill of the people who helped me, and just the wonder of it all."

Bob explained the challenges as he saw them: "I knew she was experienc-

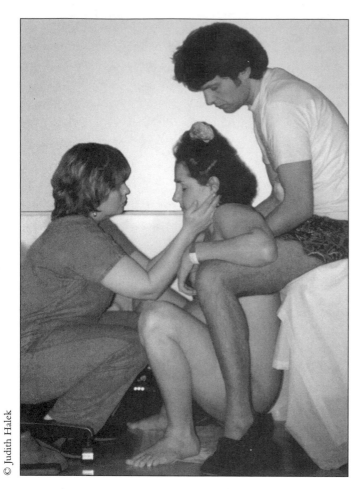

The mother is supported by her husband in the squatting position (the Dangle), readying for delivery.

fidence I had in their ability, and the determination to follow through with our plan. Perhaps what helped me the most was feeling the incredible strength Kay displayed. We were in this together. This was *our* baby. I believe that physically and emotionally we needed each other to see this through. While, of course, Kay endured the contractions and delivered the baby, I believe my support and the support of our doula helped keep her focused, motivated, and resilient."

Kay had a ten-hour period of intense contractions but very little "progress." We asked Bob how the doula helped at this time. "The period of no progress was perhaps the most challenging part for me. Our doula was very reinforcing, suggesting a myriad of techniques (the Dangle, the Double-Hip Squeeze, the Tub, stair climbing, the shower, etc.) to try. This not only proved helpful in managing the contractions but also distracted us from focusing on the clock and lack of progress. It was extremely

ing great pain, and I couldn't make it go away. I needed to accept that and just focus on using the techniques we learned in class to help manage the contractions. It's hard to see the person you love in pain. What helped was the support of our midwife and doula, the con-

comforting to know that we weren't alone in troubleshooting. I know that as helpful and attentive as I was to Kay, it was reassuring to me to hear the calm words and advice of another person, particularly someone who is very knowledgeable and trained in the birthing process."

"The biggest thing she did during that time was to stay with us," added Kay. "When she first arrived, I was so focused that I couldn't even look up, but I knew she was there and she just melted into the action, whispering in my ear, reminding me at every turn how strong I was and simply that I could do it. And our doula kept trying new things; she seemed to have an endless kit of things to try, and that helped. Just keeping us moving forward with positive ideas and input.

"Each contraction seemed to wipe out all the others, and I felt like I was starting at zero again, like I kept being moved back to the starting line, but her constant encouragement made it possible to muster the courage to get to the top of the contraction and then to let it go. I could not see from one minute to the next what I needed, so her being there and available for whatever came up was very comforting. And at several points I remember feeling a sense of relief that my husband and midwife had

her to lean on as well, in case they were getting discouraged or tired or stumped. That helped free my energy up to focus on my work."

We asked Kay and Bob whether, looking back, they had any reservations about hiring a doula. "Going into this birth," said Bob, "I felt very confident in our base of knowledge and intestinal fortitude to make this work. I also knew I would be very actively involved and needed to be very supportive of Kay. We figured that having a doula was not only going to complement the support Kay was receiving from me and the midwife, but was also going to provide tremendous support to me in my efforts. Bottom line, having a doula did not undermine my role as husband and father during the whole process. It enhanced it. To me, birth was not about excluding, but instead is about including. They are a useful tool that helps the mother *and* the father, so why not use them?"

"In my mind I did not," said Kay. "I had seen the statistics and felt that anywhere I decided to give birth I would hire a doula, but especially at home where you really want to maximize safety. We took great pains to set everything up for every possible scenario, and I knew in my mind that having a doula and all those benefits was a vital part.

But, in my more personal self, I was not sure how it would all play out. Who would do what? Would it inhibit me? Would she be as strong as I needed? We actually hired one doula, a wonderful woman with a great background of experience, then switched during the last week. It was intuition for me. I needed to know that the doula we chose had experiences and images of birth that were similar to my idea (or ideal) of what it "should" or "could" be. I needed to know that she knew in her bones what I was striving for, sort of like having a guide/mentor or something. And as clichéd as it sounds, as labor approached and I was gathering things for the birth and starting to realize that it was going to happen, I had a strong intuition that I needed "mothering"—not my mother (who I adore) but mothering in a different, more global sense. I felt the need for someone a little older and very seasoned. As it was, the doula we had hired was my age and very much a peer. At one point I was writing on the computer and I just knew who I needed and reached out. Fortunately, doulas all know that the main thing is to go with the urges of a pregnant/laboring woman, and no feelings were hurt."

Because Kay was attended by both a doula and a midwife, we asked her and Bob whether these roles overlapped.

"Only in the sense that they both brought extensive knowledge about the birthing process," said Bob. "While the midwife was responsible for managing the birth from a medical perspective, I felt our doula did a great job of following her lead and filling in the gaps of support. Griffin's birth was like a symphony of sorts. Lots of experts, talent, effort, love, and time. Everyone a part of a mysterious perfect moment.

"While holding a flashlight to illuminate Griffin's crowning head, I still can hear our doula's soft, optimistic voice telling us you're doing it, he's right here about to be born. I also distinctly remember her suggesting both Kay and I reach down and feel Griffin's head for the first time."

We asked what role the doula played after the birth. "She and the midwife cleaned everything up and took photos of us," said Kay. "That was really great. All we had to do was cuddle and take our new baby in! By about forty-five minutes after his birth, his grandmothers, grandpa, and uncle arrived, and we were tucked up in bed to greet everyone and then snuggled down with our new son for our first night together. It was amazing to wake up with a sparkling clean apartment, only a few subtle signs of the dramatic events of his birth still visible."

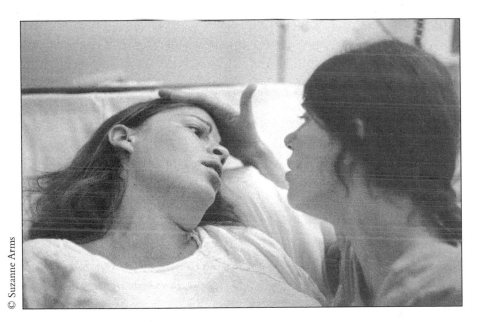

Attuned to the mother's emotional and physical needs.

About fifteen minutes after Griffin was born, while Kay showered, Bob held him skin-to-skin. "I was thankful to have that uninterrupted time alone with him to 'introduce' myself," Bob said. "I know he heard my voice while in utero, but I felt it was important to have him lying on me feeling my skin, smelling my smell, feeling my heartbeat. It provided the beginning of our own bond together."

The doula who attended the birth of Kay and Bob's child came over for a postpartum visit. We asked how that went. "I remember two really important things the doula did," said Kay. "One was that she brought food and made a point not to even let us make her tea; she got busy and set it all up herself! And then she made the important point over and over again that we should just be in bed with our baby, letting our families and friends do the laundry, make meals, etc.—and she suggested we make a list of simple tasks and directions for anyone who offered to help out. This was really good support, because our culture sort of makes you feel like you should be taking care of visitors, but really they want you to be with your baby and you really want that, too. So it helped us let others help us. The other thing she did was to write up a birth story for us, and that really helped us to come one step further out of the 'birth fog.' What I mean is that it put times and dates and numbers together to help us recreate the labor in terms of days and time. I guess the main thing she did was to keep reiterating how strong we were and how much of an honor it was to be a part of this time in our lives. That felt really great."

A number of useful techniques were used by the doula in Kay's long labor. We asked Kay and Bob to describe them.

The Dangle

"When the contraction would start," said Kay, "I felt a surge of panic, 'What to do?' And so I needed someone *very* close by to catch me. I could just lean back into Bob's arms and let all my muscles and mind relax, letting my uterus do all the work. It was all very intuitive, and I was so thankful to have people around who knew what to do, what would probably help."

"We first experimented with the Dangle," added Bob, "with me standing holding Kay. During birth class I realized that the weight and position would make it difficult to do over an extended period of time. We didn't plan on adren-aline kicking in and giving me the added strength to hold her up through contractions for hours on end."

The Shower

"We spent a lot of time here." said Bob. "To me, it felt like this became our reclusion spot when we needed to just come together and confide in each other and boost one another. We were typically left alone while in the shower. Even though we desired an open, inclusive experience, it was nice to know we could remove ourselves from others when we desired. It was beautiful and private."

The Double-Hip Squeeze

"From a supportive role," said Bob, "it was rewarding to know that this technique was clearly helping. Because of its physical requirements, it also helped me connect with the strenuous experience of the contractions. This was the same with the Dangle."

"The intense pressure people used on my hips was *so* helpful," said Kay. "For one thing, it made me feel less alone, like someone was right there with me, exerting equal effort. And it really took the pain down a big notch to where I could handle it."

8

A Father's True Role

I've run a number of marathons. I've done a lot of hiking
with a heavy backpack, and I've worked for forty hours
straight on-call; but going through labor with my wife
was more strenuous and exhausting than any of these
experiences. We could never have done it without the
doula. She was crucial for us.

A FATHER

For first-time fathers, the labor and delivery unit of a hospital is a strange place with strange smells, sights, and sounds, including the cries of women in labor. Even more stressful are the changes occurring in the mothers, the people they love most—obvious pain, anxiety, unusual sounds, and fluid discharges never seen before. The changes in the appearance of laboring women can be extremely distressing to new fathers, as can the women's sometimes dramatic changes in behavior—becoming alternately overwhelmed, demanding, desperate, and even antagonistic. Fathers also face the dilemma of what to do and where to stand, how much to touch and what kind of touch to offer, and how much loving affection to show in front of strangers. The stress is increased by the fathers' feelings of direct responsibility for the women's distress and the added responsibility, in some cases, of making significant decisions about the medical care during labor.

From the available information and our own experience, we believe that too much is expected of men in childbirth today. Fathers cannot be objective; there is too much at stake. There is anticipation and excitement, mixed with concern and anxiety about the potential danger, and the unknown. No matter how much experience a father may have had with childbirth, he cannot remain emotionally distanced enough to meet both his own and the mother's needs at this intense time. In suggesting the support of a doula, our intent is not to diminish the father's role but to enhance it, to free him up to stand by the mother. With the doula present, the father is never left as the sole, isolated, responsible person caring for the laboring mother. This vital ingredient—the support of an experienced woman—has been lost in modern obstetrical care.

A father needs to be present: a mother needs to know he is there, he is with her, loving, concerned, responsive, and taking responsibility for his new child. His presence is important for the emotional connection of the couple and for their relationship to each other and to the baby. Recognition and validation of the father's right and need to be present at the birth of his infant is not only compatible with, but also enhanced by, the presence of a doula.

FATHERS AT DELIVERY

Although the majority of births in the United States had shifted from home to hospital by the end of the 1930s, it was not until the 1970s that the majority of hospitals began to permit fathers to be present during labor. In 1973 only 27 percent of women delivering in a U.S. hospital were accompanied by the baby's father; by 1983, 79 percent had such accompaniment.

Though fathers have been permitted to come into the labor and delivery suite, they have not always been welcomed openly. Often this shift in hospital policy has been dictated by marketing pressures, to maintain or increase the number of deliveries. This policy change, attributed to the current interest in family-centered maternity care, has often given only lip service to the father's presence. Obstetricians and nurses display a wide range of comfort levels with fathers during labor—from easy acceptance to grudging toleration of their presence. During any given labor, a father may be greeted warmly and accepted by some caregivers and almost rejected by others. Complicating the father's role as a steady source of emotional support for the mother is the routine practice of some medical personnel to ask the father to leave every time a medical procedure, such as a vaginal examination or the starting of an epidural, takes place—just when the mother may be needing someone the most.

In addition to the varying degrees of acceptance of the father by the obstetrician and hospital staff are variations in the father's own ability to be supportive, as well as in the woman's desire to have him be her main emotional support. Drawing on the strong evidence now available from fifteen separate randomized trials in which doulas have been the supportive companions, we can compare doulas' and fathers' behavior and kind of support. Do the father and a doula care for the mother in a similar fashion during labor? Is there a difference in their roles, or is there a difference in the type of support a woman in labor needs from a woman and that which she needs from a man? Are the needs of each parent being addressed during labor and delivery? Are fathers being pushed into a situation where they do not feel comfortable? And are they excluded from meaningful moments?

Current views of the ideal role for fathers vary tremendously: from fathers as mere observers to fathers as fill-ins for busy personnel, as "advisers" or as actual decision makers about the birth process. For example, some doctors address the father and ignore the mother when discussing what is happening and making decisions about what procedure to do next. In other sit-

The beginning.

© Suzanne Arms

uations some anxious fathers take the prerogative to go to the nurses' station and ask that a nurse perform a particular procedure, such as providing pain medicine, as soon as possible. Sometimes fathers and medical personnel do not communicate clearly. For example, confusion may arise when the obstetrician tells a father, "I believe we possibly should give an epidural." The father may interpret this statement as a question, whereas the obstetrician has, in fact, just made a decision to give an epidural. The other side of the continuum is that a small number of caregivers consider all fathers to be in the way. Sadly, some fathers also believe this description.

DOULAS AND FATHERS: TWO DIFFERENT ROLES

To help understand and compare the roles of the doula and father during birth, we have closely observed and recorded their behaviors during early and late labor. The information was gathered in two studies: In one study the behavior of twelve fathers was observed in a Cleveland hospital, and in the other study three doulas were observed caring for thirteen mothers in a Houston hospital. The same techniques and forms were used to record the findings from the two studies.[1] The investigators in both studies assessed and then later compared behaviors during one hour in early labor (less than seven centimeters cervical dilatation) and one hour in late labor (more than seven

centimeters dilatation). The behaviors of the fathers and doulas were analyzed only for the periods when the mother was uncomfortable or having a contraction.

Overall, fathers were present for somewhat less time during the labor than were the doulas. In early labor fathers were in the mothers' rooms 78 percent of the time, while in late labor they were in the rooms 95 percent of the time. Both in early and late labor the doulas remained with the mothers almost 100 percent of the time.

Throughout early and late labor the doulas remained closer physically (less than 1 foot) to the mothers 85 percent of the time, while the fathers were that close for only 28 percent of the time. During actual contractions, the doulas were again closer to the mothers than were the fathers, both in early and late labor. Fathers held the mothers' hands a greater percentage of time than did the doulas in early labor, but this reversed in late labor. Overall, the fathers and the doulas held the mothers' hands about the same length of time. Both fathers and doulas talked much more in late labor than in early labor.

When all forms of touching were tallied, a difference was noted. (Touching here included rubbing, stroking, clutching, and holding.) During both the early and late periods the doulas were touching the mothers more than 95 percent of the observation time, compared to less than 20 percent for the fathers. The fathers watched the fetal monitors much more than did the doulas.

Interestingly, another ongoing study of fathers has noted that their behavior is altered when they are not the only person responsible for support. When a doula supported a couple throughout labor, the father was freed to offer more personal support and did much more intimate touching of the mother's head and face.

In yet another study the supportive behaviors during labor of eleven first-time fathers were compared with those of eleven women relatives or friends.[2] Fathers again remained significantly farther from the laboring mothers than did the women labor companions. When the pain of labor became more intense, the fathers remained where they were or moved back, whereas the women companions moved closer and often increased their physical contact. The women used more phrases of a specific nature—either calming, instructing, or explaining—regardless of the laboring mother's state, whereas fathers did more general talking when the laboring woman was in pain.

The differences between doulas and fathers need some explanation. This was the first time these men had been present with a woman during labor, in contrast to the doulas' extensive labor and delivery experience. The fathers appeared uncertain about what to do, and they were deferential to the nursing and medical staff, often retreating from the mother when a nurse or physician entered the room. Later in labor when the contractions were more painful, fathers may have retreated because of exhaustion and an intolerable level of concern. A doula with experience and no personal tie to the woman in labor could pace herself and not become anxious about behaviors and events that she knew were part of normal labor. We suspect that in some cases the father's behavior, like sleeping or leaving late in labor, was a consequence of anxiety that his wife might die.

We actually make demands on first-time fathers that exceed those made on medical students. For many years we have taken groups of first-year medical students who have had some experience in hospitals or emergency rooms into special hospital divisions such as the neonatal intensive care unit, the coronary care unit, or the burn unit. In almost every situation there are two or three medical students who become pale and sweaty and need to leave.

Although the fathers performed differently than the doulas in these studies, in the same and other studies more than 90 percent of the mothers stated, when questioned after delivery about the presence of the father, that it was extremely important that the father had been able to be with them. All of the fathers replied that it was extremely important for them to be present during this experience. In the majority of cases both parents found positive meaning and mutual support in the sharing of childbirth.

On many occasions we have observed the following: The mother in labor was so interested in having the father remain with her throughout the delivery that she was devoting much of her attention and energy to his comfort and well-being. She would often turn to him as he sat in a chair and say, "You must be hungry—why don't you go to the cafeteria and eat a meal? I'll be all right while you are away." And then later, "You look tired. You got up very early this morning. Perhaps you should take a nap." We have been impressed with the sensitivity and thoughtfulness of obstetric nurses to this reversal of support roles during labor. Often the nurse, overhearing the mother, would

promise to look after the father, and would also emphasize that it was the mother who needed support and that she needed to focus on her needs. The doula supporting the couple always thinks about what will be most helpful for both the mother and the father.

We noted in Chapter 5 that the doula's presence has various beneficial effects on the medical outcome of the mother's labor and delivery; we might also ask what effect the father has on the birth process. Two studies show that the presence of the father significantly reduces the pain medications (such as Demerol) required by the mother.[3,4] However, no study with fathers alone has yet reported a decrease in the length of labor, the incidence of forceps use, the rate of cesarean sections, the incidence of epidural anesthesia, or the use of oxytocin.

In the only randomized controlled trial comparing fathers' support with and without a doula, the women laboring with both their partner and a doula had a significantly lower cesarean-section rate, 14.2 percent versus 22.5 percent, as well as fewer requests for epidural analgesia, 68 percent versus 77 percent, respectively, than women laboring only with their partners and no doula.[5] All fathers and mothers in the doula-support group separately reported that the doula's presence during labor and delivery was extremely valuable. Many commented that they could not have gone through the childbirth experience without the doula.

HOW FATHERS EXPERIENCE BIRTH

Because of the opposing and sometimes confusing messages today, couples are often pulled in two directions about childbirth. One message is rugged individualism, "We can do it alone," and the other is cooperation and collaboration, "We can use help from others." The emphasis on bringing fathers into childbirth, with its many benefits for the couple's relationship and the father's relationship with the baby, has prompted a number of fathers to say, "I can do it; we're in this together. She needs me. I've learned how to help her. We don't need another person. And the wife to say, "My husband will be my support person."

Underneath these words often lay the worry that one father spoke of when told about doulas: "You mean I'm not good enough?" and the wife would say, "Gary will be my support," with her concern not only of offending her partner by suggesting they have a doula, but also that someone else may take over and her partner will be left out, feel uninvolved, or in second place. Women may also worry that the father will be less involved with their baby if he doesn't have full responsibility in the birth. Fathers have expressed worry about not doing the job well, being unimportant, losing face, or failing in some way if they are not the main support person.

It is important to remember that each father and mother comes to the delivery with different life histories, and that birth evokes within each of them different feelings and responses that are often unexpected not only within themselves but with each other. The following reports illustrate the problems and the complexities fathers encounter when participating at birth.

One father pointed out that, "A husband can give a tremendous amount, but there's no limit to the type of comforting, affection, and support a woman deserves and needs in labor, and she needs this not only from me, but from a caring, knowledgeable woman, too. While I know my wife benefited a lot from me, I was not only not jealous, I was relieved and delighted to have the help. Given all the events and the hours and the time involved in her labor, we were all needed. It was a team effort. Seeing what Sally was going through, I wanted her to get as much help as pos-

Early labor on the porch with the support of the father and doula.

sible. It felt so good to see the doula help my wife relax and be eased through each contraction. We ended up with myself, two doulas, and the midwife to help Sally. We were all needed. One doula was there just to take pictures, but after a while she was needed, too, and put aside the camera with our agreement. It was this doula's natural sensitivity to the circumstances that led her to do what she intuitively knew how to do. The baby was angled in such a way that it took many hours to get him to descend. This made me realize that labor doesn't always go as intended. If we had not all helped, Sally's labor might have taken a more interventive course. Sally had also learned self-hypnosis and was guided to move into her inner visualizations through the contractions.

"We were in early labor at home for many hours. Our main doula came to the house to work with Sally, to take turns with me, and to offer her special knowledge of massage. This was so relieving for Sally. Many times we would be walking or resting, and then with a contraction, Sally would lean into me while the doula would press or massage her back. When we arrived at the hospital, our second doula arrived to be our photographer, but it became apparent that she was needed as a doula. She put the camera aside, and all of us worked together.

The whole experience was magical and wonderful. I was amazed at the endurance of my wife and of our doula helpers. I always felt valued and involved, and I knew I was important to Sally and to our son. We realized that in another setting without this type of support, or without caregivers willing to go the extra mile with us, Sally's labor would have been handled quite differently."

This father also remarked that as partners learn about the specific benefits of labor support, they would become enthusiastic about it, just as women and their partners now have learned about the important health benefits of breast-feeding.

George, thirty-two, a clerk in a small store, had been prepared for the birth of his first baby by taking childbirth classes with his wife. The doula observed, how-ever, that he looked out the window during most of the labor. The doula made many efforts to engage him in activities with the labor but was unsuccessful. After the birth George said to the doula with great feeling, "This has been the most wonderful experience of my life." The doulas realized at that moment that this father had done all he could do, which was right for him.

Tony, thirty-five, worked in computer technology when his first baby was born. Tony had grown up in a culture where fathers did not participate in delivery and where physical modesty in hospitals was very much respected. Although he had taken childbirth classes, he attended the birth only reluctantly. These parents had a male obstetrician and no doula. Six months after the delivery, he and his wife sought help for marital and sexual problems. After exploring some of his strong negative feelings, the father realized that he was very angry at his wife because he had a deep cultural belief that his wife should not be exposed in his presence in front of other men. He felt that physical exposure at birth verged on being almost pornographic, and he was personally humiliated. Intellectually he knew this was wrong, but emotionally he could not alter his response. Much distress and several therapy sessions were necessary to work this out. A number of fathers have reported variants of this problem. It is helpful to remember that for some men birth mixes sexuality and paternity in a sometimes confusing manner. Intimate involvement in the care of a woman in labor is not right for everyone.

Similarly, another father, a twenty-three-year-old airline clerk who had been present for the birth of his first baby, said, "It was the worst thing that I had ever seen—to see my wife in that kind of pain." He felt that he had helped create this situation: "How can I have made her go through this pain?" But he also said that all fathers should be there to see their babies born and to understand what their wives go through. This couple did not have a doula.

A new mother, thirty-one, an accountant married to a lawyer, thirty-three, noted after the birth of their first baby: "We both didn't want any outside help, but I was lucky. There were no other deliveries on the floor at the time I came to the hospital, and the obstetric nurse was able to stay with me and my husband during the entire labor. I couldn't have done it without her. My husband was helpful, but the nurse was essential." In this case the nurse functioned as both a nurse and a doula.

Another mother, thirty-five, experienced feelings of depression while facing her third pregnancy. Her husband, thirty-seven, worked in real estate. In uncovering the source of these feelings, she revealed how angry and abandoned she had felt because of her husband's passivity during the previous two births. She had wanted him to be more helpful, participative, and involved. He, on the other hand, had believed he was truly involved just by being there and by saying nice and encouraging things to her. He was surprised at her distressed feelings and did not know what more he could have done. We believe that the presence of a doula might have prevented this situation.

Another father, a twenty-nine-year-old physician, stated, "With our first baby I was so overcome emotionally that I could not make any rational observations about what was happening, and I truly believed there was imminent danger at every stage of labor." Again, this couple had no doula.

A thirty-five-year-old mother, married to a skilled carpenter in his thirties, wrote the following to us after the birth of their first baby: "The doula's support was effective and meaningful. She eased a great burden from my husband, as well as myself. She freed up my husband to be exactly where I needed him, when I needed him. My first response to having a doula was negative, my husband's positive. I must admit I did not like the idea of having a third person, a stranger, in on one of the most personal experiences of our lives. My husband felt he could use the support to keep him going in the right direction. The outcome of our experience is positive to both of us. The team of my husband and the doula kept me relaxed and focused. My husband was able to tend to my needs of touching and sharing, and the doula was able to coach me and encourage me at the same time. My husband felt this was a great help to him and let him be closer to me and stay relaxed."

The complexity of the father's role and the expectations given to the father in our society are illustrated by these couples. The wide variation in life experiences and cultural backgrounds makes any simple prescription for the role of fathers at birth impossible. Fathers and mothers need to know the difference in types of support that may be available to them during childbirth.

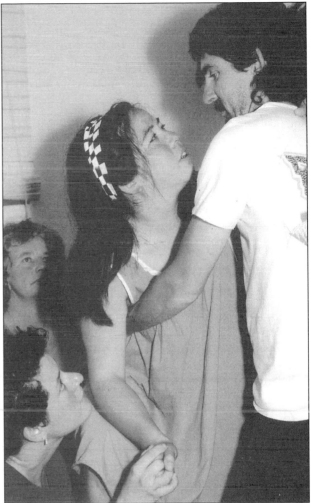

The father gives strong support during a contraction while the doula massages the mother's hand.

This information could give them permission to make the appropriate choices that are best for their particular situation.

Can a Father Be a Doula?

We are frequently asked if a father can function as a doula. After all, he loves his wife and cares for her dearly, he has had childbirth classes and has learned what relieves pain for her, and he is especially sensitive to her needs. What if a father and mother believe anyone else present during the labor might interfere with the unique intimacy between them? "We want privacy; we want to have this experience for ourselves. My partner is going to help me, coach me."

When labor begins in earnest, many of these intentions fall away, and both mother and father are greatly relieved when a nurse remains and helps. We strongly believe that a father cannot be a doula for the mother. A father is rarely able, moment to moment, to appreciate what is happening with the mother and whether each change is a normal part of the actual events of labor. An easier role for him is to give emotional support to the mother while the doula is there to support them both through the labor.

Michel Odent, the pioneering French obstetrician, noted that certain men have a beneficial effect on labor, while the presence of others only slows it down.[6] As an example, he mentioned a particular father who acted overprotective and possessive, continually massaging and caressing his wife. Odent commented that "this father anticipated her demands rather than responding to them. The woman in labor required calm, but he could only provide stimulation." Men sometimes find it hard to observe, accept, and understand women's instinctive behavior during labor and delivery. Instead, they often try to keep laboring women from slipping out of a rational, self-controlled state.

The anxiety that accompanies labor causes some men to react in counterproductive ways. For example, the father may lose touch with the mother's emotional state as he becomes more anxious and feels a need to take control. Performance anxiety, overactivity, excessive talking, or passivity may also occur. Any of these reactions may be exactly the opposite of what the woman needs. The doula can help him be in better harmony with the mother's emotional state.

As labor progresses, even fathers experienced in childbirth and trained in classes will often leave the labor room for increasingly long periods of relief (to get coffee, make telephone calls, and so on). While other fathers remain, they may distance themselves from their wives as a result of their fears. These episodes can generate unconscious anger or disappointment for the moth-

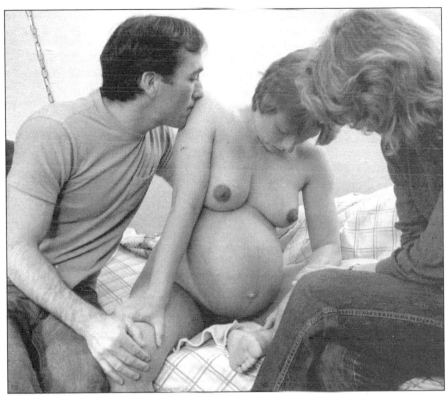

The tender affection of the father and the quiet support of a doula.

ers, because they, too, have bought into the belief that the fathers should be able to do everything. When a doula is available to both the man and the woman, they are able to fulfill their individual responsibilities: for the mother, going on with the birth, asking and receiving what she needs in the way of appropriate and empathic responses; for the father, being as supportive as he can be, yet responding at his own level of comfort and competence without losing face.

A doula needs to be sensitive at all times to the couple's relationship. When all is progressing well and they are interacting successfully, she steps away and remains present but in the background. She also helps involve the father appropriately, for example, by showing him how to massage the mother's back.

Often the doula will have to take time out to support another family member. In one case we heard about, where the mother and father were doing quite well together, the mother-in-law broke down because the couple's first pregnancy had been a stillbirth. The doula's main role at that moment was to help the mother-in-law and to protect the mother from added stress.

If the father is the only support and labor is not progressing easily and ends in a cesarean section, the father may feel that he failed in his role as coach and failed his wife. This sense of failure and guilt may affect his self-esteem. Sometimes men and women unconsciously harbor feelings of guilt or anger toward each other or toward themselves when the outcome is not as they expected.

There are other potential risks to the relationship. For some fathers, a cesarean section exonerates them from guilt or failure, for they can consciously believe that it is their wives' fault: a disproportionate pelvis, for instance, and not their inability to be good coaches. A father may also become angry at the mother for not doing her part in what they were both taught. The reality might, however, have been a dysfunctional labor. Such feelings can be prevented or ameliorated with support from an experienced doula. The doula

can help both parents understand the need for a cesarean section and feel positive about the safe outcome for their baby.

A birth happens in the context of an ongoing relationship, which can be complex. A father may be struggling unconsciously with unresolved issues of mortality, sexuality, identification with the birth process, paternity, and confusion about his role.

So many variables of an emotional nature can be projected into the birth situation. In contrast, the doula's role remains relatively constant. She is there only as a supportive and informed birth assistant. Women who choose to become doulas want to help other women and have a certain empathic sense of childbirth. They have an opportunity during their training to understand their own personal issues associated with childbirth, and they learn not to project onto the laboring woman their own emotional needs. (See Appendix A in regard to the training of a doula.)

The experienced doula knows when to be a strong presence and support as well as when to sit quietly by as the woman moves into her own body process. It is easier for the doula than for the father to shift from a guiding, directing, or suggesting role to a quieter, encouraging role, or to any other role needed as the events and drama of labor shift and change. Such a shift can be difficult for a father's self-esteem. Like the father's role, the doula's is not medical, but her experience with birth gives her a comfort and a knowledge about labor that can be extremely useful. She can be the interface between the woman or the couple and the medical staff as she applies her skills and sensitivity throughout the long hours of labor.

HELPING A FATHER PARTICIPATE

The presence of a doula complements a father's role and strengthens it. A doula often can give suggestions and encourage the father to touch, to talk, and to help in ways that feel truly comfortable to him and comforting to the mother. In conversation with the authors, Dr. Martin Greenberg, an expert on fathers and author of *Birth of a Father,* has commented:

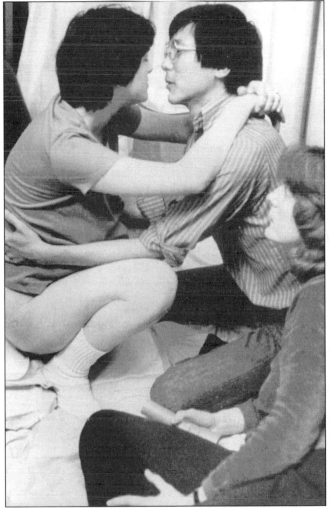

During the second stage, the squatting position increases the bony outlet of the pelvis by 28 percent. The doula respects the couple's moment of affection.

The mother has a biologically based task which is driven by a time clock, while the father feels like he is floating in air without a connection, uncertain about his tasks. A support person during this time can reach out to both of them, decrease the father's anxiety, give him support and encouragement, and teach him specific tasks, allowing him to reach out to his wife in a more caring and nurturing fashion.

Over and over again women say that "just knowing my husband was there, just his holding my hand, was the most important thing for me—while I could trust the doula's words and actions and let myself go, feeling safe that her experience would see us through."

An analogy that helps to clarify the distinction between the doula's and the father's role is the acceptance by the medical profession of the fact that doctors cannot objectively treat or care for their own families. Their strong emotional involvement leads them to judgments about diagnosis and therapy that they would not make with other patients.

Fathers, with the support of the doula, should be able to participate at any level that feels right and natural for them. In this way they can experience fully the joy and wonder of watching their babies come into the world. For father and mother, birth can then be a truly shared event—mutually moving, inspiring, and loving.

9

The Dublin Experience

Women in general have . . . [much] to gain from the
presence of a female companion who is not just sympathetic but is informed as well, and therefore in a much
better position to provide the sense of firm reassurance
which is so sorely needed at this time.

DRS. KIERIN O'DRISCOLL AND DECLAN MEAGHER,
Active Management of Labor

"You're great—you're doing well. That's right, relax. Breathe easily—breathe out through the contraction like this." In a soft voice, leaning close to the mother, a hand ever present on her arm or abdomen, the nurse-midwife continues: "That's good. Breathe out, like this—good—look at me." The midwife guides the mother through, speaking slowly in rhythm with the out breath. "Look at me. That's good, that's it. Breathe out. Let it go—out. It's easing now. Yes, good—you're marvelous."

The words of this nurse-midwife capture the warm, devoted care women in labor receive at the National Maternity Hospital in Dublin, Ireland. We traveled to Dublin to observe this care because we had heard of the extraordinarily good results—in terms of length of labor, use of anesthesia, and cesarean-section rates—that this hospital has shown.

The major emphasis of the obstetricians at the National Maternity Hospital is on the one-to-one personal attention of the nurse, and we wished to see how similar this was to support by a doula. The innovators, Drs. Kierin O'Driscoll and Declan Meagher note:

Mere physical presence is not enough, the nurse must appreciate that her primary duty to the mother is to provide the emotional support so badly needed at this critical time and not simply to record vital signs in a detached clinical manner. A guarantee is given to every expectant woman who attends this hospital that she will have a personal nurse through the whole labor, from the time of her admission to after her baby is born without regard to the hour of day or night.

THE PREVENTION OF PROLONGED LABOR

Early in his career Dr. Kierin O'Driscoll, began to question why dystocia (arrested labor) would arise in perfectly normal women after they came into the hospital. In the 1950s labors often lasted seventy-two hours or longer. Why did this prolongation of labor happen to normal women with a single fetus? He also observed that no one ever knew exactly when labor started. He began to observe what helped a woman in labor and what practices led to prolonged labor. His primary goal was the prevention of prolonged labor. By 1972 he had reduced normal labor of a first-time mother to no more than twelve hours.

Dr. O'Driscoll explained that some of the key factors included proper diagnosis of labor, one-to-one care, touch, and special treatment for first-time mothers. "If you look after primiparous (first-time) mothers properly they will deliver themselves next time. If not, they could be made an obstetrical crip-

ple for the rest of their life." Birth, he pointed out, must preserve a woman's dignity, and must remain a joyous event with a woman feeling in command of herself. When he began practice, women were left screaming or were put asleep. In the United States the problem of dystocia has been solved to some extent surgically: a 9 percent cesarean-section rate in 1970, 20 percent in 1980, and 30 percent in 1990. (By 1999, it was down to 22 percent.)

The standard of nursing in the National Maternity Hospital includes exceptional caring and good humor. The nurses are trained to touch the mother, to have eye and hand contact, to use the *en face* position (nurse and mother eye-to-eye in the same horizontal plane). Dr. O'Driscoll goes on to explain:

> As we began to understand and made a more rational approach to contain labor, we found we needed to change the organization of the labor ward, giving every woman a midwife to monitor her labor closely. This began to result in shorter and shorter labors. We found that we could deliver 225 babies [a year] for every midwife (where before it was 95 babies per midwife). So for every 200 deliveries we needed one less midwife.

The "charge midwife" (called sister) and the consultant physician are colleagues. All others, including the other doctors, answer to this midwife in charge. Midwives in Ireland have a different status than do those in the United States. The Irish midwife has a complementary role, not competing with the physicians. The physicians are consultants to the sister and are very respectful; there is no suspicion or antipathy.

© Marshall Klaus

The mother feels safe with the nurse-midwife and her husband.

Dr. O'Driscoll explained that another key factor is the education of the patient: this is education in the truest sense. The antenatal education teaches the mother to understand the process— what happens when she is in labor, how the labor graph used in that hospital works, how to help herself, and how to gain confidence in the support she will receive.

This system, which differs from that in the United States, vividly illustrates the potent effects of continuous emotional support.

This system of labor management began with the express purpose of reducing the length of labor and thereby its complications, and it is a comprehensive way of thinking about and facilitating the entire labor and delivery experience for a woman and her partner. It includes understanding the progress of her labor, her family history and number of pregnancies, and the complete organization of her experience in the hospital. Managing the labor in a thoughtfully orchestrated way allows the woman to feel attended to at all times—allows her to feel that she will be able to handle her labor, that she will be safe, that her dignity and experience matter, and that her body's responses are natural and normal.

THE DIAGNOSIS OF LABOR

The obstetricians at the National Maternity Hospital emphasize that the management of labor requires a complete understanding of the *diagnosis of labor.* A woman is either in labor or not in labor: the clear-cut criteria are known by the midwife in charge, who examines each woman. The childbirth education program also educates the woman to recognize true signs of labor. If a woman comes in having contractions or believing she may be in labor, but examination reveals that she is not in labor (20 percent of women who present to the delivery ward are not in labor), she will be sent to stay for a day in the antenatal ward, where she may go into labor at a later time, or be sent home the next day to wait until labor begins. In this hospital, until ten years ago, labor was very rarely induced.

When the diagnosis of labor is made, each woman is assigned her personal nurse-midwife, usually a nurse who is training to become a midwife and who will remain with her throughout labor. Each mother is assured that she will deliver within twelve hours, or in rare cases, shortly afterward. In this hospital, 50 percent of the first-time (primiparous) mothers have babies in five or fewer hours, and 84 percent of primiparous mothers have babies in under

eight hours. A few first-time mothers (less than 2 percent) have babies at twelve hours or a very short time thereafter.

A diagnosis of labor is made if a woman has been having strong and regular contractions every eight to ten minutes that last thirty to forty-four seconds each, if her cervix is dilated and thinned out (effaced), and if she has a bloody mucous show. The latter alone is not sufficient to diagnose labor, nor are contractions alone (since they may be Braxton-Hicks contractions). Only when she is diagnosed as being in labor does the "counting" or measurement of her labor progress begin.

This is not just a matter of labeling. If labor is incorrectly diagnosed and the measurement of labor begins too soon, a misperception of "labor lasting for hours and hours" is accepted. In that situation women will feel overwhelmed and out of control, and their anxious caregivers may feel compelled to initiate obstetric interventions such as oxytocin to increase uterine contractions. One thing can lead to another, and the mother can often end up many hours later with a cesarean section. Had the diagnosis been made correctly, she could have returned home and rested, knowing that the sensations she felt were not yet true labor. One to ten days later she would go into actual labor and most likely would have a natural delivery.

We have gone over this description of the diagnosis of labor in some detail because we think this is a critical element in the National Maternity Hospital's management of birth. If labor has indeed started but the mother's cervix is not dilating at a rate of at least one centimeter per hour, first-time mothers (only) will be given oxytocin after a number of hours. Only 41 percent of primiparous mothers are given oxytocin. (In U.S. hospitals the percentage of women receiving oxytocin varies widely.) Their management of labor may also include rupturing the membranes (the "bag of waters") once the baby's head is engaged appropriately, if the membranes have not ruptured spontaneously.

ONE-TO-ONE CARE

This kind of management of labor has spread to many parts of Europe and the United States. Unfortunately, in most hospitals the one-to-one nursing component has been left out. Judging from our research and that of others,[1] this is a fundamental error. These hospitals have not appreciated the importance of this continuous care in easing and shortening labor. We suspect that this particular ingredient of the program—the presence at all times of a caregiving nurse (or midwife or doula)—has the greatest influence on a successful outcome. As we saw in Chapter 5, in our studies we have been able to demonstrate almost the same results using *only* the component of a woman giving continuous emotional support. In the National Maternity Hospital in Dublin, birthing is women's work. Women caring for women continue an age-old tradition. The midwife practices her craft with skill, care, and intuitive and experienced knowledge.

Drs. O'Driscoll and Meagher designed the active management of labor based on their perceptive observations of a large number of women experiencing the old style of "hospital labor." In that period in Dublin before 1967 a woman in labor was often alone and was not carefully checked, and labor could last a long time. "It was sometimes chaos, with no one knowing when the woman had started her labor; sometimes a woman was in bed for days without any sense of management or containment." They believed that this was inhumane and that if each woman could be helped by another woman from the beginning to the end of her labor, her outcome could be quite dif-

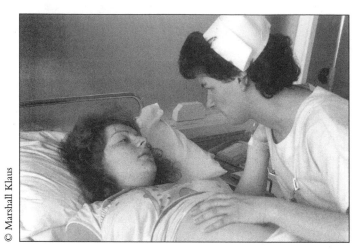

The midwife aligns her face with the mother's (en face) and holds her for full support.

ferent. They saw labor as a natural event and believed that the earlier hospital system disrupted this natural process. They also observed an imbalance in the use of personnel. For example, many more nurses were available during the day, and only a skeletal crew was on duty at night.

Keeping in mind the necessity of providing one-to-one care for each mother, these doctors created teams, each consisting of a charge midwife, two senior midwives, and five student midwives. To help them understand the process of labor, medical and nursing students who rotated through the labor ward would also be put to work providing the same kind of continuous support on day or night shifts. Being quite aware of the differences between a primiparous mother and a multiparous mother, Keirin O'Driscoll created a two-color chart system so that everyone on the floor (including the maintenance people) would know whether each mother was having her first baby or a subsequent one.

With these approaches as a guide, graduate nurses in training for midwifery are now the main supportive persons for a mother throughout her labor. These nurses are the model for care and instruct the medical students and beginning nursing students in the techniques, manner, and attitudes useful while attending labor and delivery. Obstetricians and other physicians respect the role and importance of the midwife.

After the midwife in charge determines that a woman is in labor, she assigns a nurse-midwife to the mother, and the work of support begins. The father is welcomed in whatever level of involvement he wants. He is encouraged to be present at all times, to feel comfortable about taking a break, or to leave while an intervention takes place if he wishes. He is not put in the role of

© Marshall Klaus

being the main support. It is clear that he is there as an emotional support, but not as an expert in facilitating labor. The nurse-midwife's focus is on the mother, but she is respectful toward the father; the nurse has him sit next to her and hold the mother's hand as the contractions get harder. She also asks him to hold the mother's arm while walking— the nurse-midwife on one side, the father on the other. The nurse-midwife works with the mother through each contraction, whether the mother is walking or remaining in bed. She says, "Tell me when you start having a pain." The nurse-midwives' continuous presence has an innate relaxing effect. A mother said: "I couldn't have done it without the nurse. When my husband started looking green, I sent him out for coffee. The most important thing for me was looking at the nurse's face, listening to her, holding her hand. My own sister was so nervous that I couldn't look at her. The nurse got me through it."

When the mother has a contraction while walking (as mentioned before, walking greatly helps accelerate dilatation of the cervix in early labor), the nurse-midwife has her lean against a wall, sigh out, let herself get loose, and focus her attention outward. Quietly guiding the mother through the contraction with relaxation breathing, the nurse-midwife reminds her to look at the nurse-midwife's face or at something in the hall. Focusing outward is a way for the woman to distance herself from focusing only on the pain. This attention to her natural breathing process, with focus on the exhalation, is different from any structured technique such as Lamaze. Every fifteen minutes during the walking, the nurse-midwife helps the mother return to bed to listen to the baby's heartbeat. Whatever the nurse-midwife does, she informs the mother beforehand, and while proceeding she explains what she is going to do and why, and what the results are, in simple language. For example, "I'm going to listen to the baby's heart." (She waits until after a contraction to press on the abdomen with the fetoscope to listen). "The heartbeat is perfect, strong—a healthy, normal rate of 140 beats. I'm going to time this contraction now: Good, you're doing great—nice and strong. Breathe it out—good; let it go. You're really great."

The nurse-midwives use different methods of managing pain or discomfort. The most frequently used and reinforced approach is the relaxation, exhaling, and focusing as just described. The nurse-midwife responds to a woman's questions about pain medications and

Stopping for a contraction.

informs her that she can have Demerol two times (fifty milligrams each time) up to the time her cervix is dilated to six centimeters. There is also a mask with nitrous oxide (laughing gas) or, if the mother is very distressed and unable to cope, an epidural anesthetic. The nurse most often helps the mother work through the pain. Twenty percent of women select an epidural. The nurse-midwives praise the mother throughout labor, whatever the choice. Even though there is a great deal of praise, what we heard always seemed appropriate and genuine. As labor progresses and transition, at eight to ten centimeters, occurs, the nurse becomes even more intensely involved, helping the woman manage the power of the contractions. She may hold her close and face-to-face. She will continue to talk the mother through the contraction, reminding her again and again of breathing out and letting go, and telling her how great she is doing.

Within the first two days of observing at the National Maternity Hospital in Dublin, we met one couple having a first baby, one couple with one baby at home, another with two babies at home, another with three other children, another with seven other children, and one family who had had a stillbirth with their first child. In each case the fathers were trying to be as supportive as they could. The father would sit in a chair next to the mother (the nurse-midwife would be standing at the head of the bed quite close to the mother). Typically, the father had frightened eyes, a worried look, and sweating, clammy hands. He usually held the mother's hand. The mother would squeeze the father's hand as she had a contraction; that was important for her. After one-half to one hour or so, the father in some cases went out for a break. Some felt more comfortable leaving whenever there was an internal examination of the mother. Although most of these fathers had been through labor before and, except for one family, had had good outcomes, they would tense up as the mothers had pain. If left alone for a few minutes, they would feel unsure of how to help. Afterward, they all echoed what one father said: "I was really worried. You know, you don't know how things will go. It's a blessing, really, the baby's okay and my wife." One mother of two children, now having her third, said, "I hope Paddy doesn't come before the baby's born. He always makes me more nervous than I am."

A BIRTH AT THE NATIONAL MATERNITY HOSPITAL

The following scene was typical of many we observed. The mother and father arrive at the hospital. The mother has been having contractions, and she thinks she is in labor. The midwife in charge greets her, helps her get comfortable, puts her in the examining room, and invites the father to come in or wait in the waiting room. As the mother has a contraction, the midwife gently but clearly starts her guiding instructions, even before examining the mother. "Lie on your side, breathe in through your nose, and long slow breaths out through your mouth. Keep your eyes open; look at me—good, keep doing that, nice and slowly, that's good (she models for her). Purse your lips, make a swish sound as you breathe out—good. Take a big breath in through your nose, keep your eyes open—look at the window or at my face, blow and release, breathe out through your mouth. Again; now look at me—keeps your mind off pain. That's right, you're doing great, you're doing marvelous. What time did the pain start?" The mother says she had pains all night. "Did you sleep?" She dozed. "Was there a bloody show?" Yesterday, she indicates. "How much blood? Show me in my hand." The midwife explains everything before she does it. "I'm going to examine you to see if you're in labor. If you are, I'm going to break the bag of waters to check the color of the water and to accelerate the labor. Okay? Tell me when you are getting a pain. Now I'll set you up and tell you what's happening." (She has checked the mother's pulse, blood pressure, and temperature.) She examines the mother. "You're in labor—three centimeters, a very good start. I haven't broken the waters yet because the baby's head is not yet down. I want you to walk for one hour. Walking helps get the head down. Walk with your husband and nurse

© Marshall Klaus

This photograph and the following four photographs were taken within five minutes in late labor.

now. The best way to get the baby's head down is by walking. Then it'll be very quick. I think you'll have a short labor. I'll examine you later." She introduces the mother to her personal nurse-midwife.

The three of them proceed slowly up and down the corridor. The nurse-midwife almost always has her hand on the mother. It is quiet, peaceful, and calm. They pass a similar trio. The nurse-midwife says, "Tell me when you feel a contraction starting—we'll stop and I'll help you through it." The woman says, "Yes, now." They stop; the nurse-midwife suggests that the woman lean easily against the wall, and she helps her through the contraction. The time passes quickly in this fashion: they walk, they listen, and as contractions get stronger or the mother feels any change or wants to get in bed, the nurse-midwife follows at the mother's pace: staying with her for every moment of the experience, reassuring, validating, comforting, appropriately respecting the father's position, and being the stable presence of experience and confidence for both the mother and the father.

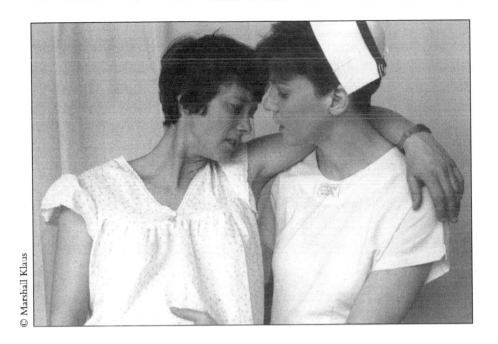

© Marshall Klaus

The midwife in charge comes periodically throughout the labor to help the training nurse-midwife who is providing support. She checks what is happening, reassures the mother, and at appropriate times checks for dilatation.

As the second stage gets under way (when the cervix is fully dilated and the head is descending), many women sometimes lose their sense of direction and control. They feel overwhelmed and even after having delivered several children may say, "I can't do it. No, it's really too hard—I can't do it!" At this point, both midwives help the woman in pushing the baby out, with the charge midwife reminding the mother how to push through the contraction, but only when she feels like pushing. Here is an excellent example of how this intense one-to-one communication is essential. The nurse-midwife says softly, "Just one person talking so as not to cause distraction. We're going to make use of that contraction. When it comes, let's use your own power to push this baby out. Good, good, take a big breath—no talk or sound. Put your chin on your chest and push that breath into your bottom as long as you can hold it, then quickly two more times within this contraction. In three contractions you're going to push that baby right out. I can see its hair—great, good, you're doing great."

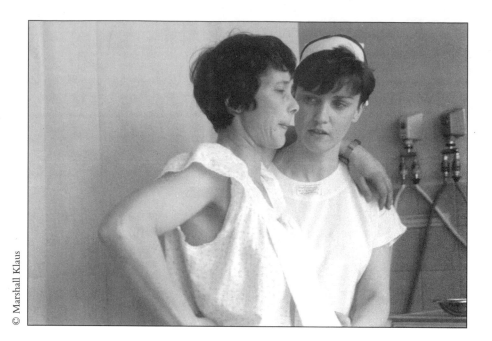

"Now, rest in between contractions." She helps the woman into position. Sometimes the mother gets leverage by holding her own knees, or the two midwives let the mother push her feet against them to brace herself. It was unusual to us to see such close physical contact—so much more humane than the old stirrups. The woman either sits up in the bed, as high as possible, or is on her left side. The midwives often use a bed-wedge pillow behind her back.

As the contraction starts, the nurse-midwife reminds the mother: "We're going to make the best use of this push-ing energy. Now another contraction; take a big breath, mouth closed, chin on chest, and push into your bottom and forward. Hold the breath as long as pos-sible. Good, now a second big breath. Good, go along with the urge to push. Now a third big breath—good, push into your bottom, and stay forward. Good, good, the baby's come forward a lot. You're great. Now rest. Let me know when the urge to push starts—that first push is the best push. Good." She has the father stand just behind the mother with his arm around her shoulders, letting him support the mother as she pushes. The midwives recognize the mother's incred-ible need for encouragement in order to

keep going. Even when any of the team or family is tired, the midwives keep going cheerfully, reminding the mother that she has all the power she needs to push the baby out and that she's feeling pressure now, not pain. When the head has crowned, the midwives guide the mother gently to relax and look at the focal point, just breathing in a light and slow breath to let her body do the rest of the natural pushing out of the baby.

A MODEL OF HUMANE CARE

Sitting as quiet observers in the corner of the room for an extended period, we saw an entire system geared toward supporting the mother and father through their baby's birth—without anxiety and with gentle caring, encouragement, warmth, and displays of real affection. Never in the entire week, after attending forty deliveries, did we hear any mother spoken to, or about, gruffly.

The mothers were treated with unusual sensitivity. We saw a warmth develop between the nurse-midwife and each mother—a component we think is extremely valuable. The mother is held both physically and emotionally. Every caregiver seemed aware that this was a very special time for each couple, and each mother was treated as a special individual, whether the mother was sad, grumpy, or upset. The equanimity of the nurses and midwives is a valuable model for all obstetrics. The cycle of nurturing and empowerment that occurs in this process makes a woman feel valued and enhances her self-esteem. If an extra nurse met a mother even for a few minutes, for example, while delivering something to her room, she would come back after the delivery, if she could, and ask, "What did you have—a girl or boy? That's great—congratulations!"

The whole system used accurate and appropriate observations of fetal heartbeat, maternal blood pressure, uterine contractability, and, only when necessary, fetal scalp sampling and fetal monitoring. Modern medical care, humanism, and warmth were balanced in the proper proportions, without overreliance on high-technology interventions to manage labor.

As we mentioned earlier, many of the units in the world that purport to employ this same management of labor use the same definition of labor, rupture the membranes, and use oxytocin, but they disregard what we consider an essential ingredient of the method— the personal nurse. This personal, continuous one-to-one care is so naturally ingrained in the personnel of the National Maternity Hospital that they themselves may not appreciate its immense value and may not have emphasized this ingredient of care when teaching or explaining their method to visitors from abroad. Because rupturing of the membranes appears to shorten labor by thirty to ninety minutes, and only about 41 percent of the mothers receive oxytocin, the one-to-one midwifery care accounts for much of the remarkable results at this hospital. This is in agreement with a separate analysis,[2] which concludes that the effective ingredient in the management of labor in the Dublin program is not rupture of the membranes or large doses of oxytocin, but the presence of a continuously supportive labor companion.

Visiting several of the classes, we saw how the childbirth educators—experienced midwives who have worked closely in the system—cheerfully and warmly help the mothers prepare for labor. The whole emphasis is on assuring the mother that her labor will be under twelve hours, that she will never be left alone in labor day or night, and that everything is geared toward that goal. This important message is a powerful subliminal suggestion, in itself helping to bring about a short, normal labor.

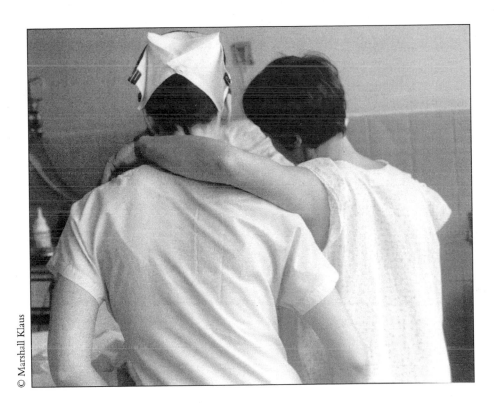

© Marshall Klaus

Another important achievement at this Dublin hospital is the unusually low complication rate for both the mother and the baby. When we visited the National Maternity Hospital fifteen years ago the cesarean-section rate was between 5 to 6 percent, and the mean length of labor for first-time mothers was slightly less than six hours. However, in 1997 the cesarean-section rate rose to 11.6 percent of all first-time mothers giving birth at full term. Some analysts of this figure[3] have suggested that the increase is due to higher rates of induction, pre-labor cesarean section such as for breech births, and a response to changing maternal attitude in Dublin. At the same time, the statistics on the health of the babies delivered continues to be most impressive. The cesarean-section rate at the National Maternity Hospital—even at 11.6 percent—raises many questions about the over-20-percent cesarean-section rate in the United States.[4]

In summary, our observation period at the National Maternity Hospital vividly demonstrated how significant every component of care and organization is in normalizing the birth experience. Theirs is a unique model that can help us all in reducing the complications of labor and in making delivery of a baby an easier, healthier, and more joyous experience.

10

Postpartum Care

A mother . . . finds it very hard to give up the nurses' care
of her, and to be left alone to care for her infant in the
very way that she herself needs to be treated.

D. W. WINNICOTT,
Babies and Their Mothers

Parents' need for support does not, of course, stop at the moment of birth. When first-time parents come home from the hospital with their new infant, they embark on a task for which they have little preparation or experience. While almost all societies have a system for helping parents through this period, in the United States the lack of a widely accepted cultural tradition for giving the necessary support to families after childbirth is a major deficiency. In the past a mother's mother and other female relatives provided this assistance and guidance. But today the mother's mother is often at work and there may be no one to fill the void.

It is often difficult for a new mother to recognize her needs and feelings and give herself permission to ask for help. Usually neither parent has a good understanding of the needs of a young infant and therefore cannot anticipate the endless demands of a newborn child. To shift from an active life where a mother has had social and work contacts with a large number of friendly and supportive associates to meeting the never-ending demands of a young infant is a momentous change. The burden of continuous responsibility with no letup and the unusual and unexpected degree of fatigue can make a mother feel desperate about whether she can survive and how she will manage.

LEAVING THE HOSPITAL

During the first days after the birth of a baby, the mother is experiencing major physical and hormonal changes.

During this time, the next day, or perhaps in two days, she goes home. In our work with new parents it has always been surprising how little of what we told mothers the day of delivery was understood and retained. Even though they appeared to hear and understand and sometimes asked appropriate questions, a day or two later it would be as if the subject had never been discussed. We learned to save our explanations until later. This lapse of memory was due to the exceptional physical and emotional demands on the mother during labor and in the early hours after delivery, which made it impossible for her to process the directions that were being provided.

Nowadays, the task of adequately preparing parents for the care of their baby is formidable. There is no time for mothers to establish a satisfying interaction and learn to breast-feed their babies in a safe, supportive environment before being discharged. Concerns about jaundice and the behavior of the baby may not be resolved before the infant goes home.

When asked to comment on any problems during the postnatal stay in the hospital, almost every mother answers, "I have not had time to get to know my baby, and to know what to do with my baby at home."

Reviewing the events of labor and delivery with the doula (or nurse-midwife) is very helpful. We have found that the mother and father frequently have different ideas about what occurred and that these may differ significantly from the observations of others present. The parents' misconceptions are understandable, given their lack of experience with the hospital environment and their intense emotional involvement. However, they need not carry misconceptions about one another's performance or about hazards or damage to the baby when these can be clarified in the early postpartum period.

Short as the time in the hospital may be, it is extremely important for the nurses, midwives, and physicians to do their best to prepare the parents for what they will encounter when they take the baby home. First, before the mother is discharged, every effort should be made to be certain that she knows she has a normal, healthy baby (if this is the case). Initial questions about the baby's breathing or general behavior should be answered clearly and fully before discharge, or else a definite follow-up course of action (such as checking the baby's bilirubin level the day after discharge) should be planned. The hospital staff and the doula need to offer basic breast-feeding information. Studies have shown that the sooner after delivery mothers start breast-feeding and the more frequently they nurse their babies in the first two weeks, the more abundant their milk supply and the greater the babies' weight gain.[2] If there are any difficulties with breast-feeding, such as cracked nipples, a call to a lactation consultant or the local La Leche League will usually answer the question or problem.

AT HOME

The vast majority of first-time parents have had no experience with a young infant. We have seen that new mothers who have cared for younger siblings or have baby-sat young infants usually know how to handle the common problems of infants and generally feel somewhat confident in the early care of the infant.

After a mother has a baby, her mind tends to go back to an early time in her life, and many memories come to mind. These memories may evoke in her a special need to be cared for and protected. As part of this psychological regression a mother needs to feel safe, to be held, and to be cared for. When this need is not met, a woman may feel abandoned, lonely, and insecure. In our culture the husband's support is essential for a mother, but he too has similar needs during this period. As we saw earlier, the doula's presence makes both father and mother feel safe. The father, too, is relieved of the heavy weight of responsibility that the doula carries.

Having a baby can place an unexpected strain on a marital relationship. For couples to bear up under the fatigue, the role and work changes, and the disruption of eating, sleeping, sex, and social activities, each partner needs to make a major effort at being understanding, supportive and communicative. It is hard to imagine how very tired parents can become when their baby's feeding schedules and needs do not follow any normal day-night cycle. Taking

turns with the "nighttime watch" can help, but a couple's most important step is to share feelings. Also, the father needs to show an awareness of the strain on the mother's system after giving birth, which is natural.

Couples do best if they already communicate well before the baby is born, if they have similar ideas about parenting, and if the father has truly wanted the baby. If conflicts arise, the couple can benefit from discussing these feelings and differences with an objective person, such as a counselor or other professional.

The parents need assistance and support with the new baby and any siblings, but they do not need to fight old battles. The more the mother is cared for, the more easily she can manage the baby. The more praise and support she receives, the more love and patience she will have with the infant. Praise and understanding from the father have been shown to enhance the mother's positive feelings about her baby and herself.

PRIMARY MATERNAL PREOCCUPATION

As we were developing our concept of the process of parent-to-infant bonding, we were attracted to the writings

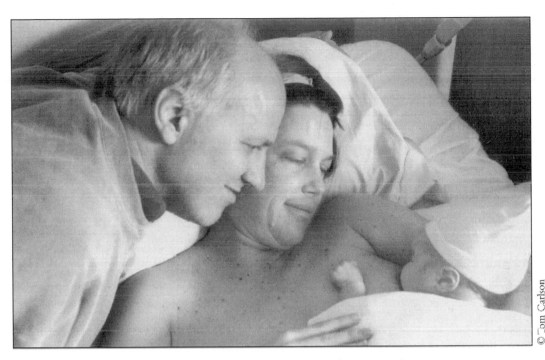

A father and mother begin to "take in" their new infant.

of the psychoanalyst D. W. (Donald) Winnicott on "primary maternal preoccupation."[3] He noted that in the perinatal period there is a special mental state of the mother in which she has a greatly increased sensitivity to and focus upon the needs of her baby. Such a state begins toward the end of the pregnancy and continues for a few weeks after the birth of the child. Mothers need support, nurturing, and a protected environment to develop and maintain this state.

"Only if a mother is sensitized in the way I am describing," wrote Winnicott, "can she feel herself into her infant's place, and so meet the infant's needs." In our own research, we have observed many examples of the special sensitivity of the mother in picking up the subtle signals of her infant, whether a fragile, tiny, premature baby or a robust, healthy, full-term one.

Using the term "holding environment," Winnicott indicated that a mother shows love to her infant through physical and emotional holding, which is crucial for the child's physical and emotional development. He felt that mothers who have the capacity to provide "good-enough care" will be helped by being supported and cared for themselves in a way that recognizes their important maternal task.

In the hectic atmosphere of a modern hospital, the heightened sensitivity of primary maternal preoccupation is sometimes misinterpreted by physicians and nurses as excessive anxiety. Once the parents are at home, the importance of this period may not be sufficiently recognized. Mothers have expectations of being perfect mothers—handling baby, work, and life as usual—and fathers need wives to be back to normal quickly, back to handling home, job, and their usual relationship. When this does not occur, a mother may feel guilty, and a father may be critical and unsympathetic.

Many women feel distressed that they cannot do everything as easily as before, or they may wonder if life will ever return to normal. Sometimes a mother in this period may question her own desire to return to work: "I'm so in love with this baby, I never want to leave him. Will I ever want to go back to work? Is something the matter with me?" Women have even told us how they have held back on becoming fully attached to their babies because they knew they would have to go back to work soon, or because they had such severe, sad, and upsetting reactions when they went back to school or work early with the previous baby that they did not want to go through this wrenching emotional reaction again.

POSTPARTUM DEPRESSION

The "baby blues," characterized by a short period of emotional lability, commonly occurring between the second and fifth postpartum day, affect between 80 and 90 percent of new mothers. In contrast, the term *postpartum depression* refers to a group of poorly defined, severe, depressive-type symptoms, which usually begin at four to eight weeks postpartum but, sometimes, later in the first year and which can persist for more than a year. In the past, women with these symptoms rarely sought treatment or were hospitalized. The incidence ranges from 10 to 16 percent of new mothers.[4]

The symptoms of postpartum depression cover a wide range, including exhaustion, irritability, frequent crying, feelings of helplessness and hopelessness, lack of energy and motivation so that the woman's ability to function is disturbed, lack of interest in sexual intercourse, disturbances of appetite and sleep, and feelings of being unable to cope with the new demands placed on her. Anxiety, a very frequent feature, is often related to the infant's welfare and may persist in spite of reassurance by physicians and nurses. It shows up in some mothers as lack of affection for the baby and, in turn, self-blame and guilt. Mothers may be concerned that they are not able to measure up to their own image of the ideal mother. It is not uncommon for a woman suffering from postpartum depression to have psychosomatic symptoms such as headache, backache, vaginal discharge, and abdominal pain for which no organic cause can be found.

It is important to point out that mothers working to meet the demands of their new babies and missing sleep may find that some of these symptoms fit their own situation. A mild appearance of one or more of these feelings is normal. When they are many and continue over a period of weeks, help is needed. The outlook for mothers suffering from postpartum depression is good if the diagnosis is made early and treatment is started. When there is a long delay in starting treatment, the depression may be prolonged. Often short-term psychotherapy is all that is needed. Simply having someone to talk to is very helpful in working out these symptoms. In some cases, mothers may need medication for depression and/or anxiety, if rest, support, and being well listened to do not relieve symptoms.

Most studies show that a person's previous history or a family history of psychiatric problems increases the chances of postpartum depression. However, in most cases psychosocial factors are very important. The effects of unfavorable life events or chronic problems such as bereavement, unemployment, inadequate income, unsatisfactory housing, or unsupportive relations may be intensified by the fact that the new mother feels trapped and unable to change her circumstances. The experience of childbirth may bring back to her the emotional reactions related to unresolved grief for a previous stillbirth, miscarriage, or abortion, or for the death of her own mother. When a mother has had a poor relationship with her own mother or was separated from one or both parents before the age of eleven, she is more likely to be depressed and anxious, according to research. The mother's inability to confide in her partner or a friend has been noted as a factor in depression. Women are often embarrassed to tell anyone how bad they feel.

Loneliness, isolation, and lack of support are serious problems for today's mothers. At the same time, mothers find it hard to reconcile the discrepancy between the hoped-for fantasy and the reality of motherhood.

Recognizing postpartum depression is important not only for the understanding and treatment of the mother, but also because of its negative effects on the relationship between the mother and the baby, and on the child's learning and social and emotional development. Preventing postpartum depression is the best way to avoid such effects, and social support is one of the most vital factors in prevention.

Help at Home

It is most important for the parents to arrange for someone they are comfortable with to help at home after the birth. This person can be a relative or an experienced friend who shares the parents' ideas about the care and feeding of the infant and will let the parents handle the baby while the helper manages the household. Parents should plan to have someone who can nurture and support them for as long a period as possible. In addition to help from friends or relatives, there are postpartum services available, such as postpartum doulas, nannies, or housekeepers.

If the father can arrange to take time off, he can perform many important tasks and provide much support, but the mother may wish to have the help of another woman. She may find it easier to talk with another woman about her most personal fears and anxieties, her emotional reactions—positive and negative—and any physical discomfort such as the episiotomy pain. After a cesarean delivery, a mother's needs will be intensified because her fatigue and discomfort will be greater. In all cases, the more the mother is cared for, supported, and protected, the better she will be able to care for her baby.

The father or other helper should have the responsibility for making sure the mother is not overwhelmed with too many visitors or phone calls for too long. The mother who can rest during the day, who does not feel the need to entertain with conversation and refreshments, faces the little ups and downs of her baby's course with infinitely more equanimity, adaptability, and good humor than a stressed, fatigued mother who talks on the phone for long periods and must entertain guests until they go home at 11:00 P.M. Relaxation exercises continue to be useful in the postpartum period.

GETTING STARTED WITH BREAST-FEEDING

The more frequently the mother breast-feeds her baby in the first two or three weeks and, as we said, the more she carries the infant in a Snugli-like carrier on her body, the less the baby will cry. Studies have also shown that if the response to a baby's cry or fuss occurs within ninety seconds, the baby will quiet rapidly.[5] To get to know her baby and get off to a good start in nursing, a mother needs plenty of time, as well as extra support, protection, and care during the first two or three months.

Along with the encouraging increase in breast-feeding in the United States, there has been an improved understanding of how to guide mothers to get started successfully. The early introduction of the breast to the newborn and the "latch on" technique are extremely helpful for successful nursing. Reducing pain medications given near the end of labor, particularly Demerol, as well as decreasing their concentration in epidurals and starting the analgesia late in labor and at lowered doses significantly improves the chances for successful breast-feeding.

After birth the infant's body should be dried thoroughly with three cotton blankets but *not* the baby's hands, because the amniotic fluid dried on the hands has an enticing smell for newborns and is useful as they find their way on their own to the breast. To improve the chances of this early suckling the injection of vitamin K and eye ointment should both be delayed one and a half hours while the infant is in the quiet-alert state.

Newborns, alone with their parents and placed on the mother's chest between the mother's breasts, often begin latching on at 60 to 90 minutes of age, if not sleepy from maternal medications. When babies "latch on," they open their mouths widely to avoid the tip of the nipple, placing their lips on the areola. *The face of the infant should never be pushed into the breast.* Sometimes after this is done the infant becomes aversive to the breast. The newborn should always be the one to decide when he or she would like to take a first drink. Many infants will manage on their own to find the breast and begin to suckle effectively because normal infants have built-in programmed systems in their brains to achieve this.

A DEVELOPMENTAL APPROACH TO LEARNING TO LATCH ON

Some mothers and their infants have difficulty with "latching on." We have

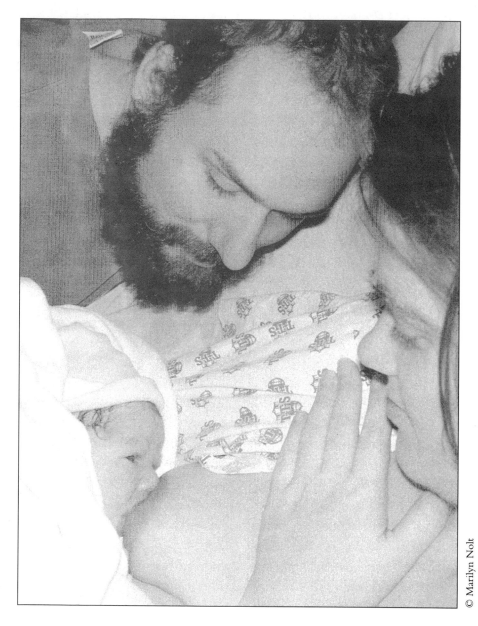

An early "latch on." Getting it right!

asked Dr. Christina Smillie[6] to describe her unique approach to preventing or resolving such difficulty. She points out that newborns and babies of all ages have the ability to find the breast by themselves, just as kittens and puppies do. We don't "make" our babies learn to latch; we simply "allow" them to learn.

To do this, the key is to start with a calm and focused infant. Babies have more control over their movements when they are calm. How can a mother do this? We start with the baby asleep, or only in very mild hunger, with mother and infant undressed and skin-to-skin, with the infant's chest on her upper chest, usually between her breasts. It's often helpful to hold the baby in a vertical position. The mother doesn't have to start with the baby's face near the nipple at all, simply with the baby well snuggled comfortably on her body.

If at first he just wants to sleep, that's fine. Mother and baby are on "baby time." As the baby stirs, his mother can keep him calm by talking to him, getting his attention, even making eye contact if he looks her way. As he gets hungry, he will start twisting his body toward one breast or the other, and may begin bobbing his head up and down, looking for the breast. Or he may throw himself rapidly toward one breast, or he might fall gently backwards toward the nipple. As he moves his head toward one breast, his mother may want to help him a little, by moving his rump up toward the other breast, and helping him keep his face in contact with her skin.

At this point, a mother can help by continuing to talk to her infant. Her encouraging voice helps him stay focused and in control. She can also help by assuring that his whole body is against her in such a way that his nose, rather than the mouth, is heading toward the nipple, and by allowing him to keep his face in contact with her skin. The infant knows the breast by feel, not by sight, and knows the nipple by smell, not by sight. Without that contact, the infant may arch, wondering where the breast went, even when it is a half-inch away!

It is helpful for the mother to avoid having a hand on the back of the newborn's head; instead, her hand can support his neck and shoulders. The infant needs neck support but also freedom to move. The baby himself—when he feels the breast against his chin and lower lip and smells the nipple under his nose—will then reach with his upper lip up and over the nipple to an off-center latch.

A comfortable latch allows the infant to swallow milk, and that teaches him that he is holding his mouth correctly.

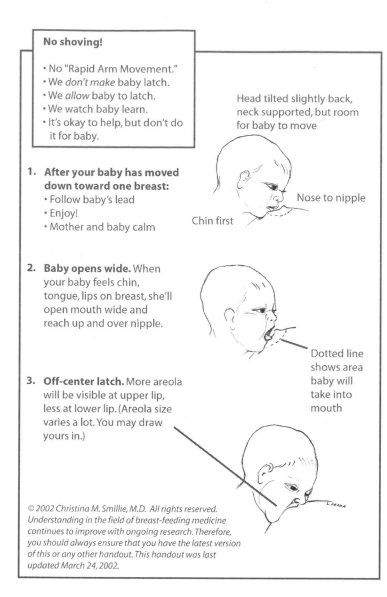

1. **After your baby has moved down toward one breast:**
   - Follow baby's lead
   - Enjoy!
   - Mother and baby calm

Head tilted slightly back, neck supported, but room for baby to move

Nose to nipple

Chin first

2. **Baby opens wide.** When your baby feels chin, tongue, lips on breast, she'll open mouth wide and reach up and over nipple.

Dotted line shows area baby will take into mouth

3. **Off-center latch.** More areola will be visible at upper lip, less at lower lip. (Areola size varies a lot. You may draw yours in.)

encourage her to fix it. If it hurts a lot, she can let him start again by putting his cheek on her breast near the nipple. If it only hurts a little, she can fix the latch by pulling gently on his chin while he sucks. A good latch is always comfortable.

POSTPARTUM DOULA

A special kind of help now available for mothers is that of a postpartum doula. The training of a postpartum doula includes CPR, lactation training, common infant health problems, knowledge of what to look for in the mother that may need medical attention, and communication skills often dealing with emotional concerns. For the safety of the infant, these doulas have TB testing and hepatitis immunizations.

The postpartum doula helps the mother keep track of the infant's urine,

After a little practice, these steps are no longer necessary, and feeding is easy.

If the baby doesn't get it quite right, there will be no milk flow, and the baby may pull off to fix the latch. Or, his mother may feel pain, which should

stool, and number of feedings and watches for increasing jaundice, if the mother wishes. She is also ready to meet other needs of the parents, such as shopping, taking care of other children, light housekeeping, and cooking nutritious meals. She helps organize the household and keeps appropriate emergency and family numbers available for the parents. In other words, a new mother's Mary Poppins.

An important skill for a postpartum doula is her ability to listen. The doula must avoid the temptation to recount her own or other women's stories. The main goal is to be present while the mother is the one talking. By listening to and acknowledging her feelings and memories of the birth and what she is experiencing in this postpartum period, the doula helps the mother process these significant events. Having someone mirror and validate her gives the mother an opportunity to make sense of the events. She then feels heard and can let go of the self-criticism that sometimes accompanies a woman's perception of her performance. A mother benefits by being able to talk about her positive and/or negative memories. During this early time, the mother may be going through a number of emotions, and being listened to gives permission for expression, sorting out, and healing.

The postpartum doula should be fully familiar with an infant's six states of consciousness or awakeness, and the special talent of a newborn to respond with interest and with finely tuned sensory abilities.[7] The doula can illustrate for the parents how the newborn responds to their voices, their touch, their faces, as well as how the infant needs to close down when she is tired or overwhelmed. Learning how to become attuned to the infant's signals is a major task for both parents in this early period. It is a process of discovery and takes time. Their sensitive responses help the baby develop a sense of self. The doula can remind parents that they cannot spoil their infants by picking them up when they cry or by being immediately responsive to their needs.

There are numerous ways the postpartum doula can engage the father to feel included in this early adjustment time. A father often feels he has nothing to do when the mother's main occupation is breast-feeding several times a day. However, a father has an important role in supporting the mother physically and emotionally in this tender time.

A father should be instructed on how to help position the infant at the breast. Here, a second pair of hands can be most useful. Bringing pillows to support different positions of the mother is essential for breast-feeding comfort. When the mother is sitting up, the partner can arrange the pillows under the baby or under the mother's arm, or while in the side-lying position in bed, the partner can prop pillows behind the mother's back, under her head, and behind the baby's back. The partner can bring her something to drink because breast-feeding makes her quite thirsty. Breast-feeding can be challenging, and a mother may cry or feel like it's not working or feel like giving up. The partner's understanding, support, love, and encouragement are especially meaningful at these times. Until feeding becomes established and the mother does not need help, being with the mother during nighttime feedings is unusually supportive to her. It is surprising how these seemingly simple actions on the partner's part can make such a difference to the mother's comfort and confidence.

Additionally, helping with routine activities lifts the burden from the new mother. A father needs to have his own time to bond with his baby. He can bathe the baby, change the diapers, dress the baby, nap with the baby on his chest, sing to the baby, and rock with the baby. The doula can encourage or instruct the new father in a variety of ways to learn about, take care of, play with, hold, soothe, comfort, and interact with his infant, always attuning to the infant's comfort and responses.

The doula can help the mother with stress management; simple exercises such as passive-progressive-relaxation techniques; slow, quiet breathing, relaxing muscles throughout the body; and using visualizations for deepening her ability to relax. In one study in which women who continued relaxation and visualization exercises after birth (similar to the exercises used in labor) were compared to a group of women who just rested, the relaxation group had 50 percent less depression and anxiety six weeks later. When the body and mind are calm, healing is enhanced, mental tension is released, and more inner peace and confidence can develop. Relaxation also enhances breast-feeding and milk flow.

We asked Tracy Fengler,[8] a postpartum doula, to explain her role:

"When you are a postpartum doula, much of the time you need to be a very quiet, calming person. You come into the home, and into the lives of these people who are at one of the most incredible times of their life. Many parents are worried about what this new person is going to be like. What are they going to do with my baby? They're

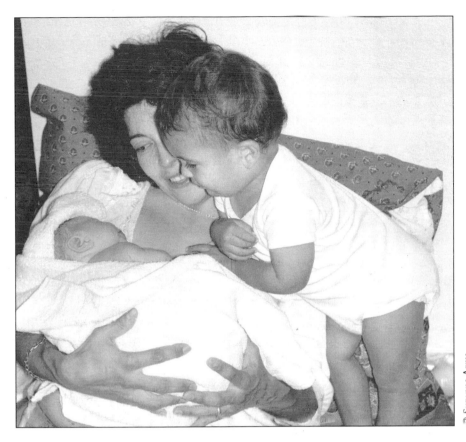

A brother meets his sister.

often afraid of a stranger being in their home and taking over. I know exactly that feeling. When I had my baby, my mom said she'd get me a baby nurse, and I said no thanks.

"I do a lot of listening. When I first come, I sit in a chair, and usually the mom is with the baby, either in her arms or nursing. If they want to tell me their birth story, great. I take my cues from what the parents tell me. I try not to come in like gangbusters, giving all sorts of directions. You don't want to overwhelm them. They've already had so much overloading, classes and reading, and the birth, and their heads are

Portpartum Care   183

spinning. I want to see how I can meet their needs.

"I tell parents that I do everything, kind of a jack-of-all-trades. I can help with all the baby care, the breast-feeding, taking care of the mom, the dad, meals, errands, and pets. I can walk the dog if they want or take the dog to the vet. I can play with other children, and I can help them with the transition of having a second one. I tell every parent when I start that every family has different needs. Some really care about food; some don't care at all about food, and I take my cues from them. They'll say, 'you know, I'm really, really interested in the baby and the baby care, and I'm really worried about my not getting enough sleep,' and so when I come in and I see them with the baby, and they're nursing, we'll work just on those items. When I come, I'll look at the baby, I'll look at the mom, look at the situation and see how I can gently help. I'll say, 'How have things been going? How do you feel? How does your body feel?' If she says 'my body feels really bad, my back is killing me, my neck is killing me, my nipples are sore,' I'll say 'okay, then let's work on positioning the breast-feeding for you and the baby. You need to be very comfortable. You need to have your back straight up against the chair; you need to have pillows around; we need to find the best place for you. For right now, the best place is a nice big area, either your bed or a couch. We're going to do this now for a couple of days, and I'm going to make sure that the baby is on right and everybody's comfortable. In a week you may be getting up and trying the rocking chair, or trying different positions.

"Lots of parents say to me, 'this is a lot harder than I thought. No one ever tells you that it's like this.' We need to make sure that the baby is on right. If the baby does not have enough of the nipple or the areola in its mouth, it's not going to get most of the milk out. It's going to be rubbing in the wrong part of the mouth, and it's going to be very uncomfortable for the mother, and it's not going to be the best way for the baby. So we'll work on that, and then I'll tell them that some discomfort is normal; for the first couple of weeks it's not pain free. It does hurt for the first ten, twenty seconds once you're on. Once we get the baby on, you can feel some pain. That should go away. If it doesn't, we need to get the baby off and try again. It really is a learning experience.

"The most common problem is letting the baby fall asleep at the breast and thinking that it's eating. Eating is usually what's going on in the beginning, but the baby might be on nearly an hour, and the mother thinks the baby is eating the whole time. The baby is not eating; it's just hanging out. Then it finally pulls off or they take it off, wondering why it's hungry again so quickly. The problem is to keep newborns awake and interested. I let them know how hard and tiring it is for newborns; they become tired out, even after five minutes. You need to keep them going, keep them active, burp them. A lot of parents are afraid of the burping; they just go from one side to the next breast without getting the baby awake. We don't want the baby to sleep at this moment. We need effective breast-feeding; you don't want a baby that's just snacking.

"I tell them some babies will pull off on their own and let you know when they've had enough, and some babies won't. Some babies are just very happy being there, and, if they're allowed, will just hang out. With these babies you really need to know when to stop them, take them off, wake them up, change their diapers, burp them, get them in different positions, positions that aren't so relaxing. Usually over the shoulder is relaxing. I tell them to place the baby sitting up on their lap and crawl your fingers up their spine to keep them awake.

"When we start, it's not just let's go right to the nipple. Let's check everything on the way to getting there. We've got the baby in the right position; are you comfortable? You need very good control, so what you need is one hand on the back of the baby's head, not too high up, right behind the ears, and you need the other hand, the one that's closest to your breast, to support that breast because it's heavy. It could slip out of the baby's mouth. People don't usually think of that; they want to go right to putting the arm around the baby, and I tell them, you know, those things will come later. Right now you need a lot of support; you need a lot of control on your breast and on the baby's head to get the positioning right because it's tricky in the beginning. But I tell them if you're doing this right and getting the baby on right, within a couple of days or a week, maybe two weeks, you're not having to do all this preliminary work. You're not having to worry about it so much. It's really important to let them know that this is not going on forever. Sometimes a new parent feels like oh, my gosh, this is my life from now on; this is the way the baby's going to eat. I tell them no. Things are constantly changing, and it's going to be different in several days. Shortly, the baby's going to become really good at breast-feeding; it's going to get a lot easier; it's going to be really great. You just need to get a really good start.

"When I meet them before delivery and I have a discussion with them, I tell them 'after you have your baby, you're going to need someone to help you with breast-feeding.' Some hospitals are really great and have lactation consultants; those are the parents I don't really have to worry about, but there are major hospitals that don't have any lactation help. You have to find a really good nurse who is going to help. Some will give you instruction from across the room, and they are not going to help you as much. You want a nurse or someone in the beginning to come and physically help you with your breast and with the baby.

"Sometimes they'll want to tell me their whole birth story. Usually, I sort of know what kind of birth it was, whether it was a very difficult one or how long it was. I usually just wait and take my cues from the mom, and they will eventually come around and tell me. Sometimes I feel kind of uncomfortable. I should be up doing something, but then I think no, I am doing something. Usually when they sit and tell me this, they go 'oh, are you bored? Just tell me.' And I'll say no, not at all. They just love being able to tell their

story, to relive it again. And then their friends call on the phone. They go through the whole story again, and I'm doing something, and they'll say gosh, you must be sick of this. I'll say no, I'm not sick of it at all. This is your story, and you should be telling it to everyone that you like. It usually makes them feel good to be able to.

"In the beginning, they can even still be in the honeymoon period where for a couple of days they don't think they need sleep. They can't sleep, they're not really feeling things yet, so I try and let them know. Before the baby comes they figure oh, how much work can it be, the baby eats, sleeps, it poops. I'm going to have my life, my life is going to be fine. And then they get the baby, and their lives change. I tell them it's okay, that's the way it should be. You should have a lot of time where you're resting, relaxing, laying in bed with that baby, just staring at it. I tell new parents your new job is going to be sitting there and staring at that baby, feeding the baby, taking care of the baby, but then who takes care of you?

"After all that time with the baby, you feel like there's no time left for you. If you're hungry, you're going to just grab something like a bagel. I tell them you need nutrition, hydration, some rest. Sometimes it's easy for parents to

© Suzanne Arms

sleep, to take naps, sometimes it's not. Sometimes people are not big nappers, but if you can, just even put your feet up. If you want a nap with the baby, great. Nap with the baby—have the baby there with you. But if you want some time to yourself where you can just shut the door, I will watch the baby. I will make sure that you're eating well when I come in the morning, and the first thing I'll usually say is: Have you had breakfast? I start at 9:30 in the morning; I work from 9:30 to 4:30, and that's a really good time to start because it gives them time to sleep in and be with the baby, and then I show up. They usually have not had breakfast; they have not had a shower. What is most important? Let's say they've fed the baby, or the baby's sleeping. I ask them what would you like to do? Can I fix you some breakfast? Would you like to have a shower? Do you want to sit and talk about the baby? What do you want me to do today? People appreciate being taken care of but it's sometimes a hard thing for them to imagine or to feel comfortable with being cared for.

"When I first start, people tell me 'it's hard for me to tell you to go get something from the kitchen. I'm not used to this,' or 'I'm the kind of person that I'm so good at my job, and I'm an executive, and I'm not used to this feeling of being so helpless and having people do things for me.' I'll let them know that the first week is really recuperation, getting to know the baby, just taking it easy, and working on the breast-feeding, and working on getting their strength back, and keeping their life calm. New moms and dads don't really understand until it's happened to them, and they have that friend who comes over and stays two hours and their afternoon or morning is totally messed up.

"I'll tell them we really want to see something in the diaper every two hours. Let's say it's been two hours and nothing has happened. Those disposable diapers trick parents, and they'll say I think it's wet because it's really hard to tell. I'll take out the diaper that has not been used. You tell by the weight. . . . If it's mooshy and crackles and moves a lot, there's nothing in there. If it pouches out a little bit and sounds heavy when you thud it, it's wet. I'll show them the different ways that they can check it.

"In the beginning this is a major issue. I can tell whether the diaper's wet or not. How do I know? Or they'll say the baby's pooping a lot, but it's not peeing. And so I'll say that's really good, the baby's pooping, and sometimes it's peeing, too, and you just don't know. It's kind of getting mixed in there. As long as they're doing the pooping, that's good; the peeing is going to come.

"I ask whether, when they left the hospital, they were told that the baby was a little jaundiced! Sometimes they won't know it at all, and they'll say 'Oh, I just thought that it had that nice olive skin.' I'll tell them that jaundice is really, really common, especially with breast-feeding. It comes about the second or third day, very normal, a lot of babies go through it, 60 percent, but this is what we need to look for. We need to make sure that the baby wants to nurse every two to three hours, that they're having real awake time, that they're not lethargic. You don't want a baby who's jaundiced to be lethargic, when you can't wake them up, and they don't want to eat. What the baby needs to be doing is eating more frequently, eating well, and passing the bilirubin through its poops. So every time you see a poop, have a party; that's a good thing.

"Sometimes I'll show up, and they're laying in bed, and the baby is crying, and the mother doesn't know what to do. So I'll say, what did you just do? Well, we just fed, and we've been laying here for a half hour, and everything was great. Then all of a sudden the baby started crying. I'll say well, the first thing you want to do is pick the baby up and burp it. That never hurts; you can always see if a burp comes out. In addition, if you pick up a baby within ninety seconds after it starts crying, it will stop. Babies like to be walked, to be close to you, and they especially like the parents' attention. So you need to get up and walk with the baby and move it around. And they'll say 'Oh my gosh, I can't do that. I'm very tired.' And that's when someone else comes in handy, either the dad or me, to help.

"Babies are very, very smart, and they know their surroundings, and they get used to and know their homes very, very well. So sometimes it's just changing them into a different part of the house, showing them a different room, taking them outside. Talking to them, singing to them helps. Babies eventually end up loving the changing table, and that's a great place where you can do a lot of interaction. Put the baby on the table because they learn pretty quickly after a week or so that on that changing table they are being attended to, being loved, and enjoyed. This is a place where you can bring them and hang out if they're fussy. And a way to help with the diaper change and the whole crying thing is to make sure that the water is warm that you're changing them with, having a soft wipe, keep the baby covered, talk to them, place the hand over their tummy, just give them some reassurance.

"Babies turn their head to one side, and they're going to want to look at something. If you have something there, they're going to know that the black-and-white picture on the wall is always going to be there, and they're going to turn toward that picture and that's going to give them something to look at and comfort them. We can buy something, we can make our own bull's eyes, or we can just get a picture from a magazine.

"If the baby is crying constantly, that really should not be happening. After a couple of weeks, once the baby is awake more and has more wakeful times, it may have cranky times at night when you're not quite sure what to do. In the beginning, under two weeks, the baby usually is crying for a reason. What the parent is trying to do is catch onto the cues of the baby, because most babies will actually signal before they cry. You will see them smack their lips, rub their eyes when they're sleepy. They really give a signal. It usually takes about a week for the mom to begin to understand a few signals.

"Mothers always feel really good about rooting and breast-feeding. They say they saw it in a book or on a tape. Another way the baby can show hunger is sticking its tongue out, shoving its fist in its mouth when putting it up to your shoulder. If that baby gets up there and it's pecking around like a little chicken, I say that's a good sign that it is really hungry. If they do know one or two signals, I'll try and clue them in on three more signals.

"I tell the father what he needs to look for when nursing begins. I'll move the mother's breast; she's still got her hands all busy with her breast and the baby's head. I ask the father to come over here. We need to see those lips flanged out. If they're not, we can help the baby with that, and this is how you help. Okay, let's first look at the top lip. Usually, the top lip is pretty good; this is what the flanged out top lip looks like. Let's look at the bottom lip. You have to physically move the mom's breast to get in there and see. You can tell when that lip is kind of tucked under and close to that nipple, this is going to hurt the mother. So you put your finger on the baby's chin, and you pull down. When I do that, the mom goes uh, that's so much better, and you end up with more of the nipple in the mouth."

Parents who can afford the help of a postpartum doula like Tracy are very lucky. However, many of the ways she helps parents, so well described here, can be done by a sister, mother, or experienced friend. The tips she gives here, about rest, asking for help, taking time to get breast-feeding right, are useful for all new parents.

Most women also find it very valuable to meet with other new mothers during the first six months postpartum. It is useful to look for new mothers' groups in the local area. As during the birthing process, mothers can benefit immeasurably by sharing experiences with others who understand their feelings and appreciate their new challenges. Emotional and physical support of new parents that continues after the birth will enhance the well-being of the whole family.

APPENDIX A:
THE TRAINING OF A DOULA

CHOOSING TO BECOME A DOULA

Women who have the interest and develop the special skills to become a doula may come from a variety of backgrounds, but they share a single goal: to help other women through the major life event of giving birth. Some doulas are childbirth educators who like to continue assisting couples through birth. Some combine both childbirth education and labor support and also offer training to other women. Some doulas come from the home-birth or lay-midwifery movement. Some women seem to have a natural bent for the whole birth process, just as some people are born with perfect pitch, and they seek a role in which to express this talent.

Many women who choose to be doulas had support when they themselves gave birth and are so grateful for the kind of support they received that they want to "give something back." Some feel that the support they received during labor and delivery was unique and invaluable—more special than any other support they have ever received.

Other women who want to become doulas express a desire to give this kind of support because they did not receive emotional support at their own childbirth, and they realize how isolated and frightened they felt and how much they would have benefited from that support. Still other women, regardless of whether they have been previously interested or involved in birth or whether they had support during the birth of their own children, are drawn to helping other women after experiencing childbirth themselves.

Whatever the impetus or motivation to become a doula, it is essential for the doula to have a period of training and/or apprenticeship.

THE NATURE OF DOULA SUPPORT

Perhaps the most important insight needed by a doula-in-training is that every woman comes to labor with a different set of life experiences, needs, coping mechanisms, and responses. Each comes with a particular set of birth stories, information, worries, and histories. She approaches birth with her individual expectations and varied abilities to deal with pain or other difficult situations. The father, partner, close relative, or friend who accompanies the mother also comes with past life experiences and concerns. For this reason the doula must be adaptable, resourceful, and often creative to meet the different needs of each woman and the person accompanying her at birth.

Doula support is, by definition, personalized. Through a dynamic interaction with the mother and father (or other partner) the doula adjusts her care to the individual mother's needs. For this reason, doula training must be designed both to specify minimum support standards and to provide the trainees with a wide variety of techniques to use as required. In addition, basic information about hospital procedures and about labor and delivery is clearly important.

The doula's communication to the laboring woman occurs at a visceral level. She breathes with the woman; she feels with the woman; she tends to the emotions of the woman. Medical caregivers often communicate only at an intellectual level. They are responsible for medical outcomes and must monitor for possible risks and be familiar with the technology available for complicated births. Both roles, of course, are important.

BASIC TRAINING

The content and scheduling of training programs vary, but each contains both courses and actual experience. Courses include discussions and introduction to the basic physiological, psychological, and emotional changes during pregnancy, labor, delivery, and the early postpartum period. Discussions also include descriptions of the layout of the labor and delivery area and, if possible, introductions to the medical and nursing staff of the local hospital. The training will include experiential exercises in communication skills, empathy training, and ways to create comfort through touch and words, as well as role-playing of common situations and ways to empower women.

Training includes how to support women in several variations of normal labor; helping women with vaginal births after cesarean sections, complicated labors; multiple births; and immediate needs in the postpartum period.

Literature for the training will vary, but we urge all trainees to read the basic medical studies that support the beneficial effects of the doula. See Chapters 4, 5, and 6, and the list of recommended reading at the end of this appendix.

Training sessions should allow trainees to experience a variety of supportive techniques used by doulas; the mothers' varied responses to the support; interactions between the doulas, the fathers, and the medical staff; and changes in support when necessary as labor progresses. After observing or assisting with several births, trainees should have a chance to discuss not only alternative techniques in a given situation but also their feelings about each technique and about the laboring woman's behavior. In this way they can develop confidence and comfort in their own abilities to become doulas. We believe that most of the training should center around hands-on experience and the development of communication and counseling skills. After the initial training and for their first solo, doulas may gain much by discussing each case in detail with another doula (if possible, within a day or two after the birth). This type of continuing dialogue will remain useful over an entire career. Periodic small-group discussions with three to six doulas have proven especially helpful. Doulas, whether volunteer or paid, will benefit from and appreciate ongoing skill development, continued training, and interpersonal support.

GENERAL GUIDELINES*

- A doula helps and encourages a mother to deal with labor *as best she can.* There is no right or wrong way for her to do this and no ideal against which she is being measured. Take time to assess how the mother is working with her labor, and then build on it. Help her call on her inner strength to deal with labor; help her help herself. Demonstrate your confidence—through your words and facial expressions—that she *can* cope with labor and birth.

- When labor is intense, she may need constant reminders that she is feeling and experiencing the normal sensations of labor, not something to fear. Remind her that she is managing and that she will continue to be able to cope with each contraction as it comes. However, the doula must always be real with the mother and not minimize her feelings.

---

*Special thanks to Susan Rose, an experienced and sensitive doula, doula trainer, and certified nurse-midwife, for her guidelines on the doula's role during the stages of labor.

- Help the mother stay focused on the present (not on how long it has been or how long it will be). Help her deal only with the pain of the moment. The experience in a given moment is rarely so intense that it can not be accepted.

- It may help the mother and her partner if you describe what is happening inside her as she has contractions. Create an image for her to focus on. Some laboring women find it very effective to close their eyes and visualize what they want to have happen in their labor (the cervix opening, contractions getting stronger, the baby moving down).

- Be ready at all times with a touch, words, or a look. If the mother gets lost or overwhelmed during a difficult contraction, tell her to blow out and breathe with you. Establish both eye and physical contact (while facing her, hold her right hand and her left shoulder, for instance). Tell her she can get through this and you will help her. You may need to be firm and directive. Use massage, touch relaxation, and stroking to encourage any tense body parts to relax during and between contractions, just like a "wet noodle."

- Between contractions, ask the mother what she liked or did not like. As labor progresses, keep communication simple and watch for her nonverbal cues. Don't take offense if the mother is less than polite during the intense portions of her labor. To labor effectively, she must be able to let go of the many inhibitions that rule behavior in everyday life.

- Acknowledge pain when it exists. This is essential. If the mother shows you or tells you she is hurting, acknowledge her feelings. You might respond with, "Your uterus is working very well and hard," or, "That was a good strong contraction," or, "Your baby is pressing down just the way she should be." This is pain with a purpose. Remind the mother that what she's feeling (such as pressure, pain, or stretching) is normal for labor. Remind her of what the feelings represent (for example, the cervix opening, the baby moving down).

- As labor progresses, what feels good and what is needed will change. Sometimes nothing feels good. At these times in a labor or birth, you need to help the mother accept the way she feels, keep it in perspective, relax more, and be open to other possibilities such as a visualization.

- Give the mother your total, undivided attention. Your emotional support can take the place of drugs for pain relief. Minimize distractions during the more intense parts of labor. Try to be aware of any people or things that may be upsetting to the mother and deal with them for her. Better still, support the mother in dealing with them in an appropriate manner—another facet of empowerment.

- Try to stay calm and relaxed. Your tension and anxiety are easily communicated. Deal with your fears and concerns before labor begins so that you are free to focus on the mother during labor. If you feel yourself tensing up, take a slow, deep breath and relax.

- Don't feel out of place or intimidated by the hospital setting, the staff, or the equipment. You are essential to the mother's well-being. Be sure to ask questions and get the information you need to feel at ease. At the same time, don't give medical advice or interfere with the medical staff's care in any way. Labor is not a time to attempt to change the practices of a maternity unit. Doulas must submerge their own beliefs about hospital practices during a birth. Be diplomatic with hospital personnel. (You are working in their territory.) Encourage the father and mother to communicate their own needs to the hospital staff.

- Focus on the mother's and father's needs, not your own. Mothers' needs come first, but many fathers also need your support and encouragement. Be sensitive to any relatives or friends who are present. Always maintain a positive attitude and model supportive behavior for the partner to use. Encourage the father to be close to and supportive of the mother at his comfort level. Add praise whenever possible.

- Adjust your support to each mother's needs and alter your care to her changing requirements as she progresses through pregnancy, birth, and the postpartum period. Concentrate on relaxing and reassuring the mother and helping her with specific individualized childbirth techniques.

Early First Stage of Childbirth

The efforts of the doula or childbirth assistant during the first stage (when the cervix thins and opens) should be geared toward helping the mother have a relaxed body and a mind at peace. This allows the mother's contracting uterus to open her cervix while she conserves her energy for pushing. You can help her with the following measures.

- Have the mother stay home as long as possible. Options for comfort are much greater at home. Going into the hospital will not make things happen faster, and labor may even slow down in a strange environment. (See "Knowing When to Go into the Birth Center or Hospital," later in this appendix.)

- During this early time in labor a woman can gradually get used to the feeling of contractions. Later, as contractions become more intense, they will hurt. This pain is a normal part of the birthing process. Remind the mother that there is a purpose for the pain: It is a sign of the work her body is doing to thin and open her cervix. If the woman is familiar with the trance state of self-hypnosis, this is a time to suggest to her: "Go deeper and deeper . . . relax with each wave . . . "

- It is essential for a woman to take nourishment in the form of fluids or easily digestible proteins and carbohydrates. A dehydrated or starved body cannot labor as effectively as a well-nourished one. Also, the baby continues to be totally dependent on her for nourishment throughout labor. Suggest that she eat a good meal early in labor, and have her continue to drink plenty of liquids and avoid high-fat foods and concentrated sweets (candy). The mother might wish to try juice, fruit,

yogurt, whole-wheat bread or crackers, nourishing soup, and other foods that appeal to her. As labor progresses, she may not feel like eating, but encourage her to *drink*. Labor is hard work, and she will need lots of fluid to meet her body's needs. If fruit juices (or fruit-juice Popsicles) do not appeal to her, suggest noncaffeinated soft drinks, which will give her the energy she needs without making her feel jittery. Nausea is normal for some women in labor and is not the result of drinking or eating.

- Suggest a warm bath (if the membranes are intact) to help her stay more comfortable and relaxed. Fill the tub as high as possible. Have her kneel in the tub or lie back against pillows. Put the pillows in a garbage sack to keep them dry and place a towel over the plastic. Keep a comfortably hot, wet towel over her belly and groin during contractions. She might want a cool drink and a cool cloth for her head. Be sure to give this a try, especially at times in labor when the mother feels that nothing will help.

  If the woman's membranes have ruptured, suggest that she try a shower. Put a chair in so that she can sit or lean on it. If she does not feel like bathing or showering or if a bathtub or shower is not available, apply warm, wet towels to her abdomen, groin, or back.

- Have the mother *walk*. Walking tends to shorten labor, reduce the need for pain-relieving drugs, decrease fetal heart-rate abnormalities, and improve the baby's condition during labor and birth. A doula and other support people may need to keep encouraging the mother (strongly!) to walk.

- Women in labor should change positions often—at least every thirty to sixty minutes. This can help to avoid or correct fetal distress, as well as speed labor. Changing positions can increase uterine activity, shorten labor by helping the cervix dilate more efficiently, and reduce discomfort. Other good positions for labor include sitting, lying on the side, and being up on the hands and knees. Use lots of pillows to help the mother feel comfortable. She should *not* lie flat on her back because this can cause a drop in her blood pressure and a decreased blood flow (and therefore decreased oxygen) to her baby.
- Laboring women should urinate every hour. A full bladder can inhibit uterine activity and be an obstacle to the baby's birth. If a woman is having trouble urinating during labor, try having her listen to the sound of running water, pour warm water over her vaginal area while she sits on the toilet, or have her relax on the toilet with her hand in a bowl of warm water.

Late First Stage of Childbirth

During the late first stage of labor, most women strongly need other people (their support people) to help them cope with and accept the intense contractions that are normal for this stage. Labor is truly easier when a woman has people to encourage and reassure her during this time. If she is going to a hospital or birth center for her baby's birth, the best time to make the trip is usually late in

the first stage. Whether at home or in the hospital or birth center, the following measures will continue to be helpful.

- Have the mother continue with warm baths or showers, hot towels, position changes, walking, nourishment, and frequent urination. Try other comfort measures such as cold compresses, pressure on the back, pelvic rocking, massages or stroking. Let the mother use extra pillows, a birth ball, a bean bag, or you or the father to lean against for added comfort. What feels good often changes as labor progresses, so remember to try again with comfort measures that may not have been helpful earlier.
- This is an intense time. The mother may need to maintain contact with you through every contraction. You can talk and breathe her through contractions, use a loving touch, and maintain eye contact. Then help her rest, relax, and refresh herself between contractions. Visualizations and imagery are also extremely useful to help the mother work through the contractions.
- Ask the mother to show or tell you not only how and where to touch her but also what feels good and what does not.
- Help the mother stay upright and walking as long as possible. Alternate periods of activity and rest as needed. She may need a lot of encouragement to change positions, walk, or urinate. Remember, these activities will help her labor progress normally.
- Many women experience a time in labor when they are in a lot of pain and cannot get comfortable. If the mother

experiences these feelings, help her concentrate on releasing tension and yielding to the intense contractions. Emotional support and focus on relaxation (in spite of the intensity of the contractions) will get her through this difficult time. Reassure her that she *can* do it. Have her deal with her contractions *one at a time* and not think about how long it has been or how long it will be.

Knowing When to Go into the Birth Center or Hospital

Experience with previous births and close contact with the midwife or physician enables you, the doula, to help the mother interpret what she is feeling and what is happening during her labor.

In deciding when to have the mother go to the hospital, be sure to consider what the weather is like, how far the mother is from the hospital or birth center, whether this is a first baby (labor and birth are often longer than with subsequent babies), and how strongly the mother feels about being settled in at the place where the baby will be born.

Several signs can help you and the mother decide when to leave home to go to the birth center or hospital. For most women these signs tend to be present in the late first stage, but every woman is different. The mother may experience none of these signs or one or more of them:

- The mother's face may become deeply flushed (red). This flushing, which looks like what some women experience after orgasm, may extend to her upper chest. This sign alone does not mean it is urgent to get to the hospital.

- The mother may have an increase of bloody, mucousy show. Again, there is usually no rush, and you might wait for other signs to develop. (This is not heavy, bright red bleeding with blood running down her leg. Have her consult with the doctor or midwife if she has constant bleeding or any questions or concerns about the bloody show she is experiencing.)

- Long, strong contractions with little rest in between, combined with shaking legs or arms, nausea or vomiting, or hiccups are typical late-first-stage signs. If these appear, consider going to the hospital.

- After a period of long, strong, close contractions (usually with increased bloody show and a deep flush on the face), a woman may experience a lull in labor, with contractions slowing down and easing up. This may be the normal resting point or plateau many women seem to experience after becoming completely dilated and before an urge to push develops. Help the mother enjoy the rest; go to the birthing location. Be aware that there are other plateau points in labor. Some women experience plateaus at around three or four centimeters of dilatation and/or around seven or eight centimeters.

- She may find herself pushing or feeling an urge to push with contractions. She may feel increasing rectal pressure (as though she needs to have a bowel movement) during or between contractions. If so, have her breathe or blow through these contractions, and go straight to the hospital.

- A mother may feel she needs to go to the birthing location. Sometimes she may feel or sense something that you do not see. If she wants to go to the birthing location even though she may still be in early first stage, and you are not able to help her feel more at ease or comfortable at home, she should go in. If she is in early labor (less than four centimeters dilatation) and everything is fine after she is checked, consider going back home (if she is close by) or for a walk in the building or neighborhood until labor has progressed further.

Transition to the Hospital

Moving out of the familiar surroundings of home into the unfamiliarity of the hospital can create feelings of anxiety and fear. These feelings heighten the perception of pain, and they can help elevate stress hormones (adrenalin and noradrenalin), which may slow or stop contractions. It is common to hear reports of labors progressing well at home but stalling when the mother arrives at the hospital. Animal studies have shown that when animal mothers are frightened, labor stops. This may represent nature's way to let the laboring female flee a potential danger. Fear may be reduced by the sense of trust and empowerment a woman develops during pregnancy while working with a doula.

Some couples who are familiar with the hospital's practices because of childbirth classes or former positive birth experiences may arrive with confidence that the experts will take over and relieve the mother's dis-

comfort or pain. However, almost all women arrive at the hospital with a vulnerability peculiar to the state of childbirth—the unconscious feelings of fear, anxiety, and insecurity about the unknown. Many women associate hospitals with illness and the role of a patient, as well as with a potential for danger, use of unexpected procedures, a lack of privacy, isolation, and confusion about high-tech equipment. There may also be rules that prohibit a woman from following her own instinctive body positions such as walking or crouching. Women in labor are particularly sensitive to harsh or brusque words or an impersonal tone of voice from busy, harassed, or tired personnel.

The most important factor in alleviating the anxiety that most women feel upon arrival at the hospital is the attitude of the people helping her. The presence of a doula makes a difference here. Having already established a relationship with the mother in advance, a doula gives the mother the confidence and security of knowing there is one person who will remain and be committed to her. The calming presence of the doula, combined with the mother's own sense of confidence achieved by prenatal preparation, can keep her focused on her labor and continue to relax through contractions even in the car, at triage or admitting, and through the often disruptive activities, interventions, and general business typical of a hospital.

The Hospital-Based Doula

If support is given by a hospital-based labor doula called on to assist a newly arrived woman who is accompanied or unaccompanied by another person, she will have to start creating that calm and comforting presence as soon as she is introduced. She can put her hand on the mother's hand or arm and let the mother know that she will be with her throughout her labor. Whenever the doula first meets the mother, her role remains constant: creating a continuous presence and offering reassurance, touch, verbal and nonverbal comfort, relaxation, and praise.

If the woman has never met a doula and seems frightened, the hospital-based doula may address the fear, asking the mother if she is afraid, acknowledging that the mother may have heard all kinds of scary stories, and responding quietly but confidently. The doula then explains what is happening in the woman's body, how normal and natural it is, and how capable her body is of having a baby. She can begin to encourage the mother to trust her body, to let it do what it wants to do, to not be afraid, to let the fear go, and to not fight against her body. She teaches the mother to breathe through the contractions and lets her know that she will help her. A frightened mother will often look at the doula and begin to feel much calmer and will start to relax. Reducing a mother's fear and anxiety lessens her stress responses, which include the secretion of adrenalin. Since adrenalin decreases uterine contractions and lengthens labor, any reduction of fears and anxiety by the doula will permit labor to progress more normally.

In this first encounter a doula may repeat words similar to those used by Nadia Stein, an experienced doula: "Nothing to be scared about—birth is normal and natural and your body knows what to do. Remember, let your body go through, let it go through, just breathe it through freely, quietly, letting go. Relax as much as you can; just breathe it

through. That's it, you see—that's just the only thing you have to do; that will help you through." A doula can repeat this same pattern of words quietly, in a rhythm, three or four times. Nadia noted: "As the woman is gaining control, the fear begins to leave. This whole sequence may take only five or ten minutes through two or three contractions—the mother begins to understand what you mean, and she knows you are helping her and that it becomes easier. So even a frightened woman begins to gain confidence in what she is doing, and even knowing that it is painful, she feels she can stand it and she understands how much being relaxed helps her."

This initial contact and the mother's initial sense of letting go and being in control of her own labor (in the sense of not being panicked) become powerful unconscious foundations for the rest of labor. As the doula continues to stay, maintaining physical contact and using a comforting voice, these important elements get reinforced.

The Second Stage of Childbirth

The doula's efforts and those of the father during the second stage (when the cervix is completely open and the mother pushes her baby out) should be geared not only toward helping her cooperate with her body but also toward providing a calm, peaceful atmosphere into which her new child will be born.

During this stage you, the doula, can help in the following ways:

- There is nothing magical about a woman being at ten centimeters or completely dilated. Some women feel an urge to push before ten centimeters, and others feel it considerably after this point.

- If the mother does not feel an urge to push, try getting her into a gravity-assisted (upright) position and continue to breathe with her through contractions. Walking, squatting, or sitting on the toilet often helps at this time. Remind the mother to be patient, relax, and wait for a pushing urge to develop as her baby moves farther down her birth canal. Waiting until the urge to push develops allows her to coordinate her pushing efforts with those of her uterus. If her physician or midwife feels it is necessary to birth her baby quickly, she or he will direct her on how and when to push.

- Have the woman urinate before she begins pushing.

- Any positions used for labor can also be used for pushing and for the baby's birth. Each position has advantages and disadvantages. A mother who has practiced during pregnancy and experimented during labor may know the most comfortable and effective position(s). Help her change positions at least every half hour if she has a long or difficult second stage. Upright positions that use gravity may be helpful. Squatting uses gravity and allows maximum opening of the pelvic outlet. Standing sometimes helps if the baby is still high in the pelvis. Sitting on the toilet is excellent for opening up and releasing the whole pelvic area. Lying on one side can be helpful in slowing a quick descent, but less helpful if the baby is coming slowly. Upright positions can

aggravate hemorrhoids; lying on the side does not. All-fours positions do not use gravity, but they do take pressure off the back and allow spreading of the hips and pelvic bones. Both all-fours and squatting positions are good for a large or posterior baby. The doctor or midwife may suggest different positions for the mother to try while pushing.

- Avoid letting the mother lie flat on her back. If she is semireclining, you or the father can sit behind her to prop her up, or you can use pillows or raise the head of the birthing bed or delivery table so that she is not lying flat.

- The mother will need frequent assurance that the intense and painful sensations she may feel—backache, nausea, hot flashes, trembling legs, spreading sensations in the pelvis, intense pressure on the rectum, an urge to empty the bowels, involuntary bearing down, intense pressure as the baby descends through the birth canal, or burning and stretching sensations as the vaginal outlet opens to accommodate her baby—are normal and that she *can* stretch and open enough to give birth to her baby.

- Remind her to work with her body—let her body tell her what to do to get her baby out. She can bear down (push) when, how, and however long her body demands that. Encourage her to ease up on pushing if it hurts or if burning sensations occur. She may want to see and touch her baby's head as it emerges from her body. This contact may renew her spirits and energy, and help her focus on bringing her baby out.

- When pushing, she might at times breathe out, make noise, or hold her breath. Many women have found that certain kinds of noises like grunts and moaning sounds help them give birth to their babies. Help her not to be inhibited about making sounds—that is a natural part of the birthing process for many women, and she will find what works for her if she goes ahead and tries it. Many women find that releasing sound opens the throat and subsequently the birth canal. Whatever works for her is fine. However, have her avoid prolonged breath holding.

- During a long second stage, a woman needs nourishment to keep up or restore her energy level. Spoonfuls of honey (or drinks sweetened with honey) or juice will provide a quick source of energy.

- You can encourage her to release and open for the birth. If you watch her mouth, shoulders, and legs for signs of tension, you can help her release these areas.

- She may be so intently focused on the work of giving birth that she does not hear what others are saying. You can help by keeping the mother informed of what is happening and conveying instructions from the doctor or midwife.

- Try to keep the atmosphere calm and peaceful, so that the mother and father can enjoy the birth (and the end of labor) and especially the new life they have brought forth.

Handling Problems and Answering Questions

Even when a labor does not proceed as planned, the doula still plays an important role. For example, if oxytocin is administered, contractions sometimes become more intense and painful. This is a time to help the mother relax even more, by leading her in breathing through the contractions or by engaging her in more deepening relaxation visualizations.

If there is a possibility of a problem and the mother requires constant fetal monitoring or more than the usual monitoring, further calming of the mother may reduce the problem and will certainly reassure her.

If there is a cesarean section, the doula will need to reassure the parents that she will remain with them. Also, she will need to remain positive and make sure that the parents understand step-by-step what is going to take place. The doula can also help a mother realize that having a cesarean section is not her failure.

When a mother is given an epidural, it is important to give her gentle encouragement to make the birth hers. A doula can remind the mother, "Your baby is getting everything it needs. What a great mom you are going to be. You know exactly what's right for your baby. You're doing just fine." Both the common as well as the uncommon situations that can arise during labor should be discussed during training.

Many doulas find it useful with each delivery to keep a record that includes the length of labor, the place of birth (at home or in the hospital), the delivery outcome (vaginal or cesarean section), the use of any drugs, the use of forceps, and any complications for the mother or the infant. A short questionnaire for parents has provided useful feedback for doulas in evaluating the effect of their services. Questions can include the following: Was having a doula helpful to you and your partner? What aspects of support helped? What aspects of support were not useful? What changes or additions of support would you make? Would you use a doula again? Do you have any other suggestions or comments?

Though the work can be exhausting, there are unusual rewards. Doulas describe a barrage of powerful and positive emotions after a birth. They describe a unique euphoria that often lasts up to twelve hours. They feel good in a way they have not previously sensed. They cannot just walk out the door. The images keep coming for a long time afterward. They and the families share a sense of warmth and connectedness. Being part of such an intense, intimate, and critical experience has been very satisfying and valuable for all the doulas we have known. One doula said: "It's hard to believe how close we become. It's the most important thing I do. After I go home, I feel close to my children. I relive my own childbirth experience. I want to talk to another doula. I need to talk to someone, to debrief, to share how it was."

Immediate Help for Postpartum Care in the Hospital

Right after birth, the mother needs tending to. Most obstetric units have nurses who take over the postpartum care of just the mother. Others have nurses who care for both the mother and baby. A mother needs someone to assess and understand the physical and emotional state she is in. If she is exhausted, she needs support to rest; if she is thirsty or hungry, food and drink; and she needs help to deal with the physical discomforts of the perineum, uterine afterbirth contractions, fluid loss, and an achy body.

A first-time mother is often insecure and uncertain how to take care of the baby. Her body is tired and sore; she needs time to rest and recuperate, and guidance on breast-feeding. Meanwhile, the mother and father are going through enormous emotional shifts. Both parents also need time to discover their baby—to take in the real baby from the dreamed-of baby.

In some units where this immediate care is less available, a doula (as agreed upon beforehand) may plan to stay a bit more than the usual two hours after the birth to fill in with some practical help. In either case the doula can help parents plan for this very early period by keeping in mind the following considerations.

If possible, baby and mother should be together at all times, but with due consideration of the mother's state. If she is overwhelmed and exhausted, help her have the baby with her but give support. For example, the mother may not be ready to hold the baby, but wants the baby in her bed. The baby can be next to her with appropriate protection of safe pillows against a secure railing that the baby cannot fall through. Parents should be told never to leave the baby alone in an adult bed. A baby can crawl to an edge and get caught or roll in a way in which it cannot extricate its face. If the mother needs to get up for the bathroom, the baby can be placed in a bassinet, or be held by the partner. Do not leave mother and her partner completely alone unless they wish to be. Ask them what you can do or sense their needs. If the mother is not ready to hold the baby, have another support person available to tend to the baby, so mother knows the baby is being held. Although she may have planned for particular aspects of the immediate postpartum period, these may have changed from her original plan. Be sure to check with her and her partner, make adjustments as needed.

Other simple steps can enhance the mother's early postpartum care and adjustment with the infant:

1. If the mother wishes, lay the baby on her chest. As we mentioned earlier, many newborns will crawl toward the breast. A light blanket can be used to keep the baby warm.
2. Respect privacy and individual timing.
3. Keep interruptions by staff or family to a minimum (if possible, suggest avoiding taking the baby away for examinations right away. Use the mother's or father's chest to keep baby warm rather than a warmer; wait on procedures if possible).
4. Allow one and one-half to two hours of uninterrupted time.
5. Be unobtrusively present if mother needs assistance. Recognize her needs with toileting, eating, or handling the baby.
6. Recognize, listen to, and acknowledge unexpected outcomes and feelings in the mother (disappointment in birth, in her performance, and lack of control).

While understanding her experience, one can still acknowledge and validate the mother on her birth and validate her great baby, and plant seeds of accomplishment, even in difficult situations. "What a difficult time you had, what a trooper you are." There are always features of the baby's appearance or a behavior that you can praise.

7. Listen to her partner's experience, if appropriate at this time. Help them talk to each other. Listening is a key factor in understanding not only what the parents may need but also in acknowledging the range of emotions and changes they are experiencing.
8. Recognize that even with a cesarean section or other interventions, a mother can nurse, if ready.
9. When the parents are ready, and if appropriate in this early period, guide them to notice how the baby listens, recognizes their voices, especially the mother's, and how the baby quiets and gives other cues. This is a way to begin to help the parents become attuned to the infant's feelings, responses, and needs. It is good to show these abilities while the baby is in the quiet-alert state.
10. If needed, give information on the effect of medications or epidural on the baby's ability to suck or latch on, to help the mother avoid feeling as though she failed. The effects of the medication will take longer to clear in the baby than in the mother.
11. Inform and give encouragement that these discomforts will pass, and that the baby will be okay.

The Birth Doula's Follow-up or Home Visit

All women can benefit from the opportunity to integrate their experiences of labor and delivery, fill in the missing pieces, or clarify and process their unspoken feelings or impressions. If the birth was a positive experience, then recalling the details and reliving the joyful feelings will deepen a new mother's satisfaction and enhance her self-esteem. However, if the birth left her with some negative memories, she will benefit by having a chance to make sense of the birth by reconstructing the events and putting into words what happened and how she felt. Partners will equally benefit by having help to resolve the childbirth experience. Having an empathic, caring listener who acknowledges their feelings may help both the woman and her partner gain a more comfortable or positive perspective. Early processing may prevent these events from escalating and avoid postpartum distress later. As a birth doula coming for a follow-up home visit to process the birth, consider the following:

1. Use reflective and empathic listening, which provides an opportunity for the parents to talk about the birth. Take time to ask the mother how she is doing, feeling, adjusting (eating, sleeping, body returning to normal. How she feels about baby, support system, partner).

2. Ask how the baby is doing and how feeding is going. Does the mother have any feelings that have surprised her? and the like. Use very open-ended types of questions and give plenty of time for her responses. Recognize that she is very vulnerable to your words.

3. Review the birth (listen nonjudgmentally). Encourage her to tell the story.

4. Include the father so that he can express his feelings and experience and help develop couple communication.

5. Help her recall aspects that surprised her, that she felt good about; acknowledge how well she did.

6. Use a variety of methods to help her release, grieve, and heal any unexpected or disturbing events.

7. Allow the parents to tell you how you helped them and what were some things that did and did not work for them. The doula must listen nondefensively and be willing to hear fully the parents' side of the experience.

8. Recognize the importance of healing the mother's expectations for the birth and any negative beliefs. For example, if she says, "I couldn't do the birth, how can I breast-feed?" By listening to her feelings, one can always find a way to validate how hard it was for her and how strong she was to make it through a difficult time. She can use that experience to tackle this next phase. Help her know that you understand that often birth does not go as planned, but there are many ways to work that through and to find new ways to cope. She can probably recall other times that did not go as planned, and then she found alternative ways to handle a difficult situation in a new, creative manner.

9. Role play (if this feels appropriate to your role), saying what she needed to

say to different people involved, and so forth.

10. Using visualization, the mother may want to imagine re-doing the experience the way she would have wanted it to be. Help the mother recognize her strengths and abilities to handle whatever she could under trying circumstances.

11. Other ways to recreate the birth and release feelings can be to (a) write in a journal, (b) use art to draw the memories, (c) write letters to one's own self, validating one's experience, or letters to others involved that the mother would not send.

12. After telling the story and finding some sense of completion, the mother might wish to tell the birth story to her baby in a calm, easy way. This often calms babies.

13. Encourage and teach stress management and self-care (for example, relaxation techniques, rest, time out, support, new mothers' groups).

14. A doula can educate herself and inform mothers about other resources in the community.

STRATEGIES TO HELP WOMEN WITH A HISTORY OF TRAUMA OR ABUSE

During her interview with the parents before birth, the doula may inquire if there is anything in the woman's history that the doula should know about that may affect her comfort in labor or in the early postpartum period. The goal of this type of discussion is not to invade the woman's privacy but simply to plan ways to help the mother feel safer, more present, and secure in the doula's desire to offer the best support she can.

Some factors that may cause the woman to fear labor or parenting, activate physiological or emotional stress levels, and affect her ability to labor freely are: past traumatic births, pregnancy problems, marital or partner distress, losses, other hospitalizations, and childhood sexual, physical, or emotional abuse.

A woman with an abuse history may have difficulty trusting; fear loss of control, pain or damage; worry about invasive procedures and being exposed; have concerns about her own emotional reactions such as anger or flashbacks of memories; experience distress with touch; and may worry about parenting and breast-feeding. In these situations, the doula's role is to create emotional and physical safety, be present empathically, help the mother develop her own choices for as many aspects of birth as possible, use imagery to contain or manage her fears, and facilitate the mother's ability to communicate her current needs and feelings to her caregivers. Arranging specific times for those conversations may be helpful so that the mother becomes secure and the doula is able to schedule her days.

As the doula listens sensitively, she becomes aware of the woman's fears, for example, of typical procedures during labor, and attempts to understand the mother's feelings, and then works with her to plan specific ways to manage the situation. Here is where the doula goes over carefully the events of labor, describes in detail what occurs, informs about the pros and cons, elicits the mother's feelings, and helps the mother develop a birth plan that meets the mother's choices. Many traumatized women need more extensive information and education about the physical aspects of pregnancy and birth, because many women are alienated from their bodies. They may be negative or ambivalent about their bodies' ability to birth. They may need more affirmation and help to correct misperceptions.

During labor, the doula should be aware of common defenses such as dissociation (numbing out, going away) or flashbacks to abuse memories or body sensations. The doula should be prepared to give verbal encouragement, eye contact, and reassurance and help in staying in the present.

a. Giving the Woman Control

Control is a major issue for all women. Loss of control for a woman with an abuse or trauma background is the thing she fears most. The doula can give the woman control by creating a partnership with her, informing her at all times of what is happening by the caregivers or in the environment, and involving her, within the doula's purview, every step of the way, in decisions about the management of her care.

The doula can share information as she understands it from the caregivers about what's going on in the mother's body and with the baby.

b. Creating a Safe Environment

Whether you know about the woman's history or not, you want to avoid as much as possible triggering traumatic memories or causing negative events that could retraumatize her. Remember that every intervention can appear intrusive and elicit reminders of the past. Some of the following methods may help women through the experience and feel empowered.

1. Provide an emotionally and physically safe environment.
2. Take time to make acquaintance, build rapport, and trust.
3. Create an atmosphere of attentiveness, openness, of unhurried listening.
   A. Ask her how she is feeling now.
   B. Use reflective listening.
   C. Let her know you hear her feelings and help her express her concerns or fears. Let her know that you will be with her.

c. Watch for Concerns about Touch

1. Touch may trigger memories of abuse, so always ask permission first, and start with nonthreatening touch: hand-holding, for example, before offering massage.
   A. Acknowledge and assess her reactions if she is shaking, withdraws, or becomes tense.
   B. Ask her what she is feeling or thinking, and reassure her you want to work with her at her comfort level.
   "How can I help you feel safe, in control, more in charge, powerful?"

(Take a moment and ask her to take a nice deep breath to help her become more relaxed and explain that breathing can often reduce stress and help the body work better with contractions.) Get a sense from her of a place where she could imagine really relaxing or a time when she felt most successful at something. Ask her if she has some ways that help her feel safe, protected, comfortable. She may have a religious or spiritual figure or image, or a memory of an inner guide or nurturing figure that she can elicit to imagine being protected.

d. Dealing with Issues of Privacy, Body Boundaries, the Body's Ability to Birth

1. Be aware of the discomfort of exposure, nakedness, being observed by strangers.
2. Do not leave her alone. Being alone she may wait nervously, uncertain about what is going to happen. She may feel unprotected, apprehensive, and anxious.
3. Many women are ashamed or frightened of being exposed, of secretions, of stool. Respect and protect her modesty and, as appropriate, suggest wipes or draping to the caregiver.
4. She may worry that her body is bad, damaged, and defective. Be sure to validate her health, her normalcy. The doula can reassure the woman that all the sounds, feelings, movement, and secretions are normal aspects of labor, mediating the woman's fears of her own reactions.

e. Working with Contractions

1. Observe her own way of coping; validate it and join her as appropriate, for example, with sounds. (Respect cultural differences.)
2. Reassure her of her own strength, choice, health, and safety in the present.

3. Notice behavior. If she seems quiet or not present in some way, check with her.
   "How are you doing now, feeling—what's happening?" Or
   "Where were you just now?"
   "When you have that next contraction, tell me what's going through your mind."
4. If she is dissociating, help her come back to the present. Use your voice, eye contact, reassurance, appropriate touch, hand-holding, and so forth. Remember that dissociation is a survival technique developed to be able to mentally leave during the times of pain and terror. At some point during labor, you might inquire if she notices or remembers that feeling of "leaving" or going somewhere safe in her mind. Would she like to continue to do that in labor, or would she prefer to remain more present. If she doesn't want to dissociate, design some ways with her, her partner, or other caregiver to help her stay present, as above, but also ask her to respond to you with words or actions. Continue to ask for feedback. Whether she mentally "leaves" or not, *make sure she is imagining "going to" a safe place.*
5. She may be able to use the ability to separate mentally into positive visualizations to distract from the pain. Help her develop one—images of the ocean or a rainbow, for example, but always check with her.
   "Stay with me."
   "You're here now."
   "You're safe here."
   "The baby loves you."

"The baby can't wait to be in your arms."

"Can you remember a place of safety, comfort? Tell me about it."

"Let's imagine you are there now."

6. If she acts demanding: ("Don't touch me.""Ask me when you can touch me." "I'll tell you when you can examine me.""Don't give me oxytocin.""Go out of the room." "Don't leave me.") Stay with her where she is. Don't fight her responses or feelings; validate them. Ask yourself: Why is she behaving like this? What is her underlying feeling or need? Then you can reflect back to her your understanding of what she is saying: "You're really needing to know when things are going to happen."

"It seems like things don't feel safe for you; let's look at what's happening." "What can we do right now to make it safe?" "Whom would you like in the room?"

7. Watch your language in labor. Avoid phrases like, "Just relax," "let go," "open your legs." These words can have a double meaning and remind her of times she had to surrender and was hurt. Find words with her that are comforting—images of nature, colors, sounds. Remind her of the baby. "The baby is your helper in getting rid of the pain." "The pain is coming out of the body."

8. With her permission, hold her hands, look into each other's eyes, breathe with her, and talk her through the contractions.

9. Remember that you are modeling for her partner what to do. It may help to acknowledge her pain, how hard it is,

and let her express her feelings and fears. Then, if possible, help her plan and develop more affirming statements, such as "I love this baby." "I can let the baby out." "It's safe to let the baby out." Some women who have been traumatized seem to retreat out of the body, and fight the pushing, rather than focusing downward and out. You may need to pull her back. "You're safe now.""It's your baby girl trying to come out. Your baby needs you to push her out. Look at me, I need you to stay here. Your baby needs you to stay here."

10. Each woman is unique. Be patient. There is no right way to birth. Let the woman choose her own path. You are there to provide information, support, resources, warmth, and comfort.

11. As you work on building a sense of trust, respect, and rapport with her, she may become able to separate the abuse issues from the birth. She can then feel validated, empowered, more in charge of her experience, and more ready to meet the challenge.

BIBLIOGRAPHY

RECOMMENDED READING FOR DOULAS

Enkin, M., Keirse, M.J.N.C., Neilsen, J. et al. *A guide to effective care in pregnancy and childbirth.* New York: Oxford University Press, 2000.

Goer, Henci. *The thinking woman's guide to a better birth.* New York: Penguin Putnam, Inc., 1999.

Kelleher, J. *Nurturing the family: The guide for the postpartum doula*. Philadelphia: Xlibris, 2002.

Kitzinger, Sheila. *Birth your way*. London: A Dorling Kindersley Book, 2001.

Klaus, M. H., Kennell, J. H., Klaus, P. H. *Bonding*. Cambridge, MA: Perseus Publishing, 1995.

Pascali-Bonaro, D., Ringel A. J. *Nurturing beginnings*. River Vale, NJ: Mother Love, Inc., 2000.

Perez, P. *The nurturing touch at birth*. Johnson, VT: Cutting Edge Press, 1997.

Simkin, P., Ancheta, R. *The labor progress handbook*. Asney, Oxford, UK: Blackwell Science, Ltd., 2000.

Simkin, P., Whalley, J., Keppler, A. *Pregnancy, childbirth, and the newborn*. New York: Meadowbrook Press, 2000.

APPENDIX B:
RELAXATION, VISUALIZATION, AND SELF-HYPNOSIS EXERCISES FOR PREGNANCY, LABOR, BIRTH, AND BREAST-FEEDING

Relaxation exercises, which include breathing, muscle-tension releasing, and mental imagery, can be practiced throughout pregnancy (Exercises I and II). In the last four to six weeks before the due date, women can practice the self-anesthesia exercises (Exercise III, three methods). They can also include the self hypnosis birth visualization (Exercise IV), being sure to emphasize, "imagine a time in the future going through a time tunnel to when the baby is fully grown and ready." Note the more detailed instructions for using visualizations in labor.

Women can use the power of their minds to help them relax during labor and reduce fear, tension, and pain. During relaxation, the body's natural ability to release special hormones (oxytocin) to enhance or strengthen contractions is augmented, and certain stress hormones that can slow labor are diminished. During the early postpartum period, relaxation and imagery have been shown to increase milk production, aid in the mother's healing process, and generally reduce stress during this sensitive time.

Guided imagery, which is also called *visualization*, is a method to use positive mental images or pictures in one's mind for a variety of goals. One major goal is to encourage relaxation of the mind and the body. Other goals can include reducing fear of childbirth; strengthening the mother's confidence in her ability to give birth safely, and helping the father gain confidence in the birth process and in his own ability to provide support; reducing pain and discomfort during labor; reducing the length of labor; and possibly reducing the likelihood of complications, including fetal distress and cesarean section; helping parents feel more prepared for birth and parenting; and enhancing prenatal bonding.

Labor, although an involuntary function, is highly sensitive and reactive to the mother's thoughts and feelings. If she is tense and anxious, feels unsupported, or has some fears or conflicts about birth or parenting, her labor can be affected. Learning how to condition the mind to remain relaxed and peaceful during labor and nursing can offset these anxieties. In addition, during pregnancy and birth, a woman's mind often becomes more intuitive and inward-focused as she becomes more open emotionally. This openness is important as she prepares to "take in" the new baby.

Visualization is largely a right-brain function in which one uses the creative and intuitive part of the brain. Because of a woman's openness and heightened sensitivity at this time, it is helpful to recognize that negative images can interfere with her ability to relax or to work through a contraction. Support people can inquire as to the particular concerns that the mother has after a contraction. For example, ask the mother what went through her mind during that contraction. If it is a distressing image or feeling, it is often possible to help her resolve, dissolve, or change it. To illustrate, one woman said, "The contraction feels like a ball of fire." Help her change it to: "See if you can change that to a ball of snow melting." The woman, using her imagination, began to feel more comfortable and able to handle the contractions.

In the same way, engaging the mother to express her anxieties about breast-feeding or about any negative images she has and helping her reframe those into positive or relieving images can enhance her confidence in nourishing her infant and activate nonstress hormones to produce more milk. "My milk is flowing like the mighty Mississippi." "With each touch of my baby's hand or face, the milk valves open and flow."

PHYSICAL RELAXATION

Physical relaxation can be helped by using breathing techniques and releasing tension in the muscles and throughout the body. When able to greet labor and nursing in a relaxed state, the mother can cooperate with her body to bring her baby into the world rather than fight against her body.

Contractions massage the baby, and prepare him or her for the first breath at birth. When a mother is relaxed, the stretchable birth canal opens to an amazing extent. When a mother is tense, the cervix tightens up and may contribute to more painful labor. Therefore, relaxation and visualization go hand in hand to reduce fear, tension, and pain. Being relaxed with positive feelings can contribute to a shorter, more satisfying labor.

During breast-feeding, a tense mother who worries about having enough milk, who receives mixed messages about her ability to breast-feed, or who has internal or external stress in her life, also tightens up, causes fear-produced hormones to be activated, with the result that milk flow is reduced.

The following exercise helps the body move into a relaxed state. It can be practiced as often as the woman wants—every day or a few times a week. It is helpful to be in a quiet room, in comfortable, loose clothes. If the mother wishes, she can remove shoes and glasses. Being in a comfortable position is important. Often women during late pregnancy prefer to lie on their sides with head and shoulders supported by a pillow and sometimes a pillow between the legs. Some prefer to sit in a comfortable chair, head and legs supported. If someone is reading these exercises to the mother, a soft voice, and a pause between each step or phrase will give the woman plenty of time to complete that step before going on. Some women like to put the exercises on tape.

Exercise I

Allow about twenty minutes for this exercise. Arrange not to be disturbed. Find a comfortable position, making sure all parts of your body are supported. Let your head be supported and let your shoulders drop into a comfortable position. Allow your legs and arms to be uncrossed if possible. Check the muscles of your face and head. Allow the muscles of your eyes to loosen, let the muscles around your mouth and jaw become loose. Begin the relaxation by focusing on your breathing. Take three easy, natural, cleansing breaths, pausing after each inhalation and then exhaling fully and completely . . . perhaps letting the first breath out with a nice big sigh . . . Notice how slow, rhythmic breathing helps you become more relaxed. You might imagine that you can release tensions and discomforts as you breathe out by just breathing them away. After these three breaths, just breathe easily and naturally. Now, as you continue breathing comfortably and slowly, allow your eyelids to close, remembering that you can open them whenever you choose to, or need to. Enjoy feeling a relaxing sensation around your eyes and let that sensation of letting go gently travel right from your eyes out to your forehead—to your scalp—around the back of your head—and to your ears, to your cheeks and nose—and out to your mouth and jaws. Now relax your jaw muscles, allowing your jaw to open slightly, so that any remaining tension can just flow away.

Remember to keep your breathing slow and rhythmic. Now, relax the muscles in your neck and allow the feeling of relaxation to radiate down into your shoulders. Feel how heavy your shoulders are as you let the muscles relax.

Now let the relaxation radiate down to your arms, to your elbows, your forearms, your wrists, and your hands . . . Take a moment to relax each of your fingers and let that relaxation flow out of your fingertips . . . When your hands and arms are completely relaxed, you might notice feelings of warmth, heaviness, tingling, or pulsing . . . All these are your body's ways of telling you that you're relaxed.

Continue breathing slowly in a natural rhythm. Now let the feelings of warmth and letting go extend down your chest and abdomen, radiating around your sides and ribs, as relaxation flows from your shoulder blades down your upper back, middle back, and lower back. Let all the muscles on each side of your spine become loose and relaxed . . .

Let this relaxation continue down into your pelvis and allow your buttocks to let go . . . Feel the sensation of warmth and comfort move down your thighs, to your calves . . . your ankles . . . your feet . . . and right out your toes. Remember to breathe slowly and rhythmically, enjoying the feeling of releasing . . . letting go a little more each time you breathe out . . . Now that you are relaxed, start from the top of your head and work down, checking to see how relaxed you are. If any part of your body isn't fully relaxed and comfortable, simply take a breath in, and send healing, nourishing oxygen to that area to release the tension and allow it to melt away. As you breathe out, imagine that you are releasing and breathing out, through your skin, any tension, pain, or discomfort . . . and let a wave of relaxation roll down your body, out your fingers, and out your toes . . .

When you inhale, breathe in that wonderful healing oxygen, and when you exhale, breathe out tension and discomfort. Send your breath to help release any part of your body that needs to be more relaxed . . . more loose . . . more comfortable . . . With each breath, allow yourself to become twice as relaxed as you were before. Wherever you notice any tension, take a nice breath in and as you exhale, let the warm air melt the tension away. Notice any remaining tension in your body, focus on that area, take a nice breath in, and again as you breathe out, breathe out through the tense area, letting the comforting warm air melt and ease the tension away.

When you are fully relaxed, take a moment to enjoy the good feeling, experiencing warmth and well-being throughout your body . . . And you can imagine with that next comforting breath . . . that you are breathing in a special light or energy . . . and sending that light and energy . . . and nourishing oxygenation to your womb . . . to your baby . . . and take all the time you like to send those loving messages . . . of comfort . . . of love . . . of growth . . . of health . . . and you may enjoy placing your hands on your abdomen sending these messages . . .

Remember your slow, rhythmic breathing. To end this exercise, tell yourself that you can reach a deep state of relaxation whenever you wish simply by taking three easy natural, cleansing breaths and letting the tension go with the exhalation.

Conclude the exercise now by taking in a full breath through your nose and out through your mouth . . . and taking all the time you would like . . . Feel yourself gently and easily and slowly coming back to the present moment relaxed, alert, comfortable, and confident, and feeling energized with a pleasant sense of well-being and comfort.

Sometimes women notice a number of thoughts or feelings going through their minds that prevent them from letting themselves relax. The following paragraphs can be added into the suggestions.

Imagine any unwanted thoughts like pieces of driftwood floating away until the water is clear again. Or perhaps imagine your mind like a big room, and the thoughts are coming in one end, and you can watch them drift by. If there is anything you need to pay attention to right now, you can do so, but perhaps you can let those thoughts drift on by out the other door, and let the room become peaceful again. Any emotions that come in can flow through you with the next exhalation so your mind and emotions can become calm again.

If there are distresses and events from the past or present that might interfere with your comfort now, perhaps you can imagine some kind of container to put them in that only you can open, at another time. Imagine a safe with a lock, or a Dumpster or a rocket, and let those issues move away or be completely contained.

Exercise II: The Special Place Visualization

In this exercise, the mother creates her own personal inner refuge, based on a real or imaginary place that she associates with relaxation, comfort, security, and peace. This exercise is helpful during pregnancy and labor and later during breast-feeding to give oneself positive suggestions and affirming beliefs for labor, birth, and breast-feeding. This visualization is usually imagined after a relaxation exercise or along with a relaxation exercise, as described above. The woman may want to tell her support person of a place that comes to mind, so that the support person can add some typical details. Or the mother may just imagine a lovely place spontaneously while being guided in the visualization:

Now that you are relaxed, body and mind, you are invited to go inside . . . to imagine that you are in a very special place . . . a wonderful place . . . a place of comfort for you . . . let it be a good place . . . a place that makes you feel comfortable, relaxed, secure, and at peace.

It can be any place at all—a real place you have been to or an imaginary place, or somewhere you've always wanted to go . . . a room in your home, a cabin in the mountains . . . a corner of your yard, or garden . . . the warm sand of the beach where you can hear the ocean waves coming to shore, an open meadow clothed with wildflowers . . . a soft moss-carpeted spot in a peaceful woodland grove near a gentle brook—anywhere you feel relaxed, comfortable, safe, and at peace. (Some women may wish to feel themselves peaceful in this special place just on their own. Others may enjoy imagining their husband or another loved one with them.) You may wish to imagine taking a lovely stairway or beautiful path to go there. Imagining going down a path or stairway can deepen the feeling of relaxation. You may enjoy experiencing yourself drifting deeper and deeper into relaxation as you go down the path or stairway. Counting down slowly is another way to feel oneself becoming more relaxed, 10 . . . 9 . . . 8 . . . to . . . 1 . . . in a comfortable easy manner.

Take a few minutes to explore your special place, allowing the place to become real to you . . . Look around you . . . taking in this lovely place with your eyes, enjoying the colors . . the shapes . . . the scenery . . . notice the details . . . you may notice that as you explore the details . . . the place becomes clearer and more vivid . . .

And notice now the sounds . . . and listen to the sounds . . . whatever they might be . . . the soft rustling of the wind, the lapping of the water, a bird call . . . pleasant sounds, familiar sounds of this place . . . safe and peaceful to you.

. . . And whatever sounds you hear, let them take you further into the relaxation . . . or the peaceful silence.

And enjoy feeling whatever you are sitting against or lying upon . . . or perhaps feeling the quality of the ground beneath your feet, a pine-needle forest floor . . . or you might be in a cozy armchair . . . or resting on nice soft grass in the sun . . . or the warm sand of the beach . . .

And enjoy feeling the air on your skin . . . just the right temperature . . . perhaps brisk or breezy . . . or soft and still . . . or balmy and wet . . . or perhaps you are inside, feeling the warmth of a cozy fire on your face and hands . . . or maybe you are outdoors, and there's just the subtlest caress of a fragrant, gentle breeze . . . so just enjoy it on your skin . . . and breathe in the freshness of the air . . . smelling the soft, full scent of flowers . . . or the refreshing smell of sea air . . . or sweet meadow grass . . . or maybe the pungent smell of moss in the forest . . . or the aroma of something comforting to you. . . .

And as you become more and more attuned to the safety and beauty of this place

. . . feeling thankful and happy to be there . . . you begin to feel a kind of comfort . . . knowing this is your own special place . . . and all the aspects are created there to allow feelings of deepening relaxation to flow through you . . . at your own comfort level . . . in your own time. (Variations may be added, if desired.) . . . You may notice a pleasant, energizing something in the air all around you . . . something that contains expectancy and excitement . . . a sense that something wonderful is just about to happen . . . and with that next breath . . . you may relax . . . more and more comfortably.

As you enjoy feeling relaxed, if you would like, say to yourself the following statements . . . feeling free to change the wording of any statement or create new affirmations to better suit your own wishes or to ignore any statement that doesn't apply to you.

- My changing body is radiantly beautiful.
- My precious baby is growing and developing fully and completely.
- Our baby is filled with love and health.
- Childbirth is a normal, healthy event.
- My body is my friend.
- I trust my body to labor smoothly and efficiently in the best possible way for my child and myself.
- I am able to give birth in harmony with nature.
- I am receiving all the support I need to give birth joyfully.
- I am giving our baby the very best start in life.
- The power of birth strengthens my mate, my child, and me.

- After the birth is over, I can relax and sleep easily at any time, at home, or in the hospital.
- All my functions are normal and healthy.
- I feel calm and comfortable.
- I can close off the switches to any discomfort.
- My milk develops quickly and flows naturally from my breasts.

In this lovely place . . . you can know that you can always change whatever you want to make it even more comfortable . . . more safe . . . more secure . . . more peaceful . . . knowing that you can return here . . . to this place . . . any time you want to, anytime you need to, it will always be here . . . just for you . . . very safe . . . very comfortable. Enjoy being here now . . . for as long as you want to, or need to . . . and take all the time you need . . .

. . . And when you are ready to return to your everyday life, take a few deep breaths, stretch gently, and slowly, in a moment, bring yourself peacefully back to this present moment feeling relaxed and refreshed . . . and gently open your eyes, feeling renewed and revitalized, and comfortably present . . . bringing a feeling of calm and confidence with you . . . Remember that you can return to your special place anytime you want to feel relaxed, comfortable, secure, and at ease.

(If you went to your special place walking down a path or stairway or counting, imagine coming back up the path or stairway or counting slowly and gently back up the numbers from 1 to 10 . . . to full present-time comfort.)

Guidelines for the Use of Visualizations During Labor

It is helpful if visualizations can be practiced before actual labor. However, they can be used for the first time during labor and can be effective in helping the mother cope better.

- Choose a visualization that appeals to the mother. Give her ideas if she can't think of any herself and ask her what she might prefer.
- Use them whenever the need arises during labor. The mother may want visualizations during some contractions and may prefer just relaxing and breathing rhythmically through others.
- She may be so tuned into her own process that just your quiet presence is enough to help her stay focused.
- Check with the woman on what she is experiencing or thinking after the contraction to be sure she is not "lost" or frightened.
- Speak slowly; pause for a few seconds after each phrase.
- Check with the mother for feedback to be sure she is comfortable with your pace, timing, and phrasing to be sure you are in synchrony with her.
- Some women prefer using the same images over and over as they focus inward through a contraction (such as "riding through the wave" or "shaping the clay pot").
- Some women may prefer to vary the images or combine different ones.
- Getting in a focused rhythm with her through each contraction is helpful.

- For example, if you are walking with her and a contraction occurs, stop, let her lean against you or her partner, and help her with counting or breathing through the contraction. You might say: "That's right, breathe through it, let the wave come through, good, breathe, open, open. Yes, 20, 19, 18, 17, 16, 15, 14, 13, 12, 11, 10, 9, 8, 7, 6, 5, 4, 3, 2, 1. (Count again backwards, 20 to 1, another breath, and so on, three or four times until the contraction is over.) Good, good, excellent. Now, relax even more. That's right. The more relaxed you are, the more productive the contraction. Good. Such a good contraction."
- During late labor, as there is often very little time to rest between contractions, many women prefer short, simple visualizations, such as a shortened version of the blossoming flower, the waterfall, the ocean waves, or the radiant light breath.
- Many women use sound to help them through contractions. When a woman opens her throat, vocalizes, moans, or groans through a contraction, she opens the birth canal. Make sounds with the mother—help her feel free to make groans or sounds. Use images like wind, water, waves.
- It is helpful if the moan or sound like "ahhhh" is deeper, coming from the throat and chest, rather than from her normal or higher voice. Chanting and vowel sounds through the different phases of labor can feel powerful and freeing.
- Encourage the mother to use the sound that resonates most for her.

Appendix B: Relaxation, Visualization, and Self-Hypnosis Exercises   217

- Be sensitive to cultural differences or preferences. Some women labor in silence; others sing or moan.
- Combine vocalization with the visualizations, if the mother wishes. The mother can make deep resonant sounds as the contraction builds with the power of the ocean wave and then fade the sound away as the "wave" (contraction) ebbs away.
- She may moan or sigh deeply as she breathes out during the radiant-light-breath imagery as she pictures the out breath carrying away her tension and pain.
- Reassure her by your words and actions that being free, unrestricted, and uninhibited is normal and good, up to her own comfort level.
- Visualizations can be combined with positions and with massage as a way to help the mother relax into the contraction and focus away from the pain.
- Use visualizations with her breathing in or on the out breath through the contraction as you do a releasing massage technique, sometimes called the roving massage. Place your hands on a part of her body, ask her to take a breath in during the contraction as you press into that part of the body, and then slowly release the pressure of your hands as she breathes out as the contraction ebbs away. One can continue this way through many contractions combining breath, touch, and images.
- In general, guide the mother through the imagery using a soft voice and pausing between each phrase. Give the

mother adequate time to complete each step before going on to the next.
- Sometimes you may need to synchronize your voice tone with the energy and sounds of the mother.
- When speaking to the mother, recognize that you are communicating with her "laboring mind." Her mind is not in the ordinary everyday consciousness. Time is subjective. You can use simple images and statements. It is not boring to her if you repeat the same statements over and over again.
- Use agreed-upon verbal and nonverbal cues to help her stay relaxed.
- In your support role, remain as physically close to her as is comfortable for her. Remember your presence and your attention to her and her needs and feelings are the most important aspects of your support. Where and how she wants to be touched at different points in labor, may change.
- Hold her, caress her, stroke her arms, legs, shoulders, back; press her hips, her hands, and so on, whatever she finds comfortable.
- Be with her throughout her experience. Walk with her if she is walking, trying always to keep one hand on her; support her physically as needed. Get appropriately close to her on the bed if she is laboring there.
- Develop a cue word or phrase, such as "calm," or "deeper and deeper relaxed"; or a touch, such as stroking her arm or hand, that the partner can use to help the trance state deepen or help the woman remain in it.

- Help her with a bath or shower if she wishes to use water during late labor. Add visualizations with the shower (waterfall) or bath (floating, waves) as she has contractions.
- Let her know you believe in her strength and power to give birth.
- Remind her of other challenges she has accomplished, if appropriate.
- Trust her to labor in the best possible way for her, even if it is different from what you expect, or even if she seems afraid.
- Stay with her, encourage her, express positive beliefs and statements. Your attitude and trust in her can make all the difference because her open and vulnerable mind can be strongly influenced.
- During labor, you may shorten the relaxation exercises, but if she is using self-hypnosis, she may need your guidance or support to use what she knows, adding her choice of visualizations. Also, *do not use* the last step of "coming out" of the visualization, such as "count slowly from 1 to 5, stretch gently, and open your eyes." The mother is in the midst of labor and may want to continue using the same or other visualizations throughout labor and through the birth.

Exercise III: Self-Anesthesia Methods

After women have learned how to relax and use guided and receptive imagery, it is useful to develop the self-hypnotic skill of self-anesthesia for pain relief. Several practition-

ers and developers of hypnotic techniques for birth, including David Cheek, M.D., and William Kroger, M.D., have used a concept of imaginary "numbing" of different parts of the body that can be directed to the abdomen, the back, or the birth canal during labor.

A simple way of helping oneself move into a light trance state for self-hypnosis is a method called "eye fixation." Ask the woman to fixate her look at a spot on the ceiling or upwards to her eyebrows and allow her eyelids to flutter closed; then take a nice deep breath and enjoy letting a feeling of relaxation and comfort flow down her body as she exhales, imagining drifting deeper and deeper into a relaxed state. (You may suggest that she continue this process of relaxing with the ideas in Exercise I.)

1. (After moving into this light trance state and if you enjoy water), imagine yourself stepping into lovely, clean, safe, cool water up to your knees. When you feel the coolness, let one of your fingers signal or lift to let you know.
2. After awhile, notice how you feel a kind of numbness. When you notice the numbness, let another finger lift.
3. Continue comfortably into the cool water to right under your breasts. As you notice the coolness, your first finger will lift; as you notice the numbness around the central portion of your body, your second finger will lift.
4. To strengthen the numbness, put two fingers (thumb and index finger) together on one hand. To release the

numbness, put two fingers together on the other hand.

5. Practice your ability to create this numbness, to bring it in and to let it go.

6. Then with the doula or partner supporting you, practice the "numbness" while walking or moving into different positions—leaning, hands and knees, squatting, and the like. (However, in order to recognize how you can maintain the numbness in the central portion of your body and still change positions, imagine that your legs are "awake and normal," and that just the central portion of your body is "numb.")

7. Practice this numbing technique every day for a few minutes during the last month along with your visualization.

A second method for self-anesthesia is called "glove anesthesia."

(Using the eye-fixation technique or the special-place imagery, first let yourself drift deeper and deeper into a light trance state.)

1. Imagine that a strong anesthetic is pouring into your hand; or imagine that you are placing your hand in a jar of anesthetic cream, and it becomes number and number, similar to the feeling of novocaine at the dentist's. Or, perhaps your hand can feel as though it is covered by a thick glove.

2. As you notice the numbing quality, imagine transferring the anesthesia to another part of your body.

3. Practice bringing in the numbness and then returning your hand or body area to normal feelings several times.

A third method for relief of pain is by strengthening and enhancing one's sensory imagery by imagined activity in one's special place. Allow yourself to delve further and further into the experience of being in your special place. For example, swimming through the changing colors of the tropical waters, or imagining resting and then floating through the rich, changing colors of the rainbow. Each of these images and inner experiences are coupled with a contraction. In this way, the power of imagery distracts you from the discomfort.

Exercise IV: Imagining Birth

Guiding the mother to imagine herself going through the actual birth can prepare her to greet labor with a positive attitude, to have images to use during contractions (with the labor companion's help), and to believe in her ability to ride above the most difficult contractions peacefully, with less tension and more trust in the power of her own body to bring her baby into the world. The following exercise has been used to prepare women for labor. Always change words or aspects of the visualization to fit the individual mother's own interests, ideas, or comfort. (*Please pause for a few seconds after each phrase to give the mother time to integrate the meaning.*)

Let your mind drift ahead in time to the future as though through a time tunnel to the day your baby will be born. Imagine that the day you have waited for has come. Your baby knows when to start labor, when your baby is fully grown and ready.

Think of your baby inside you; let baby know you are ready to meet face to face.

Imagine your baby in your mind's eye. The head is cushioned against your cervix. The back is curled up. The water the baby is floating in is crystal clear. The membranes are strong and intact, cushioning the baby. The baby is resting, getting ready for the journey.

Touch your belly if you want. Caress your baby within. Find a way to send a message to your baby, telling the baby that you are ready.

When it's time, you begin to feel a rush of energy deep within your thighs. It comes up and circles your waist, tightens around your belly, and pushes down.

Acknowledge that you and your baby are the source of this power and let it come.

At the point when labor begins, the contractions may be uncomfortable, but this will be a sign for you to start timing them and following your caregiver's advice on what to look for as you move into labor. When you have communicated the necessary information, you will begin your relaxation as soon as you are ready to. Your goal is to keep yourself completely relaxed so that you can birth your baby in confidence.

You move into your self-hypnosis easily and comfortably.

You begin by comfortably settling into a chair and taking a moment to become very relaxed. Allow your breathing to be easy and natural, like a wave of relaxation that travels from the top of your head right down your body and out your toes.

You roll your eyes up, focus on a spot on the ceiling or on your forehead. You take a nice, deep breath of air, hold the breath, and then as you exhale, allow your eyelids to close.

Think about relaxing every muscle in your body. For the next few moments, think the word *relax, relax* to yourself. Each time you breathe out, think the word—*relax*—and allow your body to respond. Each breath out becomes a relaxing breath. Just allowing yourself to go deeper and deeper . . . relaxing with each breath out.

With that next breath out, allow every muscle in your body to relax as loose and limp as a rag doll—so loose, so relaxed.

With your next few breaths, enjoy letting that feeling of relaxation continue to travel throughout your body, out your arms and hands—continue to release tension out your shoulders, your neck, and feel that soothing relaxation flowing down your back—down, down, down, just letting those muscles go, relaxing more and more.

And with every breath in, breathe in that wonderful oxygenation and nutrients for yourself and your baby, and with every breath out release more and more tension and go deeper and deeper . . . more and more relaxed. Let that wave of relaxation spread across your forehead, letting the muscles in your head, your face, your jaw relax and unwind, just like letting a tight rubber band unwind, letting go, letting go, even more.

As this relaxation spreads down your arms, they become so relaxed, so heavy, so comfortable, and as you exhale, the comfort spreads across your chest—and as you take another deep breath and exhale, the comfort and warmth spreads into your stomach—calm, relaxed . . . as your legs become very, very relaxed . . .

Perhaps in a moment it would be all right for you to go even deeper, imagining that you are going down a beautiful stairway or a lovely path that will lead you to a special and beautiful place where you feel safe, comfortable, and deeply relaxed. . . . In a moment I am going to count backwards from 10 to 1, and you can imagine very gently, safely, and easily going down to this lovely place . . . and with each step or count down, you can feel your body relax more and more, deeper and deeper. . . . 10 . . . even deeper, 9 . . . 8 . . . deeper and deeper to your own comfort level . . . 7 . . . 6 . . . 5 . . . 4 . . . 3 . . . 2 . . . 1 . . . more and more relaxed. This is the most peaceful place in the world for you, and you can feel a sense of peace and comfort flow through you.

As the contractions begin, you relax, deeper and deeper. You go along with each contraction, calm and relaxed, breathing slowly and deeply. You can enjoy a pleasant sense of anticipation to replace any feelings of apprehension. As labor continues, you feel more and more confident in your ability to respond appropriately. . . . And you may notice how the wisdom of your body in the DNA structure of your cells throughout all of time knows exactly how to birth your baby . . . and you can trust this innate knowledge in your own biology.

As you need to, you can practice your self-anesthesia, feeling the whole central part of your body become more and more numb with each contraction. If you wish, you can make your hand and arm numb and transfer this numb feeling to your abdomen by touching it as if you were pulling on a thick glove, and as the glove goes over the fingers and hand and wrist, then each part becomes numb as if a powerful anesthetic is flowing through them. And you can transfer this numbness to your abdomen and to any place you need it, and the contractions will feel

even more comfortable than before, no matter how strong they become. Or you can imagine yourself floating in the cool, comfortable, crystal clear safe water, allowing the coolness to help you feel more and more numb from your ribs to your thighs, and as this coolness flows, it stops any pain impulses on the nerves because coolness flows down the same paths of the pain impulses. You are tapping into your body's natural opiates.

You welcome each contraction as a message drawing you closer and closer to your baby. You may feel the contraction as a tightening or as a hardening, and you may feel pressure or movement, but you will feel less and less discomfort. The stronger the contraction the more relaxed you become. Although you may notice them, the contractions become more and more remote, and while still perceptible, they do not bother you anymore. And you may notice that with each feeling of pressure, the birth canal becomes more and more numb. And using the skills and cues you (and your partner) have created, you can go even more relaxed with those words, (example): "deeper and deeper," "calmer," etc., or with those touches, pressure or strokes on your hand, arm, or putting two fingers together to become even more peacefully relaxed.

And as you relax, you may notice the contractions become more and more productive, and you go deeper and deeper, as you drift deeply and comfortably to your beautiful and safe place.

Whenever you feel the surge fading away, perhaps you allow yourself to go even more relaxed, totally limp, drifting into a deep comfort, a comfort you already know, and this comfort can last and last—and, in fact, you might be surprised that the rest in between surges seems to last longer than you thought—so that you experience a lovely and deeply profound rest . . . So you can feel so delightfully refreshed and energized when the next wave occurs . . . and you might not even pay attention when the next surge begins . . . because your caregivers are watching, timing, and keeping you safe, and they will inform you if they need your help, so that you can just relax more and more into that peaceful, comfortable place . . . and it might even feel as if the surge passes more and more quickly and even more and more easily . . . And you may be surprised that no matter how fast or how slow the surges come, you always feel on top of them and ride through them as though you are riding the waves, and you know that the waves always come to shore . . . and you rest and you rest . . . and during labor, you need to pay attention only when someone speaks directly to you; then you can respond . . . and you can always say what you need. If there is any pain you need to pay attention to, you will always be able to do so, and stay relaxed through any procedures necessary to enhance your own or the baby's health. And you can be flexible and adjust to whatever is best and safest and trust those whom you have chosen and who are there helping you. And whatever choices you make enhance your own ability to work with your body.

You can remain calm and confident and comfortable throughout your labor and delivery.

Since you already know there are so many sounds in the labor rooms and hallways, you don't need to bother with them at all because others will tend to whatever is needed, and whatever sounds you hear can lull you deeper and deeper like a lovely wave or the gentle sounds of a waterfall or a soothing breeze on a summer day (use the images of the woman's special place).

As you relax, the lower circular muscles of the cervix become more and more stretchy and relaxed, opening and opening, and the top long muscles of the uterus become stronger and stronger joining with the baby to push down and out. The baby helps with his or her own power to swim out as though on a water slide. Each contraction is like a hug for the baby, and with every surge, the cervix opens and opens, and the tapestry of satin threads gently pulls up and loosens and loosens . . . and you breathe through it . . . that's right . . .

And you can feel any contraction to whatever extent you wish to satisfy your need to know or experience what labor is like. You can remember any and all of the sensations connected with having a baby so you can share in the birth experience and share with others as you wish.

As you progress through the different phases of labor, you may be curious about the variety of experiences you are having. Some may be quite different from what you expected and some may seem very familiar. And you may discover how you can use your own creativity and your own skills again and again to find just the right kind of comfort or relaxation . . . At times finding yourself focusing on your calm inner place . . . at other times, tapping into your power and strength and endurance, and still at other times moving through your waves of energy . . . or something else . . . so you can be pleased with your own ability to meet the goals you have for the birth of your baby.

And throughout you can remain calm, confident, deeply relaxed, feeling in control, energetic and strong, and know that your baby and the universal plan is perfect. You can imagine each contraction like a safe and powerful wave, like waves of energy. You relax even more. The contractions surge, rise to a crest, and ebb away like waves. You welcome each new wave as it comes. Yes. Yes. You breathe through it. You take in the next breath, breathing through the contraction. Each powerful wave moves your baby down, down, down . . . And you can appreciate how well and easily and safely labor is progressing. Each time you feel the wave coming closer and closer, you can take one of those full refreshing breaths, replenishing your comfort and feeling reenergized . . . And as you exhale, you can release whatever you don't need . . . letting it go . . . And every wave brings your baby closer and closer to your waiting arms.

The baby's head easily pushes against your cervix, opening it wider, wider, wider, like a flower opened by the sun's rays.

The next wave comes—from the distance—stronger and stronger. You ride through the wave, the wave always comes to shore, and you rest, and baby rests . . . and with each surge you can feel your birth canal relaxing . . . and opening up . . . ever so easily . . . ever so gently . . . ever so persistently . . . and you rest . . . knowing the age-old biological wisdom of your body . . . and trusting . . . and releasing. But you are still the source of these waves. You welcome them . . . and you rest . . . deeper and deeper . . . relaxed through the changing progression . . . the changing nature . . . the changing intensity of each surge.

Look at your baby again. Your baby is surrounded by the warmth of the waves, coming closer and closer to you . . . to the light.

Again the wave surges. It circles your abdomen. It tightens. You let it happen, you breathe through it.

Again, a mighty surge of energy strengthens and pushes and eases your baby down, down, down. Your birth canal responds so naturally in just the right way to the waves of relaxation the contractions are sending to that area . . . and taking a nice deep breath, you relax even more.

You and your baby are grateful for this surge of power. You welcome it as a friend.

Again it comes, tightening, strengthening the surge . . . pushing down, down, down.

Take a breath. And breathe through it and . . . you may feel pressure and tightening but no discomfort as you go deeper and deeper more and more relaxed. And when your midwife or doctor and your wisdom tells you that it is time to push, you will feel so in tune with your body, with your baby, with your own surges of energy, you will find it so very easy to let your own power come through to push in just the right way at just the right time, for just the right length of time, and when the contraction eases away, you easily drift back into that relaxed state . . . resting and resting . . . gathering renewed energy . . . and even more strength for the next surge for whenever it is ready . . . and you have all the time you need.

And imagine your cervix is opened, and you think about your baby coming out.

Now look at your baby again. See the moist curly hair. Perhaps you can feel, touch the baby's head. Look down.

You feel the baby pushing down, down, down. You go deeper and deeper relaxed. As you wish, you can open your eyes and still remain deeply relaxed. You can experience as much of the birth as you wish. The perineum is easily stretching . . . and as your baby slides down, swimming through, you feel an in-pouring of waves of anesthesia as you wish . . . and you can experience the birth as you wish and can feel the head as it slides down, coming through . . . Your body is kneading and massaging . . . and hugging . . . and with the next powerful wave, the baby comes through.

You have birthed your baby. Your baby is dried quickly and placed on your breast, you are holding your baby in your arms, warm, beautiful, the child you have made, cradled in your arms. You feel, smell, touch, see this beautiful baby. You feel the love between you (and the baby's father). You say to your baby, we are grateful for this beautiful birth. Your uterus contracts healthfully. The placenta comes out whole. The vessels fully contract down so there is no bleeding. The uterus continues to contract . . . and contract . . . returning to its original size. You and baby rest . . . and sometime in the first hour or so baby finds his or her way to the nipple and latches on perfectly, healthfully activating the wonderful production of your breast milk.

You recuperate quickly, fully and completely. All your systems work perfectly. You are able to continue relaxing and resting, regaining your strength and enjoying the wonder of motherhood.

Take a moment or so to enjoy the feeling of your newborn child against your breast. Now slowly let this beautiful scene fade into the future where it belongs and very slowly and comfortably . . . slowly . . . so that all your systems are balanced and integrated . . . come back to the present as I count or you can count to yourself from one to ten.

And when you are ready, count slowly perhaps once again, and stretch gently and open your eyes and feel fully present and good.

APPENDIX C:
CHARACTERISTICS OF RANDOMIZED
CLINICAL TRIALS OF LABOR SUPPORT

Type of Presence	Trial Location	Clinical Trials Subject	Doula
Continuous	Gagnon et al.,[1] 1997, Montreal	413 primigravidas	Nurses (one-to-one)
	Gordon et al.,[2] 1999, Oakland, California	314 primigravidas primarily Caucasian, African-American, Hispanic	Laywomen trained through project
	Hodnett & Osborn,[3] 1989, Toronto Canada	103 primigravidas, primarily Caucasian, middle class	Lay-midwives or apprentice lay midwives
	Kennell et al.,[4] 1991, Houston, Texas	516 primigravidas, low-income, Hispanic, African-American	Laywomen trained through project
	Kennell & McGrath,[5] 1993, Cleveland, Ohio	555 primigravidas, middle-income	Laywomen trained through project
	Klaus et al.,[6] 1986, Guatemala	463 primigravidas	Laywomen trained through project
	Langer et al.,[7] 1998, Mexico City	724 primigravidas	Retired nurses given doula training
	Madi et al.,[8] 1999, Botswana	109 primigravidas	Untrained female relative
	McGrath & Kennell,[9] 1999, Houston, Texas	513 primigravidas	Laywomen trained through project
	Sosa et al.,[10] 1980, Guatamala	40 primigravidas	Untrained laywomen

Intermittent	Breart et al.,[11] 1992, Belgium	264 primigravidas spontaneous labor	Midwife or student midwife
	Breart et al.,[11] 1992, France	1320 primigravidas spontaneous labor	Midwife or student midwife
	Breart et al.,[11] 1992, Greece	569 primigravidas spontaneous labor	Midwife or student midwife
	Hemminki et al.,[12] 2 trials 1990, Helsinki, Finland	79 subjects in 1987 trial 161 subjects in 1988 trial	Midwifery student
	Hofmeyr et al.,[13] 1991, South Africa	189 primigravidas	Untrained laywomen

[1]Gagnon, A. J., Waghorn, K., Covill, C. A randomized trial of one to one nurse support of women in labor. *Birth*, 24:71–77, 1997.

[2]Gordon, N. P., Walton, D., McAdam, E. et al. Effects of providing hospital-based doulas in health maintenance organization hospitals. *Obstet Gynecol*, 180:1054–1059, 1999.

[3]Hodnett, E. D. and Osborn, R. Effect of continuous intrapartum professional support on childbirth outcomes. *Research in Nursing and Health*, 2:289–297, 1998.

[4]Kennell, J. H., Klaus, M., McGrath, S. K. et al. Continuous emotional support during labor in a U.S. hospital. *JAMA*, 265:2197–2201, 1991.

[5]Kennell, J. H., McGrath, S. K. Labor support by a doula for middle income couples: The effect on cesarean rates. *Pediatric Res.*, 33:12A, 1993.

[6]Klaus, M., Kennell, J. H., Robertson, S. S. et al. Effects of social support during parturition on maternal and infant morbidity. *Br Med J*, 293:585–587, 1986.

[7]Langer, A., Campero, L. Garcia, C. Effects of psychosocial support during labour and childbirth on breastfeeding, medical intervention, and mother's well-being in a Mexican public hospital: A randomized clinical trial. *British J Obstet & Gynecology*, 105:1056–1063, 1998.

[8]Madi, C. M., Santall, J., Bennett, R. et al. Effects of female relative support in labor: A randomized controlled trial. *Birth*, 26:4–8, 1999.

[9]McGrath, S. K., Kennell, J. H., Suresh, M. et al. Doula support vs. epidural analgesia: Impact on cesarean rates. *Pediatr Res*, 45:16A, 1999.

[10]Sosa, R., Kennell, J. H., Klaus, M. et al. The effect of a supportive companion on perinatal problems, length of labor, and mother interaction. *N Engl J Med*, 303:597–600, 1980.

[11]Breart, G., Mika-Cabase, N., Kaminski, M. et al. Evaluation of different policies for the management of labour. *Early Hum. Dev*, 29:309–312, 1992.

[12]Hemminki, E., Virta, A. L., Koponen, P. et al. A trial on continuous human support during labor: Feasibility, interventions, and mothers' satisfaction Part A and B. *J of Psychosomatic Obstetrics and Gynecology*, 1:239–250, 1990.

[13]Hofmeyr, G. J., Nikodem, V. C., Wolman, W. et al. Companionship to modify the clinical birth environment: Effects on progress and perceptions of labour and breastfeeding. *Br J Obstet Gynecol*, 98:756–764, 1991.

APPENDIX D: RESOURCES

American College of Nurse-Midwives
818 Connecticut Avenue Suite 900
Washington, D.C. 20006
Tel: (202) 728-9860
Fax: (202) 728-9897
www.midwife.org

American College of Obstetricians and
    Gynecologists (ACOG)
409 12th Street S.W., P.O. Box 96920
Washington, D.C. 20090-6920
Tel: (202) 638-5577
www.acog.org

Birth
Blackwell Science Inc.
350 Main Street
Malden, MA 02148
Tel: (800) 661-5800
Fax: (781) 388-8270
www.blackwell-science.com

Birthworks
P.O. Box 2045
Medford, NJ 08055
Tel: (888) TO BIRTH (862-4784)
www.birthworks.org

The Bradley Method of Natural
    Childbirth
Box 5224
Sherman Oaks, CA 91413-5224
Tel: (800) 4-A-BIRTH
www.bradleybirth.com

Cascade Health Care Products Birth and
    Life Bookstore
141 Commercial N.E.
Salem, OR 97301-3402
Tel: (800) 443-9942
Fax: (503) 371-5395
www.1cascade.com/birthlife.html

Chicago Health Connection
954 West Washington Blvd.
Suite 36 4th Fl.
Chicago, IL 60607-2211
Tel: (773) 235-5077
Fax: (773) 384-3904
www.frca.org (programs & networks/IL)

Coalition for Improving Maternity
  Services (CIMS)
P.O. Box 2346
Ponte Verda Beach, FL 32004
Tel: (888) 282-CIMS (1613)
Fax: (904) 285-2120
www.motherfriendly.org

Community Doula Program
Nadia Stein, Executive Director
7110 Tickner
Houston, TX 77055
Tel: (713) 686-4658
www.communitydoula.org

Doulas of North America (DONA)
P.O. Box 627
Jasper, IN 47547
Tel: (888) 788-DONA (3662)
Fax: (812) 634-1491

International Cesarean Awareness
  Network (ICAN)
1304 Kingsdale Avenue
Redondo Beach, CA 90278
Tel: (310) 542-6400
Fax: (310) 542-5368
www.ican-online.org

International Childbirth Education
  Association (ICEA)
P.O. Box 20048
Minneapolis, MN 55420

Tel: (952) 854-8660
Fax: (952) 854-8772
www.icea.org

International Lactation Consultant
  Association (ILCA)
1500 Sunday Drive, Suite 102
Raleigh, NC 27607
Tel: (919) 787-5181
Fax: (919) 787-4916
www.ilca.org

La Leche League International, Inc.
P.O. Box 4079
Schaumburg, IL 60168-4079
Tel: (847) 519-7730
Fax: (847) 519-0035
www.lalecheleague.org

Lamaze International
2025 M Street, Suite 800
Washington, D.C. 20036-3309
Tel: (800) 368-4404
Fax: (202) 367-2128
www.lamaze-childbirth.com

Maternity Center Association
281 Park Avenue South, 5th Fl.
New York, NY 10010
Tel: (212) 777-5000
Fax: (212) 777-9320
www.maternitywise.org/mca/bookstore

Midwives Alliance of North America
  (MANA)
4805 Lawrenceville Hwy.
Suite 116-279
Lilburn, GA 30047
Tel: (888) 923-MANA (6262)
Fax: (801) 720-3026
www.mana.org

Mothering Magazine
P.O. Box 1690
Santa Fe, NM 87504
Tel: (800) 984-8116
Tel: (505) 984-8116
www.mothering.com

MotherLove, Inc.
Debra Pascali-Bonaro, CD (DONA), CCE
584 Echo Glen Ave.
River Vale, NY 07675
Tel: (201) 358-2703
Fax: (201) 664-4405
www.findamidwifetoday.com/loves/
   motherlove

National Association of Childbearing
   Centers (NACC)
3123 Gottschall Road
Perkiomenville, PA 18074
Tel: (215) 234-8068
Fax: (215) 234-8829
www.BirthCenters.org

Pacific Association for Labor Support
   (PALS)
2524 16th Ave. South #207C
Seattle, WA 98144
Tel: (206) 325-1419
www.pals-doulas.org

NOTES

CHAPTER 1: THE NEED FOR SUPPORT IN LABOR

1. Scott, K. D., Berkowitz, G., Klaus, M. A comparison of intermittent and continuous support during labor: A meta analysis. *Am J Obstet Gynecol,* 180:1054–1059, 1999.

2. Raphael, D. *The tender gift: Breastfeeding.* Englewood Cliffs, NJ: Prentice-Hall, 1973.

3. Enkin, M., Keirse, M.J.N.C., Neilson, J. et al. *A guide to effective care in pregnancy and childbirth.* New York: Oxford University Press, 2000, p. 295.

4. Hodnett, E. D. and Abel, S. M. Person-environment interaction as a determinant of labor length variables. *Health Care for Women International,* 7:341–356, 1986.

5. O'Driscoll, K. and Meagher, D. *Active management of labor,* 2d ed. London: Bailliere Tindall, 1986.

CHAPTER 3: ENHANCING THE BIRTH EXPERIENCE

1. Erikson, M., Mattson, L. A., and Ladfors, L. Early or late bath during the first stage of labour: A randomized study of 200 women. *Midwifery* 13:146–148, 1997.

2. Cammu, H., Clasen, K., Van Wettern, L. Is having a warm bath during labor useful? *Acta Obstet Gyn Scand,* 73:468–472, 1994.

3. Fenwick, L., Simkin, P. Maternal positioning to prevent or alleviate dystocia in labor. *Clin Obstet Gynecol,* 30:83–89, 1987.

4. Roberts, J. Maternal position during the first stage of labour. In: Chalmers, I., Enkin, M., Keirse, M.J.N.C. (eds.). *Effective care in pregnancy and childbirth,* vol. 2. Oxford, UK: Oxford University Press, 1999.

5. Simkin, P. Reducing pain and enhancing progress in labor: A guide to nonpharmacologic methods for maternity caregivers. *Birth,* 22:161–171, 1995.

6. Russell, J.G.B. Moulding of the pelvic outlet. *J. Obstet Gynecol Br. Commonio,* 76:817–820, 1969.

7. Bogren, G., Lundeberg, T., Uvnas-Moberg, K., Sato, A. The oxytocin antagonist 1-deamino-2D-Tyr-(Oet)-4-Thr-8-Orn-oxytocin reverses the increase in the withdrawal response latency to thermal, but not mechanical nociceptive stimuli following oxytocin administration or massage-like stroking in rats. *Neurosci Lett,* 187:49–52, 1995.

8. Klaus, M., Klaus, P. *Your amazing newborn.* Cambridge, MA: Perseus, 1998.

CHAPTER 4: REDUCING DISCOMFORT, PAIN, AND ANXIETY IN CHILDBIRTH

1. Wuitchik, M., Bakal, D., Lipshitz, J. The clinical significance of pain and cognitive activity in latent labor. *Obstet Gynecol,* 73:35–41, 1989.

2. Ransjö-Arvidson, A., Matthiesen, A., Lilja, G. Maternal analgesia during labor disturbs newborn behavior: Effects on breastfeeding, temperature and crying. *Birth,* 28:5–11, 2001.

3. Jacobson, E. *Progressive relaxation.* Chicago: University of Chicago Press, 1974.

4. Fezler, W. *Creative imagery: How to visualize in all five senses.* New York: (Fireside) Simon & Schuster, 1989.

5. Alman, B. M., Lambrou, P. T. *Self-hypnosis: The complete manual for health and self-change.* New York: Brunner/Mazel, 1992.

6. Kroger, W. S. *Clinical and experimental hypnosis,* 2d ed. Philadelphia: J. B. Lippincott, 1977.

7. Lieberman, A. B. *Easing labor pain:* The complete guide to a more comfortable and rewarding birth. Boston: Harvard Common Press, 1992.

8. Feher, S. D. K., Berger, L. R., Johnson, J. D., Wilde, J. B. Increasing breast milk production for premature infants with relaxation/imagery audiotape. *Pediatrics* 83, 57–60, 1989.

9. Freeman, R. M., Macaulay, A. J., Eve, L. et al. Randomized trial of self-hypnosis for analgesia in labour. *Br Med J,* 292:657–658, 1986.

10. Perez, P. *The nurturing touch at birth: A labor support handbook.* Katy, TX: Cutting Edge Press, 1997.

11. Simkin, P., Ancheta, R. *The Labor progress handbook.* Malden, MA: Blackwell Sciences, 2000.

CHAPTER 5: OBSTETRIC BENEFITS OF DOULA SUPPORT

1. Kennell, J. H., McGrath, S. K. Labor support by a doula for middle-income couples: the effect on cesarean rates. *Pediatric Res.,* 33:12A, 1993.

2. Gordon, N. P., Walton, D., McAdam, E. et al. Effects of providing hospital-based doulas in health maintenance organization hospitals. *Obstet Gynecol,* 93:422–426, 1999.

3. Scott, K. D., Berkowitz, G., Klaus, M. A comparison of intermittent and continuous support during labor: A meta-analysis. *Am J Obstet Gynecol,* 180:1054–1059, 1999.

4. Kennell and Mcgrath. Ibid.

5. Gagnon, A. J., Waghorn, K., Covell, C. A randomized trial of one-to-one nurse support of women in labor. *Birth* 24:71–77, 1997.

6. Sosa, R., Kennell, J. H., Klaus, M. et al. The effect of a supportive companion on perinatal problems, length of labor, and mother interaction. *N Engl J Med,* 303:597–600, 1980.

7. Klaus, M., Kennell, J. H., Robertson, S. S. et al. Effects of social support during parturition on maternal and infant morbidity. *Br Med J,* 293:585–587, 1986.

8. Kennell, J. H., Klaus, M., McGrath, S. K. et al. Continuous emotional support during labor in a U.S. hospital. *JAMA,* 265:2197–2201, 1991.

9. McGrath, S. K., Kennell, J. H., Suresh, M. et al. Doula support vs. epidural analgesia: Impact on cesarean rates. *Pediatr Res,* 45:16A, 1999.

10. Fusi, L., Moresh, J. J. A., Steer, P. J. et al. Maternal pyrexia associated with the use of epidural analgesia in labor. *Lancet,* 1:1250–1252, 1989.

11. McGrath, S. K., Kennell, J. H. Induction of labor and doula support. *Pediatric Res,* 43:189, 1998.

12. Glink, P. The Chicago doula project: A collaborative effort in perinatal support for birthing teens. *Zero to Three.* 18:44–50, 1998.

13. Vallejo, M., Firestone, L. L., Mandell, G. C. et al. Effect of epidural analgesia with ambulation on labor duration. *Anesthesiology* 95:857–861, 2001.

14. Connelly, N. R., Parker, R. K., Lucas, T. et al. The influence of a bupivacaine and fentanyl epidural infusion after epidural fentanyl in patients allowed to ambulate in early labor. *Anesthesia and Analgesia* 93:1001–1005, 2001.

15. Howell, C. J. Epidural versus non-epidural analgesia for pain relief in labour. (Cochrane Review) In: The Cochrane Library (Database on disk and CD-ROM) Issue 2, Updated quarterly, The Cochrane Collaboration update software, Oxford, 2000.

CHAPTER 6: LONGER-TERM BENEFITS OF DOULA SUPPORT

1. Kramer, M. S., Chalmers, B., Hodnett, E. D. et al. Promotion of breastfeeding intervention trial: A randomized trial in the republic of Belarus. *JAMA,* 286:413–420, 2000.

2. Whitelaw, A., Heisterkamp, E. G., Sleath, K. Skin-to-skin contact for very low birth weight infants and their mothers: A randomized trial of "kangaroo care." *Archives of Diseases of Childhood,* 63:1377–1381, 1998.

3. Rôdholm, M. Effects of father-infant postpartum contact on their interaction three months after birth. *Early Human Development,* 5:79–85, 1981.

4. Lvoff, N. M., Lvoff, V., Klaus, M. Effect of the Baby Friendly Initiative on infant abandonment in a

Russian hospital. *Arch Pediatr Adolesc Med,* 154:474–4777, 2000.

5. O'Conner, S., Vietze, P. M., Sherrod, K. B. et al. Reduced incidence of parenting inadequacy following rooming-in. *Pediatrics,* 66:176–192, 1980.

6. Siegel, E., Bauman, K. E., Schaefer, E. S. et al. Hospital and home support during infancy: Impact on maternal attachment, child abuse, neglect, and health care utilization. *Pediatrics,* 66:183–190, 1980.

7. Gomes-Pedro, J. C. The effects of extended contact in the neonatal period on the behavior of a sample of Portuguese mothers and infants. In: J. K. Nugent, B. M. Lester, T. B. Brazelton (eds.) *The cultural context of infancy,* vol. I. Norwood, NJ: Ablex, 1989.

8. Anisfeld, E., Casper, V., Nozyce, W., Cunningham, N. Does infant carrying promote attachment? An experimental study of the effects of increased physical contact on the development of attachment. *Child Development,* 61:1617–1627, 1990.

9. Sosa, R., Kennell, J. H., Klaus, M. H. et al. The effect of a supportive companion on perinatal problems, length of labor, and mother interaction. *N Engl J Med,* 303:597–600, 1980.

10. Hofmeyr, G. J., Nikodem, V. C., Wolman, W. et al. Companionship to modify the clinical birth environment: Effects on progress and perceptions of labour and breastfeeding. *Br J Obstet Gynecol,* 98:756–764, 1991.

11. Wolman, W. L. Social support during childbirth, psychological and physiological outcomes. Master's thesis, University of Witwatersrand, Johannesburg, 1991.

12. Wolman, W. L., Chalmers, B., Hofmeyr, G. J. et al. Post-partum depression and companionship in the clinical birth environment: A randomized, controlled study. *Am J Obstet and Gynec,* 168:1380–1393, 1993.

13. Wolman, Ibid.

14. Manning-Orenstein, G. A birth intervention: the therapeutic effects of doula support vs. Lamaze preparation on first-time mothers. *Alternative Therapies Health Med,* 4:73–81, 1998.

15. Wolman, Ibid.

16. Landry, S. H., McGrath, S. K., Kennell, J. H. et al. The effects of doula support during labor on mother-infant interaction at 2 months. (abstract) *Pediatr Res,* 43:13A, 1998.

17. Winnicott, D. W. Primary maternal preoccupation. In: *Collected papers, through pediatrics to psychoanalyses,* New York: Basic Books, 1958.

CHAPTER 8: A FATHER'S TRUE ROLE

1. Bertsch, T. D., Nagashima-Whalen, L., Dykeman, S., Kennell, J. H., McGrath, S. K. Labor support by first-time fathers: Direct observation. *Journal of Psychosomatic Obstetrics and Gynecology,* 11:251–260, 1990.

2. Brooks, A. K., Kennell, J. H., McGrath, S. K. Supportive behaviors of men and women during labor. *Pediatric Res,* 37:17A, 1995.

3. Henneborn, M. J. and Cogan, R. The effect of husband participation on reported pain and probability of medication during labour and birth. *Journal of Psychosomatic Research,* 19:215–222, 1975.

4. Scott, J. R. and Rose, N. B. Effects of psychoprophylaxis (Lamaze presentation) on labor and delivery in primiparous. *N Engl J Med,* 294:1205–1207, 1976.

5. Kennell J H., McGrath, S. K. Labor support by a doula for middle-income couples. The effect on cesarean rates. *Pediatric Res,* 33:12A, 1993.

6. Odent, M. *Birth reborn.* New York: Pantheon Books, 1984.

CHAPTER 9: THE DUBLIN EXPERIENCE

1. Thornton, J. G., Lilford, R. J. Active management of labour: current knowledge and research issues. *BMJ* 309:366–369, 1994.

2. Thornton, *Ibid.*

3. Impey, L., Boylan, P. Active management of labour revisited. *British Journal of Obstetrics and Gynecology,* 106:183–187, 1999.

4. O'Driscoll, K., Meagher, D. *Active management of labor,* 2d. ed. London: Bailliere Tindal, 1986.

CHAPTER 10: POSTPARTUM CARE

1. Winnicott, D. W. *Babies and Their Mothers.* Reading, MA: Addison-Wesley, 1987.

2. DeCarvalho, M., Robertson, S., Friedman, R. et al. Effect of frequent breastfeeding on early milk production and infant weight gain. *Pediatrics,* 728:807–811, 1983

3. Winnicott, D. W. Primary maternal preoccupation. In *Through pediatrics to psychoanalysis.* New York: Basic Books, 1958.

4. Murray, L., Carothers, A. D. The validation of the Edinburgh post-natal depression scale. *British Journal of Psychiatry*, 157:288–290, 1990.

5. Korner, A. F., Thoman, E. Visual alertness in neonates as evoked by maternal care. *J Exp Child Psychology*, 10:67–68, 1970.

6. Dr. Christina Smillie, 2505 Main Street, Stratford, CT, 06615. Smillie@erols.com

7. Klaus, M., Klaus, P. *Your amazing newborn.* Cambridge, MA: Perseus, 1998.

8. Tracy Fengler, Oceanside, CA 92056.

INDEX

reviewing the events of, 49, 171
when the doula should come, 34, 35
See also positions; relaxation and visualization; stages of childbirth
La Leche League, 171, 230
Lamaze technique, 157, 230
late labor. *See* Second stage of childbirth
laughing gas (nitrous oxide), 158
length of labor, 80–83, 84, 98, 152, 154
light in the birthing room, 38
Lind, Johnny, 31, 49
long-term benefits of doula support, 101–11
 during the sensitive period, 101–3, 109
 for mothers' after delivery, 103–9
 pain after delivery and, 101
 parent-infant bonding and, 109–11
 parents' relationship and, 106–7
 See also obstetric benefits of doula support

Maning-Orenstein, Grace, 107
maternal fever, 58, 84, 88–90
Meagher, Declan, 12, 46, 149, 151–52, 155–56
medications
 Demerol, 56, 158, 177
 for depression, 175
 doula support and, 98
 effect on infants, 56–57
 medicated vs. nonmedicated births, 96
 narcotic medications, 84
 for pain, 56–67, 157–58
 vaginal deliveries without, 83
membranes rupturing, 37, 82, 155, 164
memory lapses, 170
midwives
 nurses as, 154, 157, 159–63
 one-to-one care from, 151–53, 155–59, 164
 time constraints of, 15–16
 used during early labor, 35, 36
modeling supportive behavior, 22
modesty, 39
 See also privacy
mothers
 changing needs of, 34, 38, 68–70
 dependence and independence needs of, 23
 with history of abuse, 45, 205–8
 mother-infant relationship, 96, 102–3, 107–9

mothering the mother, 22–27, 48, 91–92, 172
 psychological regression to her own birth, 23
movement during birth, 40–41
 See also positions; walking
music, 39

narcotic medication, 84
National Maternity Hospital, 151–66
 births at, 159–63
 diagnosis of labor at, 154–55
 as model of humane care, 163–66
 one-to-one care at, 151–53, 155–59, 164
 preventing prolonged labor and, 152–53
nitrous oxide (laughing gas), 158
nurses
 doulas supported by, 92–93
 as midwives, 154, 157, 159–63
 one-to-one nursing care, 151–53, 155–59, 164
 support of fathers, 138
 time constraints of, 15

obstetric benefits of doula support, 75–98
 cesarean sections and, 76, 77, 84, 86–88, 90
 emotional support and, 76–80
 epidural anesthesia and, 94–96
 financial considerations, 96–97
 induced labor and, 90
 length of labor and, 80–83
 maternal fever and, 88–90
 natural vaginal deliveries and, 83, 84
 pain relief and, 83–86
 practical application in hospitals, 92–94
 teenage mothers and, 90–92
 See also long-term benefits of doula support
Odent, Michel, 144
O'Driscoll, Kieran, 12, 46, 77, 149, 151–53, 155–56
one-to-one care, 152–53, 155–59, 164
oxygen, reducing use of, 76
oxytocin
 contractions increased with, 82, 85, 211
 doula support and, 84, 85–86, 98
 epidural anesthesia and, 95
 first-time mothers and, 155
 pain and, 42
 reducing stress and, 70, 71, 211
 released through touch, 41–42

See also relaxation and visualization; self-anesthesia
sensitive period, 101–3, 109, 173
septicemia (sepsis), 89
settings for birth, 9–10
sleep, 111, 175, 186–87
smells, 39, 177, 179
Smillie, Christina, 179–80
Snugli carriers, 177
sounds
    for help with contractions, 217–18
    importance of voice, 65–66
    minimizing, 39, 45
    music during labor, 39
    relieving tension with, 66–68
special needs mothers, 27, 45, 205–8
Special Place Visualization exercise, 214–19
squatting, 40, 41, *126*, 130, *147*
stages of childbirth
    first stage, 34–37, 136, 194–97
    second stage, 45–49, 136, 161–63, 199–201
stress, 54, 16–17, 70–72
studies
    Chicago doula project, 90–92
    Cleveland Couples Study, 77, 79, 90
    Guatemalan study, 80, 81, 85, 87–88, 102–3
    Houston study, 81–82, 83–84, 86, 87–88
    Johannesburg study, 103–9
    on labor support, 227–28
sympathetic nervous system, 70

talking during labor, 40, 137
teenage mothers, 90–92
temperature
    of the birth environment, 37, 38–39
    maternal fever, 58, 84, 88–90
time
    bonding with infants and, 105–6
    importance of, 72
    length of labor, 80–83, 84, 95, 98, 152–53, 154
    midwives and, 15–16
toilet used for labor positions, *23*
touch

concerns about, 206–7
cultural sensitivities to, 44–45
during labor, 41–42, 136–37
individual needs for, 25–26
medical touch, 41, 42
training for doulas, 191–208
    basic training, 192–93
    choosing to become a doula, 146, 191
    doula support described, 191–92
    first stage of childbirth, 194–97
    follow-up or home visits, 204–5
    general guidelines for doulas, 193–94
    handling problems/answering questions, 201–2
    helping mothers with history of trauma or abuse, 45, 205–8
    hospital-based doulas, 198–99
    postpartum care in the hospital, 202–3
    second stage of childbirth, 199–201
    transitioning to the hospital, 197–98

UNICEF Baby Friendly Hospital initiative, 48
upright position, *69*
uterine pain after birth, 48

vaginal deliveries, 83, 86–87
visitors, limiting, 39–40, 47, 176
visualization. *See* Relaxation and visualization; Self-hypnosis
vitamin K injections, 177
voice, importance of, 65–66
volunteers, doulas as, 21
vomiting during labor, 39

walking
    with the baby, 189
    cervix dilatation and, 157
    contractions and, 157
    during epidural anesthesia, 95
    pain relieved by, 26–27, 37
    for positioning the baby, 159–60
Winnicott, Donald W., 73, 99, 109, 167, 173
Wolman, Wendy, 103, 107
work, returning to, 174

ABOUT THE AUTHORS

Marshall H. Klaus, M.D., is Adjunct Professor of Pediatrics at the University of California, San Francisco. A distinguished neonatologist and researcher, he conducts research into the importance and effects of doula support. He is the author or coauthor of several standard works in the field, including *Maternal-Infant Bonding; Parent-Infant Bonding; Bonding: Building the Foundations of Secure Attachment and Independence; Care of the High-Risk Neonate*, 5th ed. (with A. A. Fanaroff); *Mothering the Mother: How a Doula Can Help You Have a Shorter, Easier, and Healthier Birth;* and *Your Amazing Newborn.*

John H. Kennell, M.D., is Professor of Pediatrics at Case Western Reserve University School of Medicine, Cleveland, Ohio. In addition to his on-going research on the doula and his teaching of residents and fellows in behavioral pediatrics, he continues to participate each year with first year medical students who serve as apprentice-physician doulas for mothers. He is the coauthor of *Maternal-Infant Bonding; Parent-Infant Bonding; Bonding: Building the Foundations of a Secure Attachment and Independence;* and *Mothering the Mother: How a Doula Can Help You Have a Shorter, Easier, and Healthier Birth*

Phyllis H. Klaus, C.S.W., M.F.T., teaches and practices at the Erickson Institute in Santa Rosa and also in Berkeley, California, providing psychotherapy and especially working with the concerns, both medical and psychological, of pregnancy, birth, and the postpartum period. She consults nationally and internationally, does research, and is coauthor of *Mothering the Mother: How a Doula Can Help You Have a Shorter, Easier, and Healthier Birth; Bonding: Building the Foundations of Secure Attachment and Independence;* and *Your Amazing Newborn.*